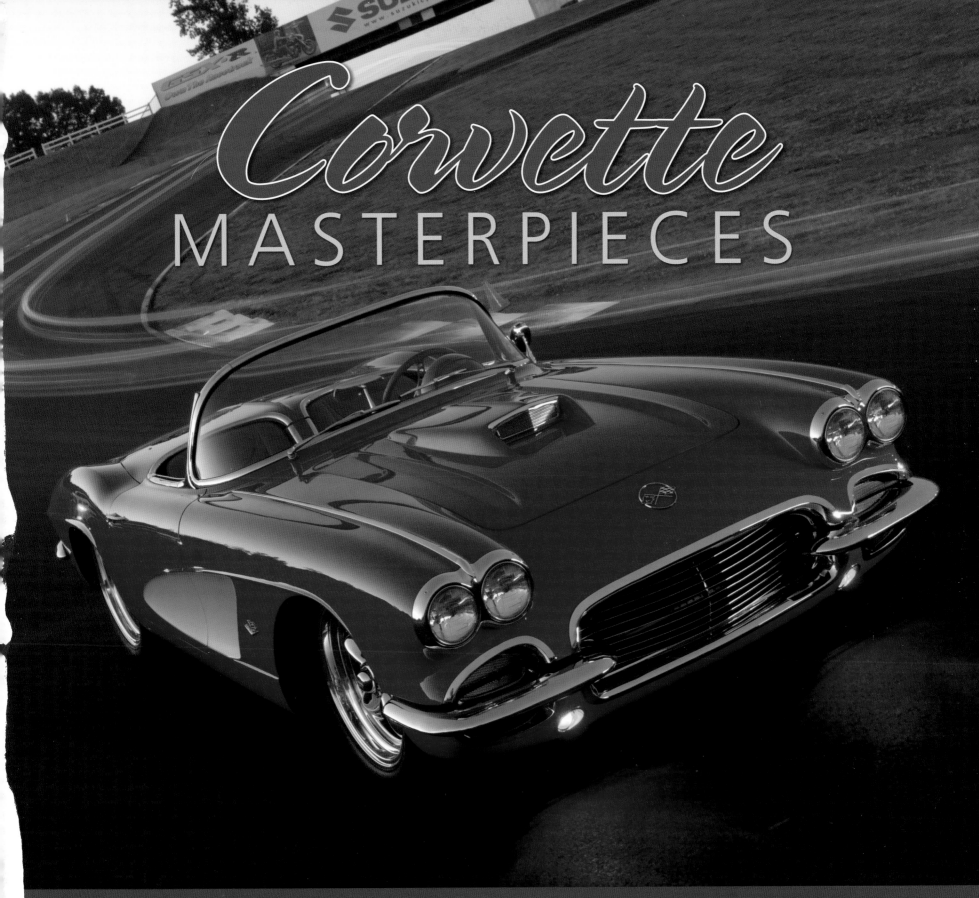

Corvette
MASTERPIECES

Jerry Heasley

Published by

krause publications
An Imprint of F+W Publications

700 East State Street • Iola, WI 54990-0001
715-445-2214 • 888-457-2873
www.krausebooks.com

Our toll-free number to place an order or obtain
a free catalog is (800) 258-0929.

Library of Congress Control Number: 2007923818

ISBN-13: 978-0-89689-554-6
ISBN-10: 0-89689-554-8

Designed by Paul Birling
Edited by John Gunnell

Printed in China

Dedication

Dedicated to…

… My father, Herbert Victor Heasley, who instilled in me an interest in cars. We'd peruse car lots looking at the different makes and models. When my dad found one he really liked, the vehicle was no longer merely a car. He'd announce, "Now, that's an automobile."

Acknowledgments

I would like to acknowledge…

… the many Corvette owners who graciously helped me photograph their cars for various magazines over the years. Without them, there would be no "Corvette Masterpieces."

… Brian Ernest, of Krause Publications, who convinced me to assemble this book. At first, I didn't want to do it. Brian liked my photos and my work, so I went ahead.

… John Gunnell, who went beyond what an editor should have to do, such as writing captions. In some instances, he knew specific cars in the book and owners, such as Kevin Mackay. He personally contacted some owners to make corrections or additions. I free-lanced for John when he was editor of *Old Cars Weekly*. I believe he knows more people in the car hobby than anybody on the planet.

7 Corvette: A Symbol of American Pride & Freedom (Corvette and the American Flag)

36 Pugesek Motorsports Revolution Roadster is a Corvette Masterpiece

61 Cascade Green '56 Dual Quad

96 Corvette Racing History: '59 Purple People Eater

107 1961 LS7 Corvette: 20th Century Meets 21st Century

Corvette MASTERPIECES

Contents

113 Concept Corvettes At GM Design

140 Custom 1965 Corvette

173 '68 yenko Racing Car — Never Titled, Never Registered

221 "Corvette Summer" Movie Corvette

233 Pop Art 'Vette: A Real Psychotic Reaction

Preface

Dreaming Big Corvette Gold-Chain Dreams

A book on totally stock Corvettes would be cool, but, a book on modified, racing, "tuner," celebrity, Resto-Mod and hybrid Corvettes — in addition to those great stock Corvettes — seems even cooler.

Over the last 25 years, I've photographed and written feature articles on Corvettes from national shows across the United States. For this book, I drew from literally hundreds of features and tens of thousands of pictures to assemble a select group of cars for your viewing pleasure. These cars comprise what I call "Corvette Masterpieces."

The model years run from the very first year, 1953, to the present. The format is a coffeetable book, which implies looking and not reading. As an incentive to read, I have inserted surprises for your entertainment, such as the story of the time an alleged drug dealer helped me photograph a ZR-1 Corvette on the streets of Inkster, Michigan. Maybe I should write a hip-hop song about what happened when the police showed up? One cop told me, "Son, Little Willie will put a cap in your head. Stay outta here in an $80,000 Corvette."

The police told me almost the same thing when I was driving around downtown Los Angeles, in a new Corvette, hunting for a photo location. As you will see, I didn't take any of my Corvette pictures in a locked studio. I shot them on the streets of America. Do you know what a *Kamikaze* shoot is?

This book will show you Corvettes you've probably never seen, like "tuner" specials from Lingenfelter, Carravaggio, Mallett, Callaway and many others. Have you ever seen a Z06 convertible built by Chevrolet's underground Skunkwerkes team headed by C5 Corvette styling ace John Cafaro?

Cafaro is a typical Corvette enthusiast and has a great, dry sense of humor. I once asked him in a serious tone, "John, what's the speed of a Corvette in a vacuum?" John laughed and told me he figured one day the Corvette could reach the speed of light.

Although non-stock Corvettes dominate this book — just like they dominate the hobby — I have included a choice sampling of stock Corvettes, as well. For example, the '57 "Air Box" Fuelie (option code 579E) is a "Corvette Masterpiece." So are many other factory-original Corvettes. Sometimes, it's their originality that makes cars fit the theme of *Corvette Masterpieces* so well.

I tried my best to make the text fun to read. Writing and photographing Corvettes is fun. The people who drive these cars also know how to have fun, too. To illustrate, I have included people and events, such as a Corvette Forum "Cruise-In." Like so many Corvette owners, these Forum members enjoy cruises, drag races, autocrosses, smoky burnouts in the parking lot, jokes, loud music, fine food and drink and in general laughing and having a fun time.

I think the character of the Corvette is wrapped up in this have-fun philosophy. If you walk into a room of Corvette people, they won't ignore you. They'll say, "Hi." If they're imbibing, chances are they'll offer you a beer. If you join their fun, pretty soon you'll be taking a wild 'Vette ride and hanging onto the "oh-xxxx" grab bar. Maybe you'll be buying a 'Vette of your own; possibly you'll soon be shopping for one of those ostentatious gold chains that the 'Vette cognoscenti strap around their neck, wrist or other visible part of their anatomy.

In the spirit of fun, I have chosen the feature cars in this book. They are the wildest most attention-grabbing, greatest, *baddest-ass* rides ever to wear the Corvette name badge. They are my big gold-chain dreams and "Corvette Masterpieces."

Corvette: A Symbol Of American Pride & Freedom

Funfest 2001 Was A Flag-Waving Celebration

"Not only do we need to hug each other today. Not only do we need the comfort of your company. We also need to show ourselves and the rest of the world that we will not permit terrorism to control our lives. To run for cover today is to surrender to those who would trample on our inalienable rights to life, liberty and yes, even the pursuit of happiness."

— Mike Yager, President of Mid America Motorworks on Saturday, September 16, 2001.

△ I ran and walked through the show grounds to get the mood. I happened onto Paul and M.J.McConnell, of Antioch, Illinois. They were walking down the fairly crowded midway. Paul gave me the scoop on Yager's talk, "It ran parallel to what was on the internet; he said that the Corvette was a symbol of America, that this isn't going to deter us. I don't think there was a dry eye in the crowd for his opening speech."

With terrorist hijackings in Boston and Washington, D.C. and crashes in New York City, D.C. and Pennsylvania, the obvious questions were, "Should Mid America Motorworks have held Funfest a mere four days later? If so, how many people would attend? And what would their mood be?

At no other time in our nation's history did the Corvette symbolize the patriotism of its loyal group of owners than after the tragic events of September 11, 2001.

9/11 was a Tuesday. The next Saturday was Corvette Funfest, one of the biggest Corvette shows of the year. I was scheduled to attend. Could I get a flight to St. Louis, Missouri? Would the airlines still be grounded? Would Mid America Motorworks cancel the entire event? Would enthusiasts drive their Corvettes to the company's headquarters in Effingham, Illinois?

Funfest 2001 began, as planned, at 8:30 a.m. Saturday morning. Mike Yager, owner and president of Mid America Motorworks, greeted attendees. Sadly, I didn't quite make it on time to hear his speech. My flight Friday night had been canceled, but I did fly to St. Louis early the next morning. I had to drive 107 miles to Effingham. I arrived at Funfest at 12:30 p.m.

I managed to get a copy of an excerpt of Yager's speech. What he said was:

"You are family. We at Mid America couldn't any more shut our doors to you this weekend than we could shut out the horror of last Tuesday. I know I speak for everybody at Mid America when I tell you of all the years we've been hosting this family reunion, we've never felt as strongly about going ahead as today."

I ran and walked through the show grounds to get the mood. I happened onto Paul and M.J. McConnell, of Antioch, Illinois. They were walking down the fairly crowded midway. Paul gave me the scoop on Yager's talk, *"It ran parallel to what was on the Internet; he said that the Corvette was a symbol of America and that people should be rallying around the symbol of America; that this isn't going to deter us. I don't think there was a dry eye in the crowd for his opening speech."*

With terrorist hijackings in Boston and Washington, D.C. and crashes in New York City, D.C. and Pennsylvania, the obvious questions were, *"Should Mid America Motorworks have held Funfest a mere four days later? If so, how many people would attend? And what would their mood be?"*

Inside, Yager was holding a luncheon for the press and answering those very questions in detail. I caught him in mid-stride, speaking boldly, *"We checked with law enforcement and asked if there was a security risk here. I think part of the reason that sporting events, like major league baseball and the NFL got discontinued was not as much the gathering of people at stadiums, but how do teams get from city to city? The majority of the teams fly. Then, the other thought is, with this many people together, is that a risk factor?*

Overall, the consensus was there was no risk factor here in Effingham and the show should go on."

Yager added, *"Walking around the show, I've had numerous people say thank you, this is a nice diversion from a diversion."*

The year before, I had gone to Funfest 2000, which was much bigger. But in 2001, crowd size wasn't an issue. The 2001 Funfest was a very special event. Everybody was united.

Rich and Karen Partlow drove their 1997 Corvette coupe from Naperville, Illinois. Rich commented, late on Saturday afternoon, *"My personal feeling was, I was hoping they would have Funfest because a lot of us needed time to get with other Americans and be away from just sitting in front of the television and feeling so helpless. Our way of life has*

△ Doug Croy and his 8-year old daughter stood beside the 1971 LT1 coupe they drove from their hometown of Lake Matton, Illinois.

△ Amidst the sea of 6,000 Corvettes and 28,000 enthusiasts, American flags waved proudly and red, white and blue-clad participants showed that their thoughts and prayers were not far from the victims and families of the terrible tragedies, along with the ongoing rescue efforts in New York City.

△ Joan Spoerndle displayed an American flag on her "Miss Mako" Corvette, a '64 model convertible. Her goal was to raise money at Funfest for the American Cancer Society.

△   Jay Janco from East Hazlecrest, Illinois set up one of the most impressive patriotic displays with his 396 'Vette, a '65 model. Jay said, *"We debated a little bit, but by coming out here we're showing our support for the country. We want life to go on and whatever we have to do, if necessary, we will do it."*

▷   Marcus Swan from Baltimore, Ohio, had a message for us. "God Bless America, let's get together and stand up," it read. He displayed his yellow C4 Corvette.

been threatened and I think we're the ones who control that. Major league baseball is a different story. A lot of people on airplanes would be nervous. I'm confident of that. I know it is good to be with other Americans and we're looking forward to the rest of the day."

The Partlows belong to Chicago's "Windy City Corvettes." They were part of a troupe of club members headed back to the hotel for a "little function" late Saturday afternoon.

"We're going to go to the pool and have a few drinks and some appetizers," someone said. *"We have over 160 members and probably about 65-70 are here today."*

△ Chuck Ring, of Itasca, Illinois, won a "Judge's Choice" award. His car was picked by the Corvette plant's quality manager. He affixed two huge American flags to the '94 'Vette.

◁ David and Connie Baxter from Roscoe, Illinois, displayed a pair of American flags from their windshield header.

Funfest is a Corvette celebration from the heartland of America and the 2001 show was a big relief for everybody.

The previous year's total attendance had been 8,230 Corvettes. The 2001 tally was about 3,500 Saturday and 2,500 Sunday. That is still a huge show, of course. Mike Yager handed out two free lunches for every Corvette and provided Saturday night entertainment.

In 2000, Funfest had featured a carnival. For 2001, Yager hired a Country & Western band. No one seemed to mind that the band couldn't make the big gig due to flight cancellations. Everybody sat on hay bales in the cool night air and enjoyed Corvette camaraderie and talked the night away.

Corvette & The American Flag

This original Corvette logo, which incorporated the American flag, is an amazing artifact that has survived more than 50 years. You can see it on display at the National Corvette Museum in Bowling Green, Kentucky.

The Corvette has been linked to the American flag and the spirit of patriotism and freedom from the inception of the marque in 1953. The original Corvette logo, designed by Robert Bartholomew, consisted of a pair of crossed flags. On the right was a checkered flag, which had links to racing. On the left was the American flag.

This emblem was affixed to the original 1953 Corvette show car, which debuted at the GM Motorama in New York City. However, during advance preparations for the show, a member of the General Motors legal staff rejected the emblem design. He noted that the American flag cannot be used on a commercial product.

As a result, a redesign was quickly done. The new design utilized the Chevrolet "bow tie" insignia and the French fleur-de-lis symbol. Two new emblems displaying the now familiar Corvette logo were quickly shipped to New York and installed on the show car just hours before the Motorama opened.

Be that as it may, this long-preserved original logo is certainly a "Corvette Masterpiece" and a great memorabilia item to start this book with.

▷ Corvette people affirmed that life would go on American-style, with truth and justice (and burgers and fries) for all.

△ Kevin and Tammy Breck-enfelder drove their '71 coupe from Germantown, Wisconsin. They expressed their emotional reaction to 9/11 by draping an American flag over the car's back glass.

▷ Dave Hill, Corvette chief engineer in 2001, was among the celebrities signing posters at the show. Also present was David McLellan, Corvette chief engineer from 1975-1992.

As Funfest wound down on Sunday afternoon, Mike Yager asked for a moment of silence and reflection as the song *"Proud To Be An American"* filled the airwaves of the entire Funfest grounds.

The 1953 Motorama ·
Waldorf Astoria Show Corvette

The Saga Of EX-122

For decades, the car seen here has been known as EX-122. This car is part of the Kerbeck Brothers' collection in Atlantic City, New Jersey. It is the car in which the first V-8 was developed for the Corvette, but this car may also be the famous GM Motorama Corvette. If so, it's the very car displayed at the Waldorf Astoria Hotel, in New York City, in January of 1953.

We also have some evidence that EX-122, although built for show, was *the* car that Chevrolet counted as the first of the 300 Corvettes numbered for the 1953 model year.

Clearly, EX-122 was re-bodied by Chevrolet. So, the unique show car features were missing when Jack Ingle bought the car from Russell Sanders on October 10, 1959. There is a photocopy of Ingle's check, which was written for $1,000.

Perhaps the re-body is why Ingle did not promote the car as the Motorama show car of 1953. Under the hood was a 265-cid V-8. The body is a '55 body. The hubcaps are '56.

Nonetheless, Ingle received a letter, postmarked December 8, 1959, that came from R.F. Sanders, Director of Engineering & Sales of Rochester Products Division. In this three-page, typed letter, Sanders explained that the car he sold Ingle was EX-122. The letter said it was built in the "Experimental Department of

△ Due to paint advances in the early '50s, white pigments became stabilized enough to avoid uneven chalking and GM design chief Harley Earl preferred using white finish on dream cars like the EX-122 to highlight their massive curved shapes.

Chevrolet Engineering" — which was located in Detroit — in the "latter part of 1952." At the time, Sanders worked there.

Sanders said EX-122 was to be the Motorama show car put on display at the Waldorf Astoria in New York. It was "carried, babied and handled" in shows in the United States. Afterward, it was parked in the lobby of the General Motors Building for public display. Later, it went back to the Engineering Department and was used as a test car.

The new V-8 was under development, so engineers installed the 265-cid V-8 in place of the straight six. Sanders indicates the car became a "plaything for the Engineering Department" and was used for "various performance demonstrations."

When Chevrolet decided to go ahead with a V-8 in the production 'Vette, EX-122 (still 265-powered and re-bodied) ran a 25,000-mile durability test. On completion, it was torn down. Each part was inspected and reports were made. Then, the car was reassembled and repainted red. A new top, new seats and a new speedometer were installed. The transmission was completely overhauled and safety items were replaced. A new set of tires was put on the car.

Sanders explained in his letter that EX-122 was next used as a courtesy car. It was driven about 5,000 miles and then put up for sale. He bought the car on April 11, 1956. His letter said he had "considerable difficulty" licensing the car in the states of Michigan and New York, due to the serial number. The VIN EX-122 denotes an experimentally-built automobile. His daughter drove the Corvette while she attended the University of Rochester. She was known as "the girl with the little red sports car." When she transferred to Michigan State University at East Lansing, she was not permitted to have a car, so EX-122 went up for sale.

In the final paragraph of this letter, Sanders addresses the subject of the first Corvette ever built. He says EX-122 was *not* the first Corvette ever built. It was the first Corvette built for show. The test cars "looked nothing like a Corvette at all, having some handmade bodies in place of the smooth, plastic body which was finally released for production."

From the facts in this letter, EX-122 is the car pictured in this chapter. The car's history is documented by the VIN plate (EX-122) and by the fact it was in the possession of Jack Ingle from 1959 until recently, when the Kerbeck brothers bought the car.

George Kerbeck recalls that he first saw EX-122 in the "Special Collection" at the Bloomington Gold Corvette show in 1993. His brother Frank was with him.

"We were walking around and saw this car. At this time it was painted Venetian Red or a shade similar to Venetian Red. It had this V-8 engine and the placard out in front of it that said EX-122."

George and Charlie were "totally intrigued." In all their searches for unique and interesting Corvettes, they never knew that such a car existed. Having a car-dealer mentality, George *had to* own this 'Vette. He says he figured it was "just too special to go through life without."

They met the owner, Jack Ingle and his son David. Jack explained that he bought the car, in 1959, from a good friend who worked for General Motors. Jack was not interested in selling EX-122. He planned to own the car until the day he died.

"Jack went on to tell us he had this house on Lake Canandaigua," George continued. "He built a living room for the car and the car sat in the living room and overlooked the lake. It was his prize possession. He loved going to shows and showing the car."

George was persistent about wanting to buy EX-122. He said he would call up Ingle "probably twice a year." George is not the pushy type; he's very polite and cordial. He would tell Jack Ingle, "You know I'm in love with your car and I know it's not for sale, but if you ever change your mind . . . "

These conversations went on for seven years. In "1997 or 1998," according to George, he almost bought EX-122, but Jack just couldn't go through with the deal. So, it was left to his family to sell the car after he died.

When the Kerbecks bought the historic 'Vette from the Ingle estate, they began a restoration to return the car to its Motorama show car looks. For the first time in over 50 years, inside and out (but not under the hood) the car looks like the original show Corvette that appeared at the Waldorf Astoria Hotel in January of 1953.

It's definitely a sight to behold with its exterior door buttons, special gold body emblems and other unique show-car features that did not make production. The Kerbecks re-produced these items by scrutinizing original photographs and transparencies retrieved from Corvette expert Noland Adams and the Chevrolet archives. (It was Noland Adams who blew up a photo of the shift knob. On a regular '53, this knob is white, but on this car it is red.) In this way, the car came back to life.

At the '53 Corvette 50th anniversary celebration in Flint, Michigan, in the summer of 2003, George Kerbeck was sur-prised when Ken Kayser, who works for GM, handed him the blueprint of the exact EX-122 body side molding. Painstakingly, the Motorama show car surfaced through the Kerbecks' restor-ative measures.

△   The "EX" indicated an experimental car and the number "122" represented the car's place in the long line of concept cars created by Harley Earl's Art and Colour Section and GM Design Studio.

△ **The dashboard on the show car is made completely of fiberglass and lacks a vinyl "roll" used on production versions. It also has two extra knobs.**

△ **After some deliberation, the Kerbeck Brothers left the small-block 265-cid V-8 in the car.**

There were actually *two* show Corvettes: the Waldorf car and another. George Kerbeck told us that the second show car was for Canadian display. Apparently, these two show cars were the same, except the Motorama version (EX-122) had two scoops on top of the front fenders.

"We had to re-create the cowl scoops. We also had to re-create the body-side spear molding. On a production '53, the headlight doors are much fatter and on a production '53 the headlight doors don't open. But, if you study the pictures of the Motorama car, you can see they are hinged into the body. And so we made the headlight doors an exact duplicate of the headlight doors that were originally in the car."

The Motorama show car also came with door buttons. The bullets on the bumpers front and rear are two-piece. By June,

in production, they had become one piece. On the Motorama show car, "Corvette" is also spelled out in script on the nose and deck lid. Apparently, Chevrolet wanted the public and press to read the name of this car when they saw and photographed it.

The interior is considerably different than on a production car. George said that the main difference is "a great big frame around the seats." The dashboard is all fiberglass. It doesn't have the vinyl "roll" that comes down the door panel and goes around the dash. The Motorama car also has a different arrangement of knobs including two extra knobs. These knobs, on the left and right of the dash, opened and closed the cowl scoops on top of the front fenders.

The Kerbecks sweated over what to do with the 265-cid small-block V-8 under the hood. They decided to leave it in place for one big reason. Historically, this car was quite possibly the first V-8 installation ever in a Corvette. (For the record, Chevrolet pulled the test engine and replaced it with a fresh 265 before it was put up for sale in 1956, but, it's still a 265 and it's still an original factory installation.)

George speaks of a "fraction" of the Corvette *cognoscenti* who think they should have left EX-122 in the configuration it left GM in 1956. At that time, the car looked like a production '55 model.

The Kerbecks did not make their decisions about the restoration without counsel. George called Noland Adams, the straight-axle Corvette guru and author of the exhaustive book, *Corvette Restoration & Technical Guide -- Volume 1, 1953-'62* for his opinion.

George told Adams, "I said, before I do this, you're like the king. What do you think?" Adams answered him, "I've told everybody from the beginning, the car never should have been put back together like a '55. It's too significant to the hobby not to look the other way." So George figured, "You know what, that's the way we're going to go."

The Corvette hobby is embracing EX-122 as never before. At the prestigious 2002 Concours d'Elegance at Meadow Brook Hall, the Kerbecks received the Matilda and Alfred Wilson Award for the "Best Featured Sports Car." In the 2003 GM Styling Dome, it won an award for "Privately Owned Concept Vehicle" in the "Eyes On Design" show. When the C6 Corvette was unveiled at the Amelia Island Concours d'Elegance in 2004, organizer Bill Warner requested that EX-122 be parked right next to the C6.

EX-122, it appears, is right back on the show car circuit where it started. Any day of the week, it is on display at Kerbeck Chevrolet in Atlantic City. Anybody who stops there can have his or her picture taken next to it. George, Charlie and Frank Kerbeck are not fussy types; they're "good old" Corvette boys. They are also the owners of a "Corvette Masterpiece."

Who Are The Kerbeck Brothers?

George, Charlie and Frank Kerbeck are three brothers who I became very familiar with when the 50th anniversary of the Corvette was celebrated, in 2003, in Carlisle, Pennsylvania. The brothers own the world's largest Corvette dealership, which is located in Atlantic City, New Jersey. They are not your normal show car people. Who else has a 'Vette worth easily into six figures – perhaps a million dollars – and lets kids touch the car and sit in it?

I can hear Charlie saying, "Hell, you only live once. Let's have a good time."

Boy, do they ever have a good time. I mentioned to Frank how much I liked their Kerbeck Chevrolet shirts.

"You want one?"

"No, Frank, that's OK."

"Charlie, go get Jerry a shirt."

"No, please, Frank … Frank."

Frank was already gone to get a shirt. These guys will give you the shirt off their back if it makes you feel a part of their team.

There was no problem getting the car to the photo location. They simply had an employee *drive* it the three or four miles. Most cars surrounded by this much history and worth tons of money *must* be put on a trailer.

That evening, I joined about 15 people who work for or are affiliated in some way with Kerbeck Corvette. We all went to dinner at Rillos, an Italian restaurant in Carlisle. I don't like to "talk shop" after hours. I started telling jokes. Everybody joined in and we laughed for two hours straight.

Note: The Kerbeck Brothers maintain a modest collection of about 30 Corvettes and various GM muscle cars at their dealership. You can see the cars at "www.kerbeck.com."

△ The Kerbeck brothers pose with some of their classics.

△ It's the largest 'Vette dealership in the land.

The first Corvettes came off the assembly line on June 30, 1953.

Mr. H. R. Yount

R. W. Thorns

July 24, 1953

- 2 -

To facilitate identification of the Corvettes, it is suggested that they be numbered as follows:

    Corvette # 1 will be the car which has been used in the Motorama and is the car with the hydraulic hood and rear deck cylinders presently installed.

    Corvette # 2. This car is the second show car which, at present, does not have the hydraulic cylinders installed.

    Corvette # 3. This car will be the first production car designated for use by the Sales Department.

There are to be eight more Production Corvettes designated for Sales Department use during August. Continue to number these cars consecutively from three up as they are received from production.

To identify the car, paint or otherwise attach a number to the underside of the glove compartment flap in the door in an inconspicuous manner.

W. W. Thorns,
Engineering Department,
Technical Data Group.

RWT/sh

◁ **This 1953 letter talks about the first three Corvettes made.**

▽ **The '53 'Vette is a real collectors item.**

ROCHESTER PRODUCTS DIVISION

GENERAL MOTORS CORPORATION

ROCHESTER 3, NEW YORK

OFFICE OF THE
DIRECTOR OF
ENGINEERING & SALES

December 8, 1959

Mr. John W. Ingle
21 Creekside Lane
Rochester 18, New York

Dear Jack:

    This letter will give you the information you desire concerning the red Corvette you purchased from me around the middle of October, 1959. This little car has quite a history and is certainly worth recording, particularly if you intend to keep the car for a considerable period of time.

    It was built up originally in the Experimental Department of Chevrolet Engineering in Detroit around the latter part of 1952. Although all the pieces were made by hand at that time, they represented the intent of production drawings being released. It was extremely difficult to say how many thousands of dollars were spent in producing the vehicle. I would guess in the neighborhood of $55,000 or $60,000. Of course, you realize that most of this was spent to pay the very high skilled labor and technicians that swarmed over these parts during their inception and manufacture. When completed, it was white and equipped with a 6-cylinder Chevrolet engine with three Carter side-draft carburetors and a special high capacity powerglide transmission. Workmanship and quality, of course, were the best possible at Chevrolet Engineering because it was to be used in the Motorama at the Waldorf in New York as a showpiece of the new 1953 model Chevrolet Corvette. This was in December, 1952.

    It was carried, babied and handled very carefully through the various automobile shows in the United States and then it stood in the lobby of the General Motors Building for a considerable period of time where it is needless to say that it drew a great deal of interest and comment. As the 1953 model became more common because it was being produced in regular production manner, the Corvette was taken back to the Engineering Department and used as a test car.

Flight Companion
to Chevrolet

A new set of AC's will provide *top-flight* performance for your car, too

STANDARD FACTORY EQUIPMENT ON CHEVROLET • PONTIAC • OLDSMOBILE • BUICK • CADILLAC • GMC

△ **AC Spark Plugs ad honored the new Corvette.**

◁ **Documents such as these are the car's pedigree.**

▷ **Here's the last two pages of the Ingle letter.**

Mr. John W. Ingle   -2-   December 8, 1959

About that time the new Chevrolet V-8 engine 265 cu. in. capacity was being developed by Engineering, and it was a natural move to see how this engine would perform in a Corvette in place of the 235 cu. in. valve in head 6-cylinder engine. The car became a plaything for the Engineering Department. The 6-cylinder engine was removed and an 8-cylinder engine installed, and it was used for various performance demonstrations. It gave such a good account of itself that immediately it was decided to abandon the 6-cylinder engine in regular Chevrolet Corvette production and supplement it with the new 8-cylinder as standard equipment.

The natural question was with this added power, what happens to the durability of the automobile? So the car was taken to the Proving Ground where it was run on a 25,000 mile durability test and then it was completely torn down and each part inspected and reports made for production reasons. After being displayed in this manner for several weeks, there was no further need for the vehicle, and it was reassembled using new production pieces wherever the experimental parts showed wear. I was in charge of the Experimental Department at that time and saw to it that the car was rebuilt in the very best of condition. It was repainted red, a new top and new seats installed, a new speedometer installed, transmission was completely overhauled, safety items were replaced and a new set of tires put on. It was used as a courtesy car for about 5,000 miles and then put up for sale. I purchased the car from Chevrolet on April 11, 1956. We were never able to put a production serial number on the car and this gave me considerable difficulty in getting it properly licensed both in the states of Michigan and New York. As you know the serial number is EX-122 which denotes an experimentally built automobile.

I am enclosing the 1957 Michigan certificate of registration which may be of interest to you with your papers on this automobile. I cannot locate the certificates for previous years. The car was used considerably by various members of my family, particularly my wife and daughter. While my daughter attended the University of Rochester here, she was known as the girl with the little red sports car. She is now attending Michigan State University at East Lansing where she is not permitted to have an automobile, and therefore, the car was put up for sale. Our family misses the Corvette very much, however, I think we will probably buy another one in the future when my daughter returns from school.

Mr. John W. Ingle   -3-   December 8, 1959

I hope you will find this information interesting as much as we have. If there is any other information you need, I will be very happy to give it to you, if it is available.

I hope that I have not given the impression that this is the first Corvette ever built because that is not so. It is the first Corvette built for show. There were other test cars built for test that were far from good looking, in fact, they looked nothing like the Corvette at all, having some hand made bodies in place of the smooth plastic body which was finally released for production. The Styling Department made up a mock-up model of the complete styling proposal which appeared to be the same as this car, however, it was of dummy construction and the body was made of clay. It was from this clay model that styling was finally approved, and this car was then built.

Sincerely,

R.F. Sanders

R. F. Sanders

mwh
Enc.

▽ **A formation of 'Vettes on the Proving Ground track.**

△ **This early press photo shows a '53 kicking up dust.**

What If?

Could the long lost and thought to be destroyed serial No. 1 Corvette actually be EX-122, seen here? A July 24, 1953 Chevrolet inter-office memo, from Mr. H.R. Yount to D.W. Thomas of the Engineering Department, is evidence to support this belief.

The memo states:

"To facilitate identification of the Corvettes, it is suggested that they be numbered as follows:

Corvette #1 will be the car that has been used in the Motorama and is the car with the hydraulic hood and rear deck cylinders presently installed.

Corvette #2. This car is the second show car, which, at present, does not have the hydraulic cylinders installed.

Corvette #3. This car will be the first production car designated for use by the Sales Department.

There are to be eight more production Corvettes designated for Sales Department use during August. Continue to number these cars consecutively from three up as they are received from production."

If EX-122 was Chevrolet Corvette No. 1 and the second show car was No. 2, and No. 3 was the first production car, then the historic photo of the first three cars coming off the assembly line at Flint, Michigan, on June 30, 1953, actually shows car Nos. 3, 4 and 5, rather than Nos. 1, 2 and 3.

This supposition is conjecture at this point, but it does make some sense. Actually, all 1953 Corvettes, especially the early units, were hand-built show cars. So, it would be logical for Chevrolet to number the show cars with the production cars. There really wasn't much difference from one to the other.

The current thinking in the Corvette hobby is that the first Corvette, which would have been serial number E53F001001, was put through a burn test. It is believed that the body was destroyed and the salvaged frame was used in the Nomad show car. The earliest production Corvette is said to be 003, which was recently restored. EX-122 is thought to be the second Corvette in this series.

Corvettes @ Carlisle:
'53 Corvette Reunion Sets World's Record

The 50th At Carlisle, 2003, Brings Out The Cars & The Memories

The best place to see the '53 Corvette as a masterpiece was at the fairgrounds in Carlisle, Pennsylvania, in the summer of 2003. It was the 50th anniversary of the Corvette. It was also an event that will remain special for another reason — it was Chip Miller's last "Corvettes @ Carlisle."

Chip, along with his friend Bill Miller (no relation) started the first Carlisle automotive event — "Postwar '74" — over three decades ago. The events grew to 12 per year and now draw over a half million visitors to the small city in central Pennsylvania. Although Carlisle covers many different marques, Corvettes were certainly Chip Miller's favorite. He owned more than 80 Corvettes before his life was cut short by complications related to the disease Amyloidosis — a rare blood disorder.

Corvette enthusiasts will never forget Miller. He was a member of the Corvette Hall of Fame and was well-known as one of the principal movers and shakers in the Corvette hobby.

Chip was one of the main reasons that the largest gathering of 1953 Corvettes ever came together at Corvettes @ Carlisle during the Labor Day 2003 weekend. For his entire life, Chip was a connoisseur of "Corvette Masterpieces."

△ **Forty-nine Corvettes in a row make quite a sight.**

▷ **Chip Miller's last "Corvettes @ Carlisle" show honored the '53 model.**

△ A total of 49 first-year Corvettes were arranged in one long row under a series of blue-and-white striped tents erected at the fairgrounds in 2003.

▷ For years, the oldest production Corvette known and recognized as such was No. 003, also known as ES-127. It was a test car and went through extensive testing at the GM Proving Grounds.

△ Dave McLellan (center) and Jerry Burton (right) talk about Corvettes at the 50ᵗʰ anniversary in Carlisle. McLellan was the Corvette chief engineer (1975-1992). Jerry Burton coined the phrase, "The Heartbeat of America." Both are inductees of the Corvette Hall of Fame.

There's something glorious about seeing 49 Corvettes arranged in one long row. When all 49 of the vehicles are first-year-of-production '53 Corvettes, it's amazing. "We'll probably never see this again," said marque historian and author Noland Adams, who owns '53 Corvette No. 284.

Just 300 of the first-year Corvettes were built and the cars are now referred to by their order in the production run. In 2003, 11 a.m. on a Labor Day weekend Saturday was to be their moment of glory at Corvettes @ Carlisle.

"We're pulling them out for a group shot," a man named Joe Clemente told us. (Clemente helped Chip Miller organize the event.) Actually, all this amounted to was edging each car, strung in a row under a continuous series of blue and white tents, into the sunlight. Carlisle officials roped off the area for two photo ops. One had the owners standing beside their car; the second included the cars only.

Alan Blay owns eight '53 Corvettes and brought six along for the display at Carlisle. He told us that the previous record

◁ Two very early and very famous Corvettes, Nos. 5 and 6, went to the wealthy du Pont family. The original Corvette was so desirable that Chevrolet reserved cars for VIPs.

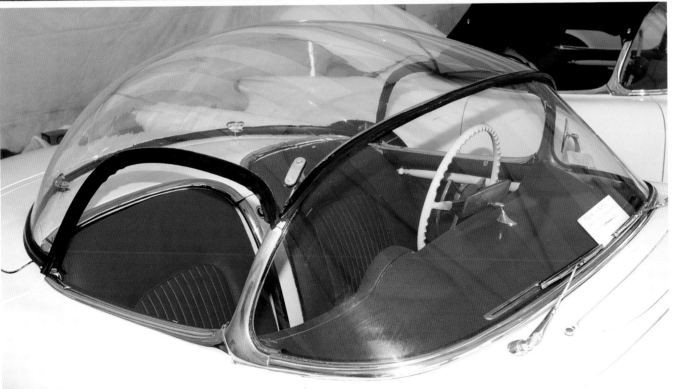

◁ The plastic bubble gives this '53 a spaceship appearance. You figure the Jetsons just landed in your driveway. Alan Blay believes about two dozen of these were made. This was an experiment with plastic in 1953.

△ Noland Adams, the famous Corvette writer, stands beside the 1953 model he bought in 1955.

for the number of cars brought back together was 26. That was done on June 30, 2003 for the 50th birthday reunion in Flint, Michigan. Blay was a big help putting together the Carlisle display. For those keeping records, the total number of cars displayed at Carlisle was 54.

Clemente gave us the tally. There were 49 cars under the tents, two in a "Chip Miller's Choice" display inside the main building, George Kerbeck's EX-122 prototype, a '53 at the GM Restoration Parts display and one in the National Corvette Re-storer Society (NCRS) gallery.

The original Corvette was a trendsetter; the first American car to have an "organic" design. The 49 cars, lined up like a chorus line, made an incredible sight, but the real fun was walking along the row of '53s and listening to the stories. Each car had a unique history.

Out of the midst of the hubbub of voices, we heard a lady bubbling with enthusiasm as she remembered, "We used to get all dressed up on Saturday night and go to dinner in the Corvette."

▷ Notice the vintage Paxton supercharger on this '53. What a masterpiece this car has become. Think of it. Paxton-McCullough did the work over 50 years ago.

▽ Pat Amendolia was one of the '53 Corvette owners at the 2003 show.

△ Annette Amendolia remembered the '53 'Vette as the couple's Saturday-night-go-to-dinner car.

◁ Not all of the 1953 Corvettes in existence have been restored to pristine condition. This one, previously owned by the Amendolias, will require a great deal of work to look like new again.

She stood with friends in front of one of the '53s that was obviously unrestored and not running. We told her we wanted to hear more. "Oh, I'll go get my husband," Annette Amendolia smiled. The lady was shy to think she could do the '53 justice. We did not want technical details. She had opened a door into the past and we wanted to look inside.

The year was 1961. Annette remembered that her two sons were "very, very small." The Vette was eight years old and a very big deal.

"Saturday nights we used to get all dressed up, get in our Corvette and drive it around. Sometimes we'd take the boys with us and people would say, 'That's not a family car. How can you stuff those two kids in that car?' And we'd say well, we're doing it, we're doing it. We're taking them out to dinner, too. It was a great car. We have a lot of pleasant memories with it."

Pat Amendolia was not your average car enthusiast. He was in the fiberglass business at the time he bought the Corvette. In 1952, he had actually built his own fiberglass body

△ **Here's an original chassis of the No. 30 Corvette of 1953. This car was in storage for many years and was this far along in the restoration when the 50th anniversary arrived.**

and installed it on a chassis made up from the frame rails of an Essex automobile. He fitted his car with a Chevrolet "Stovebolt Six" engine. Initially, the car was supposed to be a hot rod, with a '26 Chevy body.

Fascinated with fiberglass and full of the sports car mania that filled America after World War II, Pat says he went bananas and built a mock-up. He then built the fiberglass body.

The end result was a roadster. He ran that car in an SCCA road race. He still has video of it today.

Pat and Annette owned their '53 for 38 years. Four years

ago they sold their "baby." It was seen at Corvettes @ Carlisle 2003 in all of its unrestored glory. We think this '53 is a masterpiece just as it sat that day.

The buyer of the car was Alan Blay. He actually lives near Pat and Annette in New York. Blay is a virtual human encyclopedia of '53 Corvette history. He named owner's names and spouted individual car histories as we walked along the row of roadsters. When we asked him about the fascination of the '53, he gave us much more reason than its trendsetting use of fiberglass — the thing you seem to hear so much about.

▽ New Yorker Alan Blay is well versed in the history of the first Corvette and also knows the background behind many of the cars that survive today, including who owned them over the years.

△ 1953 Corvette No. 113, owned by Alan Blay, was the first Corvette sold in Massachusetts. There were four 1953 Corvettes sold in New England — No. 27, 113, 174 and 277. Blay told us, "We're doing a body-off-frame restoration and hopefully we'll go all the way to Duntov (a Duntov Award) on this car. I'm about seven years into the restoration already."

△ This '53 was radically customized in 1959. It's car No. 77. In the early 1990s, it was restored to its customized configuration.

Blay pointed out that the '53 Corvette had America's first "organic" American car design. In other words, its appearance resembles a living thing. The headlights are eyes, the grille is a mouth with teeth, the emblem looks like a nose. Many American cars after Corvette followed this theme, including the original Ford Thunderbird and the first Mustang of 1965. Prior to 1953, U.S. industrial designers working on cars followed the streamlined look of airplanes. Now, the original 1953-'55 Corvette is getting the respect it deserves. One of Blay's '53 Corvettes, No. 75, was on exhibit in the Brooklyn Museum of Art as part of an "organic forms" display.

Corvettes @ Carlisle set the record for the most 1953 Corvettes ever gathered in one place. According to Blay, even in 1953, there were no more than a dozen on the back lot at the factory in Flint, Michigan, at any one time. Only 14 cars were shown at the press party on September 28, 1953.

The Original 1953 Corvette

E ach one of the 300 Corvettes built in 1953 is special and a Corvette Masterpiece. Actually, in a way, each '53 is a show car. Master stylist Harley Earl and engineer Ed Cole were very excited by the Corvette Motorama show car. So, by the last day of June of that year, Chevrolet had set up a special assembly area to actually produce Corvettes in a little building next to the Chevy plant in Flint, Michigan. The mood was good. Earl and Cole thought that a sports car from Chevrolet would really catch on with the American public if the price could be kept low.

Chevrolet's original Corvette — the division's first sports car — was quite a contrast to the bulky-looking 1953 sedans

△ About 200 of the 300 Corvettes made in 1953 are known to still survive today. All of the first-year cars were finished in Polo White and trimmed with Sportsman Red interiors.

◁ The Corvette's rounded front fenders housed the recessed headlights with wire screen covers. The car had no side windows or outside door handles, but the wraparound windshield was modern.

△ **Below the Corvette's hood, the 235.5-cid "Blue Flame" six carried three carburetors and featured special valve covers and a one-piece carburetor linkage. It developed 150 hp at 4200 rpm.**

in the Chevy lineup. The Corvette had a novel fiberglass body resting on a unique chassis with a 102-inch wheelbase. It sure didn't look like a Chevy.

In truth, the first Corvette was Chevrolet's attempt to create an authentic sports car in the manner of the Jagaur and MG, which were so popular in America after World War II.

The new Corvette required a separate chassis. It had an exciting body that was a true roadster — it had snap-on side curtains and lacked roll-up windows. The uniqueness of the Corvette contributed to its hefty base price of $3,498.

The regular Chevys lent major mechanical componets to the Corvette. The engine was the factory's "Blue Flame" six. This venerable in-line six-cylinder engine was popularly known as the Stove Bolt Six. The Corvette version produced 150 hp from 235 cubic inches. It was backed up by a two-speed Powerglide automatic transmission.

Production totaled 300 of these "Corvette Masterpieces" that first year. The Corvette project seemed like more of an ambitious to project mass produce "show cars" than an attempt to build "assembly line" Chevrolets.

△ The 1953 Corvette's "dream car" image featured protruding, fender-integrated taillights that looked like rocket thrusters from TV personality Captain Video's spaceship.

◁ The Corvette interior featured round oil pressure, battery, water temperature and fuel gauges arranged horizontally across the instrument panel, plus a tachometer and clock.

Bob McDorman:
Legendary Corvette Collector

△   **Imagine owning 100 Corvettes! Chevy dealer Bob McDorman, of Columbus, Ohio, has over that many of the fiberglass-bodied sports cars in his 250-car collection. Here Bob poses with a few of his favorites.**

Andy Roderick, curator of the National Corvette Museum said, "You've got to go to Bob McDorman's." Bob is a Chevy dealer in Columbus, Ohio.

"Bob has over 250 cars in his collection," said Andy. "Over 100 of them are Corvettes. He is a major player in the hobby. He has one of the biggest shows in the country." Andy knows a thing or two about Corvettes, so I packed my cameras and caught a jet to Ohio to see the McDorman Car Show for myself.

Bob is in his 70s. He was driving a golf cart made up to look like a red '57 Chevy Bel Air with shiny chrome wheels. The morning of his car show we caught up to him when he stopped in his golf cart to eat a bratwurst. It was 9 a.m. Ob-

viously, Bob is not a vegetarian. After the introductions and niceties, Bob revealed his collecting philosophy in easy to understand terms. "I hate Fords!" he said.

McDorman was dead serious. Wearing a tie emblazoned with colorful C4 Corvettes contrasting with his white shirt, Bob opened his left hand and pointed at the backside of his fingers, one at a time. "I was going to have tattooed on these fingers, right here, H-A-T-E and have a Ford emblem right there."

Bob then opened his right hand. "On this hand I was going to tattoo L-O-V-E and a Chevy emblem. And every time I saw a Ford dealer, I was going to throw up my left hand, then throw up my Chevrolet hand to him."

◁ McDorman's show features mostly Corvettes, although even Fords are welcome.

The only thing that kept Bob from burning these tattoos was his wife Alice. He describes her as, "A great gal . . . an all-American gal."

Bob focused on his life and his work with cars. A far away look came over his eyes. He pointed to the back of his dealership lot and chattered, "That's me back in those buildings. Those old dealer signs are exactly what I believe in. I mean, I got over $1 million in the signs — the neon signs. A million dollars! I got enough in this car collection to buy six more dealerships. I wouldn't trade this collection for 10 more dealerships. I mean I just love, love the cars."

We had already eyeballed the immense "McDorman III" collection. (It is the third collection he's put together, so hence the name.) We spotted a '53 Oldsmobile Fiesta convertible, a '69 ZL1 Camaro, rows and rows of Camaro and 'Vette pace cars — all brand new: Novas, Monte Carlos, Cameo pickups, El Caminos and Corvairs. There were celebrity cars in one building, Burt Reynolds's 1960 'Vette, Ricky Van Shelton's '67 'Vette, George Strait's red-and-white '58 'Vette. There was one of every model year 'Vette in front of the dealership in two big circles.

We wondered if Bob had a favorite car or marquee? Clearly, Corvettes are a specialty. However, he likes anything GM.

Bob said, guys ask him, "'What's your favorite car?' I say, 'All of them.' I got a story to tell you about every car that's in here."

Bob wasn't always a collector. He didn't have the money to collect when he first started working as a parts manager in a Buick/Pontiac/Olds dealership in 1952. His dad was an International Harvester farm machinery dealer.

Bob made me laugh when he said of his dad, "I only made him cry twice in my life, when I got married and when I quit working for him. He told my mother, he says, uh, gosh, he's the only one in the family I always got along with 100 percent of the time. But you know why he got along with me? Whatever he said, I did. If he wanted me to paint the windows black, I went after black paint. I didn't question him."

McDorman is definitely old school. "Today's kids challenge you. And my kids did the same thing to me; they wanted to challenge me on everything. There's an old saying, he who pays has the say. And when a guy is paying the bill, he's entitled to have done whatever he wants, as long as he is honest and legitimate."

△ Chevrolet brings vehicles like this 1968 Astro II XP880 concept car to the show. This was the second in a series of experimental sport vehicles. It debuted at the 1968 New York International Auto Show and was warehoused until April 1993. Then its restoration began. The mid-engine car uses an L36 427. The body is fiberglass over a backbone frame.

te: Racing Around the Clock.
ng Around the World.

△ **Another Corvette Masterpiece** is this C5-R Chassis No. 02. It is one of two cars that marked the Corvette's return to racing. It last raced at LeMans in 2000. It was the first factory designed, built and financed Corvette racing car.

Bob became a Chevy dealer in 1963 at age 33. He bought 33 acres of land off Route 33 in Canal Winchester, Ohio, just southeast of Columbus. Since that day, he's had the ultimate dream job.

"This is my 37th year," Bob told me. "I'm as happy being a Chevrolet dealer today as I was the day I signed up. I just love the car business and I wouldn't trade it for anything in the world."

Corvettes are a large part of Bob's business. McDorman told me he had sold 150 brand new C5 Corvettes in the past 150 days. "We are really selling them. I bought five Corvettes out of Atlanta yesterday, brand new ones, from one of the biggest Chevrolet dealers in the country. Guess what? They'll be here this afternoon."

McDorman Chevrolet is a blending of the new and the old. It is a big, metropolitan dealership. Ninety people work at the business full time. Eight buildings on the back of the 33 acres are devoted to Bob's collection. He has 260 cars and over 200 signs and the collection is still growing.

Every September, Bob hosts his annual "Corvettes and Chevys at the Canal" show. It's his chance to pull out every car he owns and light up every sign in his collection for the weekend. He invites other enthusiasts and collectors to bring their cars, too. The show kicks off with a Friday night cruise-in and continues through Sunday with a Corvette auction, a Concours d'Elegance, a swap meet, live bands and more. Proceeds benefit the Children's Hospital in Columbus.

Bob is really the big attraction. He's a legendary figure in the Corvette hobby and he's one of us. But he's still Bob McDorman of course. For example, Bob purchased a neon sign at the Auburn, Indiana, auction and it said, "We service Fords and Chevrolets." His friends teased him about buying it, so Bob said, "When I'm done with it, I'll have a circle on the Ford side of that sign with a slash going through it before I ever put it up." What else would you expect a man with a collection of "Corvette Masterpieces" to say?

◁ **Bob McDorman** wasn't always a big-time car collector. He started out working in the parts department of a BOP dealership 55 years ago and worked his way up in the car business.

Celebrity Corvettes
From Bob McDorman's Collection

George Strait's 1958 Corvette Convertible: George Strait's dream Corvette was this '58. It is Signet Red with a white cover, red interior and a white soft top. The engine is the base 230-hp 283, backed by a four-speed manual transmission. The singer also enjoyed Chevrolet's Signal-Seeking Wonder Bar radio. Pressing a bar on the radio advanced the tuner to the next station with a good signal.

Johnny Carson's 1986 Corvette Coupe: There's really nothing special about this '86 Corvette coupe other than its celebrity heritage. An automatic transmission backs the 220-hp 350. This 'Vette is white with blue interior and has air and power windows. The famous talk show host drove this car to the studio each day.

Johnny's co-host Ed McMahon wrote in a September 2005 *Reader's Digest* article, "Devoid of visible ego, Johnny drove himself to the Burbank studio each day, carrying his lunch with him in a paper bag. It was probably the only time anyone ever brown-bagged it in a white Corvette."

Bob McDorman told us Carson pulled up in his white 'Vette only to find Leno already had his parking space. This was in the time frame Jay Leno was taking over the "Tonight Show."

Jim Gilmore's 1984 Corvette Coupe: The '84 Corvette was the hottest sports car in the world to own and drive. The name that pops out on this windshield is A.J. Foyt, the famous racing car driver. However — Jim Gilmore, A.J.'s car owner — actually held the title to this '84 coupe. It is orange with a tan leather interior and is powered by a 205-hp 350. It has automatic transmission, air conditioning, power windows, power door locks and 16-inch aluminum wheels.

Alan Jackson's 2002 Corvette Coupe: Bob McDorman got the chance to buy a Corvette and an El Camino from Alan Jackson's garage. With original Quicksilver paint and a red interior the car runs a 350 hp 5.7L LS1 V-8. It has automatic transmission and the Z51 Performance Package, polished aluminum wheels, fog lamps, the Head's Up display, memory package, and sport seats. The El Camino is a Mulsane Blue '71 model with white stripes and a white vinyl top. The stock bucket seats are Parchment vinyl.

Burt Reynolds' 1960 Corvette Convertible: Fans associate Burt Reynolds with the Pontiac Trans Am made popular in his "Smoky & The Bandit" movies. However, he's also a Corvette enthusiast. Bob McDorman owns Reynolds' Ermine White 1960 Corvette. The convertible has the auxiliary hardtop. Under the hood is a 230-hp 283 that's stock. Inside are black bucket seats, a Signal-Seeking Wonder Bar radio and a two-speed Powerglide transmission.

Dinah Shore's 1987 Corvette Coupe: In the early 1970s, Dinah Shore had a well-publicized romance with actor Burt Reynolds. Later, Dinah bought this '87 Corvette coupe. It's Bright Red with black interior and has a 230-hp 350 V-8, automatic, Bose stereo, power windows and the defogger package.

Dwight Yoakam's 1973 Corvette Convertible: Despite his hit Country & Western single, "Guitars, Cadillacs," Dwight Yoakum liked Corvettes. It's fitting for Bob McDorman to own this '73 that Yoakum owned, since Dwight graduated from high school in Columbus, Ohio, near Bob's dealership. That was in 1974. The 'Vette is a '73 model, red with white interior. The 350 is backed by a four-speed manual gearbox, but overall the car has luxury features including air conditioning, power steering, a tilt-telescopic steering wheel and power brakes.

John "Cougar" Mellencamp's 1956 Corvette: John Mellencamp's beautifully restored '56 'Vette is Aztec Copper with white covers and a beige interior and top. It has the 210-hp 265 V-8, Powerglide automatic transmission and power windows.

Mario Andretti's 1994 Corvette Convertible: A base 350-cid 300-hp LT1 was hot enough for one of the most famous racing drivers of all time. Mario Andretti did select a four-speed manual transmission and sport seats. The car is Torch Red with a black interior and top.

Miss America's 1993 40th Anniversary Corvette Convertible: Leanza Cornett was Florida's first Miss America. She won the title in 1993, the year Corvette turned 40. She drove this 40th Anniversary convertible. It is Ruby Red with a Ruby Red interior and a Ruby Red convertible top. It has the 40th Anniversary Package. The 300-hp 350-cid LT1 is backed by an automatic transmission. Inside are optional Sport seats.

Roy Orbison's 1966 Corvette Coupe: Roy Orbison's Corvette of choice was this '66 coupe done up in Mosport Green with a black interior. It has a 327-cid V-8, a four-speed manual transmission, power steering, air conditioning and tinted glass.

Ricky Van Shelton's 1967 Corvette: Ricky Van Shelton drove this '66 Corvette convertible. It's Sunfire Yellow with black interior. The car is powered by a 350-hp 327. Options include a vinyl-clad auxiliary hardtop, side pipes, a four-speed manual transmission and power steering.

Pugesek Motorsports Revolution Roadster is a Corvette Masterpiece

▷ **Pugesek Motorsports builds custom Corvettes like this Revolution Roadster, 'Vette rods, resto rods, street rods and muscle cars for drivers who want performance and show car styling combined with modern amenities.**

Sometimes, a specific make and model of automobile is so popular and so rare that the aftermarket simply makes one from the ground up. The originals just get so expensive and hard to find that the only alternative is to start from scratch.

The '53 Corvette was the inspiration for Pugesek Motorsport's "Revolution Roadster," which debuted in March of 2004.

Pugesek — a firm owned by the father and son team of Larry J. and Larry M. Pugesek — built this 'Vette rod from the ground up using mostly aftermarket and custom-fabricated components.

The company's Website (www.pugesekmotorsports.com) says the goal is to revolutionize the classic style of C1 (1953-'62) Corvettes. While honoring America's sports car, Pugesek updates the classic look with sophisticated style and show-quality details.

"What the classic Corvettes had in style they lacked in performance," says Pugesek. "We have engineered a technological makeover with the best of today's technology. Innovative engineering and top-of-the-line materials and parts make these custom Corvettes impressive to drive.

Custom engineering, hand fabrication and attention to every detail are reflected inside and out. Pugesek builds the cars in a 1,200 sq.-ft. shop in Sheridan, Illinois. The build quality is excellent. The seamless merging of old and new makes these cars revolutionary.

By all appearances, this Millennium Yellow roadster is a '53 Corvette. However, the custom chassis with a late-model drive train gives it an ultra-high-performance character quite different than that of an original '53 'Vette with a Blue Flame six.

In 2004, at VetteFest in Chicago, the Revolution Roadster scored 985 out of 1,000 points in judging. That's a "Corvette Masterpiece."

▷ Pugesek Motorsports' advertises that its quality is unmatched. The company strives for a seamless merging of the best of old and new to make its creations truly revolutionary.

▽ What classic Corvettes provided in style they lacked in performance. Pugesek engineers a technological makeover using the best of today's technology for comfort and performance. Innovative engineering and top-of-the-line materials make the cars impressive to drive.

FEATURES

Engine:	LT-1 V-8
Displacement:	350 cid
Horsepower:	350
Induction:	Electronic fuel injection
Features:	OBD II, high-performance oil cooler
Cooling:	Dual electric fans
Transmission:	4L60-E 4-speed automatic with high-performance trans cooler
Chassis:	2x4 box mild steel frame Adjustable aluminum coil over shocks
Suspension:	Tubular front suspension 4-link rear suspension with Panhard bar
Rear axle:	8.5-inch rear end with Positraction
Fuel system:	Aluminum fuel cell
Steering:	Rack and pinion power steering
Exhaust:	HPC coated headers Custom fabricated 2.25-inch stainless steel Borla stainless steel mufflers
Body:	Aftermarket 1953 Corvette Reinforced fiberglass Hand-fit and shaped panels
Paint:	Millennium Yellow urethane paint
Exterior trim:	Precision fit triple chrome plated trim
Interior:	Ultra rare soft top and side curtains
Brakes:	Power-assisted 4-wheel disc Cross-drilled and slotted rotors
Front wheels:	Custom Billet Specialties 17 x 7
Rear wheels:	Custom Billet Specialties 17 x 9.5
Front tires:	Pirelli P-Zero Corsa P215/45
Rear tires:	Pirelli P-Zero Corsa P255/40
Interior:	Hand-stitched leather interior
Steering:	A tilt steering column
Steering wheel:	Budnik billet steering wheel
HVAC system:	Complete climate control
Sound system:	Kenwood motorized CD player
Wipers:	Intermittent windshield wipers
Dash:	Custom-designed hand-fabricated dash

◁ Custom engineering, hand fabrication and attention to every detail make the Revolution Roadster a perfect alternative to a classic Corvette both inside and out.

Torch Red 1954 Resto-Mod 'Vette

△ **Vestris' Vettes builds custom Corvettes or Vettes-Rods or resto-rods for customers that are looking for that great retro look combined with today's technology.**

▷ **All of Vestris' Vettes' classic creations begin with real Corvettes built by GM in the '50s and '60s. This particular car is based on a '54 model.**

Some enthusiasts like the look of a 1950s or 1960s 'Vette, but they are disappointed in the performance. The solution is the "Resto-Mod," a car with a vintage body with the mechanicals upgraded to bring the "drivability" factor into the 21st century.

If you want the C1 (first-generation) 'Vette body style, it doesn't make sense to start a Resto-Mod project with a '53 or '55 Corvette. The first-year models are too rare and valuable and the '55 is rare, too. The '55 is a little less valuable than a '53, but still rare, since only 700 were built. In addition, the '55 offered the first V-8 in a 'Vette, which makes it desirable.

☐ Vestris promotes all of its cars as "turn key" creations so they come completely trimmed and equipped, including a T56 six-speed gearbox.

 The cars are fitted with fuel-injected 427-cid GM "crate" engines, which come with a full factory warranty.

△ The goal at Vestris' Vettes is to make a Corvette you can drive every day if you so desire. It will take you to work or the golf course and provide better performance, reliability and comfort than an original.

For these reasons, of the the three model years, the higher-production '54 'Vette gets picked on most by Resto-Mod builders.

John Vestri started a business to build Resto-Mods for other Corvette enthusiasts. Vestris Vettes is located in California. Vestri is now among the top builders turning out early 'Vettes with better handling and more power.

John found our featured car — a '54 — in San Diego. It had no engine or transmission. His company did a total rebuild from the ground up. They started by removing the fiberglass body from the chassis.

The character of the build was set with a General Motors LS6 "crate engine." This 427-cid V-8 comes with a complete warranty. It is backed by a GM T56 six-speed manual transmission.

Power is no good if you can't get it to the ground with a great suspension. Another big leap into modern times is the Jim Meyer Racing coil-over suspensions used in the front and rear. Additional features like rack-and-pinion steering and four-wheel disc brakes make this '54 a fun-to-drive Resto-Mod.

It's elements like these that make this hybrid Resto-Mod a "Corvette Masterpiece."

△ Company founder John Vestri.

◁ Vestri cleaned up the classic styling just a little bit.

◁ The Vestri Vette uses coil-over front and rear suspensions that give it a low-to-the-ground look. Tires and wheels are upgraded to provide more modern performance.

Buried Treasure:
An Unrestored Find from 1954

▷ The 235.5-cid inline six-cylinder engine still sports the original induction setup with three Carter Type YH one-barrel carburetors. Remnants of original paint hint at the factory colors used in 1954, but age has had an effect on the actual hues.

△ This weathered hood badge indicates that time hasn't treated the car overly gently, but it certainly has a patina to it.

Most of the time, magazines and books run pictures of *perfect* Corvettes that are all restored and look pristine and new. However, if you go to a car show, you'll see people gathering around "barn finds." These are cars that were stored away for years (not necessarily in a barn, however) and preserved in original condition.

The most coveted barn finds are complete and not modified. Finding one gives the enthusiast a thrill similar to finding buried treasure.

This original Pennant Blue 1954 roadster (one of 300 built

in this color) sat in a heated garage from 1970 to 2002. Its body had suffered damage in a 1955 car wreck and it was damaged again in 1958. Both times, owner Richard Hathaway fixed the fiberglass. So the car remained a pretty much complete, one-owner vehicle.

Hathaway bought the '54 'Vette brand new from a Chevrolet dealer in Bowling Green, Ohio. At the time, Chevrolet did not offer an auxiliary hardtop, but aftermarket suppliers did. Hathaway got one from a company in California and added it to his car in 1955.

△ Amazingly, the delicate screens designed to protect the headlight lens from flying stones have survived.

◁ The auxiliary hardtop affixed to the 'Vette is a period aftermarket item that the car's first owner obtained from a company in California. It was installed on this '54 when the car was a year old.

◁ As the Michigan tags behind the "funky" Plexiglass license plate holder attest, the car is road ready and sees regular use in weekend-driving and car-show visits despite its never-restored condition. Most of the wear and tear took place early in the car's existence. From 1970 until 2002 it was kept in a heated garage.

Vic Lucarelli, an upholsterer in Lamberville, Michigan, restored Corvettes as a hobby. In 1990, he finished a '57 'Vette and was looking for another project. However, it wasn't until October 2002 that he got the chance to buy this one-owner 'Vette.

Several Corvette judges have advised Lucarelli to keep this '54 in unrestored condition. Vic is having fun driving this original 'Vette and taking it to car shows on weekends. He still has his '57 for when he wants to show a restored car, but the never-restored '54 is a "Corvette Masterpiece" that really draws a crowd.

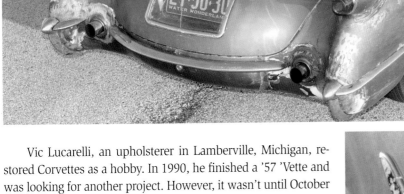

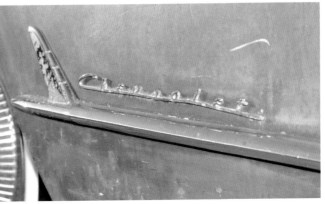

◁ Corvette experts have suggested to owner Vic Lucarelli that the car should be maintained "as is" to preserve the patina that a restoration would destroy.

Wayne Davis' 1954 Rodded Roadster

△ **Resto-Mod builder Wayne Davis liked the ground-hugging "step-aside" look of the '54 Corvette's fish-mouth grille, but decided to clean it up by removing the license plate fixture and other tinsel.**

Wayne Davis built his '54 'Vette to a "Resto-Mod" theme. The engine is a vintage 1968 'Vette 327 pumped up with a pair of Edelbrock 600s. Wayne even chose a stock dual-point distributor from a '68 'Vette. Dual quad carburetors give the car a muscle car feeling.

Wayne made a few subtle changes to the stock body. He likes the aggressiveness of the low, open-mounted grille, but he felt that the front end looked cleaner without the license plate surround and bumper guards on either side.

Wayne made one subtle modification to the exterior that is difficult to spot. The stock C1 'Vette is very plain and flat. Wayne added a 1957 hood, which incorporates a pair of raised bumps running lengthwise front to rear. They add a muscular look and were nicely integrated with the corresponding bumps on top of the dash.

Upholsterer Joe Romero covered the stock seats and door panels with red Connolly leather and covered the floors with Wilton wool carpet from Mercedes-Benz.

◁ Pirated from a 1968 Corvette, the small-block 327-cube V-8 carries a set of Edelbrock 600 carburetors that make the car a bit more muscular than a stock '54 roadster.

▽ The lowness of the stock-style body, the fat tires and the modified look of the exhaust runners definitely leave following cars with the impression that the car in front of them is no antique.

△ Trimmer Joe Romero did the stock seats and interior door skins up in Rolls-like red Connolly leather and covered the floor with Mercedes-style Wilton wool carpets. A '57 'Vette donated the 3-spoke steering wheel with punched-out spokes.

The steering wheel is from a '57 'Vette. The stock '54 wheel was a Chevrolet sedan item with a Corvette logo. On very close inspection, you will also recognize the "Davis" logo on the gauge faces, a job Wayne farmed out to Carriage Works in Grand View, Missouri.

In the "Dark Ages" of 1954, a four-speed manual was still three and a half years away from the Corvette option sheet. Wayne moved all the way up to model-year 1968 for the Corvette four-speed manual transmission and shifter that he used in his '54 Resto-Mod.

Aesthetics was important on this car and a silver-and-red color theme prevails. Kirk Cunningham — at Carriage Works — built the custom air cleaner and also finished it in the silver-and-red combination. Allen head screws secure the top of the air cleaner from the bottom side, so that the fasteners are hidden away for a clean look.

Color was a big deal for Wayne. He liked silver because he felt it has the look of polished steel and emphasizes the car's total mechanical renewal from the chassis up. However, silver was unavailable in 1954, so Wayne had to update the paint, too.

△ Center Line Wheel Corporation, of Santa Fe Springs, California custom-created the 5-spoke wheels on this Resto-Mod and it actually took eight wheels to build four of them. This was a necessity, since car owner Wayne Davis could not find readily-available rims that fit inside the Corvette's wheel wells. To get the offset just right, Center Line's Bob Devore decided to combine two sets of wheels. It was an expensive, but distinctive way to go to achieve the desired result.

The most exotic changes were made to the car's frame, which was modified at both ends to accept Corvette C4 underpinnings. The red-painted 1954 frame's X-member is easy to recognize. Wayne powder coated the aluminum C5 components an Inca Silver color to make them pop out against the red 1954 frame.

Cutting the half shafts on the rear end to fit under the fender wells was the biggest job. The half shafts are also modified to lie over the top of the A-frames. No off-the-shelf wheels fit inside the stock wells. Bob Devore, at Center Line, made four wheels from eight to get the offset right.

The brake master cylinder on Wayne's 'Vette is a work of art. Cunningham cut back a GM dual reservoir master cylinder to fit in the stock location in the 1954 engine bay. In keeping with theme of Wayne's desire for simplicity, there is no computer to engage the C4's ABS braking system, which is not used on this Resto-Mod anyway. Carriage Works also stamped the top of the master cylinder with the Davis logo.

Neither a C4 radiator fan nor a C4 steering system will fit under the hood. Wayne hooked up an electric fan to the Bee Cool radiator and chose a Sweet Manufacturing rack-and-pinion steering system designed for sprint cars.

The result of all these modifications is a C4-quality '54 roadster that represents a hybrid. It has classic looks with the amenities and detailing of a high-tech street rod. What a "Corvette Masterpiece!"

☐ The underside of the car is very "sano" looking and as detailed as a World of Wheels champion street rod. Note the C4 X-member and the modified half shafts that form the rear suspension.

1954 Stock Corvette:
This is the Way it Really Was

△ Jerry Palmer's body-on-frame-restored Polo White 1954 Corvette is like a jewel that reflects the art of automotive rejuvenation. The car was refurbished to be exactly the way it was when it was new. This car originally belonged to a local California politician.

For owners of original cars, having a car with blazing speed is considered secondary to historical preservation. Part of the joy of owning a vintage Corvette in stock condition is sampling the car's original-type ride.

Cranking the starter on a six-cylinder Corvette can be a draining experience for the original six-volt battery. Unless the sidedraft Carter YH carburetors are tuned just right and the choke is first closed tight, the car may balk at starting.

Jerry Palmer knows the early Corvette 235-cid six inside and out. He rebuilt the engine in his '54 'Vette to concours specifications, right down to the correct "Three-Dot" 155-hp camshaft. "Once you get the carburetors set right, with the chokes all the way closed, the 235 will start right up when you pull on the starter knob," he says.

If collectors and enthusiasts have trouble igniting the Blue Flame six in their lovingly-restored 'Vettes, imagine the frustrating times that the VIP buyers of early 'Vettes had, in the

mid-'50s, when driving these cars! Maybe we've made too much of the horsepower advantage the V-8 gave the Corvette after 1955. Maybe the V-8's advantage had more to do with making the cars easier to start.

Jerry Palmer has put 15,000 miles on his restored '54 'Vette and he told us that the 235-cid six has enough horsepower to spin the tires on the lightweight rear end. The car is fun to drive. It looks elegant. It must have stood out like no other American car on the road in 1953-1955.

Even today, the one and only true Corvette roadster stands out like no other car on the road and no other Corvette. I've thought for years that the shape of the fabric top resembles that of an Auburn Speedster of the Classic era. Opening the hood is a chrome show like no other.

Jerry Palmer was a Navy pilot. He flew single-seat fighter planes when he bought his '54 'Vette 10 years ago. Needless

to say, he appreciates speed and the important role speed plays in winged transportation. Throughout automotive history, airplane pilots have tended to gravitate towards sports cars. Palmer had actually been after his '54 for a decade. Then, he finally bought it and the love affair with the Polo White 'Vette really started. Now, the "relationship" is more than 20 years old.

Palmer remembers his friends in flight school buying brand new '65 Corvettes, but he couldn't afford one while he was in training. His high school ride had been a '55 Chevy Nomad wagon. That car was followed by a '57 Chevy two-door hardtop that he drove while he was learning to fly.

The '54 'Vette sat near his father's summer house in Oxnard, California. That's where the former Mayor of Pasadena had parked it outside, with no protective cover. Since it was just sitting, Jerry figured he could buy the Corvette, but the owner said he'd never sell the car. Fortunately, the politician

△ A new style of valve cover was used on the 1954 Corvette engine. It was held on by four bolts that went through the outside lip, instead of two center studs. The valve cover decals were different and decorated with larger lettering.

△ The Corvette used a full-size Chevrolet steering wheel with a Corvette horn button insert. A full array of gauges and controls were laid out horizontally across the stylish-looking dashboard. An unusual bent-to-the-side gear shift stalk controlled the two-speed Powerglide automatic transmission.

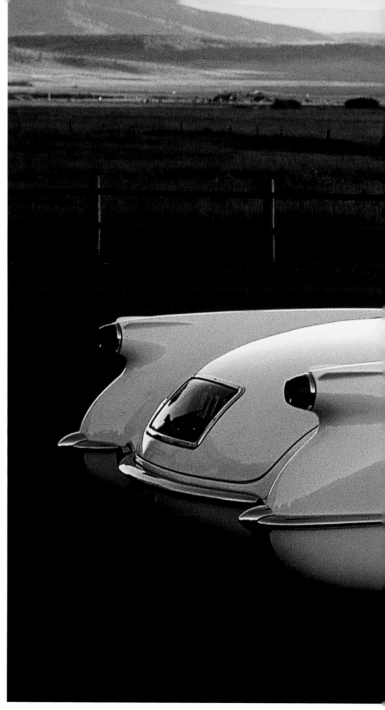

reversed his ownership oath, although he did keep his "campaign promise" to give Jerry — the pilot, who had flown many combat missions over Vietnam — the first right of refusal.

This time, Palmer had the money to buy his first Corvette, but he didn't think he'd ever restore it. The '54 was simply a neat little car to sport about town in. It cleaned up pretty nice.

Jerry shudders when he thinks of the time he gave away the original fuel pump because it wasn't working. Overall, the car was amazingly clean and original. The one modification made to it was the three-speed manual transmission — a common swap with the original two-speed Powerglide automatic.

After a few years of fun driving, Jerry started reading car magazines. After repainting his '54 and fixing up a few things here and there, restoration fever set in. Jerry joined the National Corvette Restorers Society (NCRS) and his '54 'Vette underwent a body-on-frame restoration.

In Jerry's words, "It's a 99-point NCRS-rated car, but I have never taken the body off the frame. The underside was nice and clean and I just didn't want to take the body off if I didn't have to. Instead, I laid on my back, underneath the car, and painted the frame and restored the undercarriage. So, I guess it's fair to call such work a body-on restoration."

When the car is judged in shows, Jerry loses points for using reproduction tires. He also doesn't have the original soft top. The battery in the car is not exactly original. So Jerry's '54 gets a point off here and there, but it is still one of the finest restored 1954s in existence. It has won the Duntov Award.

Attention to detail by a super enthusiast is what makes this car so great. Jerry also credits his achievements to the fact that he had a great starting point, his '54 was essentially a one-owner car when he bought it.

The Mayor of Pasadena purchased the car off the dealer's lot the first day it was offered. He owned it until Jerry managed to deal for the car over 20 years ago. The Mayor had it for only one year. (The rumor is that he traded the car in on a '55 V-8 Chevy the first time the skies over Los Angeles opened up and rained on the fiberglass body).

The Blue Flame six racked up about 60,000 miles that first year, so it wasn't all worn out. Then, Jerry added another 15,000 to the odometer before he began restoring the car.

The camshaft needed replacement. The fuel pump eccentric and the number one cylinder lobe were "history." Jerry found a shop in Fresno run by an older gentleman who said, "Young man, if it's a cam you need, I can help you."

To make a long story short, instead of regrinding the cam, the man unexpectedly pulled an identical New Old Stock (NOS) '54 Corvette camshaft off the shelf and sold it to Jerry for the bargain price of $35. This sale took place just a couple years ago and the man knew both the original and replacement camshafts were of the rare Three-Dot type.

What's that mean? The Three-Dot cam differed from the type used early in 1954 production. The later Three-Dot design upped horsepower from 150 to 155. Physically, it can be identified by three dots stamped between the No. 5 and No. 6 inlet cam lobes.

Jerry has been consulting with Corvette restoration guru Noland Adams for the past few years. Adams believes that Palmer's '54 — built in April of 1954 — is the earliest documented Blue Flame six with a Three-Dot camshaft.

Of course, it takes a true Blue Flame six enthusiast to get excited about having the correct part number on an internal engine part that an NCRS judge can't even see. Jerry Palmer fits the bill and his gorgeous '54 roadster shows it. The car is a genuine "Corvette Masterpiece."

△ Jerry Palmer's car falls into the 99-percent-perfect category in strict National Corvette Restorers Society (NCRS) judging. In the early 1950s, the Corvette was a popular car among airplane pilots and Jerry Palmer seems to be upholding tradition with his ownership of this car.

Polo White 1954 Corvette EX-87

△ "Zowie, Batman!" It's amazing how much a "little" dorsal fin alters the looks of the C1 Corvette. This fascinating experimental version of the sporty Chevy is the work of an absolutely fascinating man — Zora Arkus-Duntov. He was the first Corvette chief engineer and had a tremendous influence on the machine.

Zora Arkus-Duntov was hired as a Chevrolet assistant staff engineer on May 1, 1953. Zora was greatly saddened when he learned, in the fall of 1954, that the Corvette was no longer going to be built.

With thousands of Corvettes unsold at the end of the '54 model year, cancellation of the model appeared imminent. Zora wrote a memo to Ed Cole and Maurice Olley, asking to continue production of the Corvette. He told the two executives that drop-ping the Corvette would have an adverse effect on Chevrolet's reputation. It would be like an admission of failure, especially since the new 1955 Ford Thunderbird was selling well.

"With the aggressiveness of Ford publicity, they may turn the fact to their advantage," Zora warned. Eventually, Chevrolet reversed its decision to drop the Corvette and went full speed ahead to make a new overhead-valve V-8 standard equipment.

One hundred sixty-three miles per hour is the amazing speed this streamlined 'Vette hit at the General Motors Proving Ground, in Mesa, Arizona, in December of 1955.

EX-87/ 5951/ # 399
"ZORA DUNTOV'S
MULE TEST
CORVETTE"

▷ EX-87 was fabricated starting in October 1955 and the all-new small-block Chevy V-8 was available to stuff under its hood. Chevy engineers started with a 265-cid engine and bored it out to 307 cubic inches. With its special "Duntov" cam, the car produced 275 hp.

▽ A huge tachometer was attached to the steering column to help the driver monitor engine revs at high speeds.

▷ EX-87 looks best when it's photographed in action with Dave Landenburg at the wheel.

In October of 1955, engineers started building EX-87. They modified one of the many unsold six-cylinder '54 'Vettes to accept V-8 power. They pulled the six and replaced it with the new-for-1955 small-block V-8. This 265-cid engine was bored and stroked to 307 cid. With a special "Duntov" cam grind, peak horsepower was upped to 275.

Zora had wanted to take the car to Daytona Speed Weeks and drive it at least 150 mph on the sands at Daytona. He streamlined the body with a fiberglass tonneau that covered the passenger compartment. The large stock windshield was replaced with a small driver's side windshield. Zora also installed a headrest with a fin. Then, he replaced the two-speed Powerglide automatic with a three-speed manual transmission.

In November of 1955, EX-87 was moved to Chevrolet Engineering where it was assigned tracking number 5951. This number is visible today on a plate under the hood.

In December of 1955, Chevrolet took EX-87 to the General Motors Proving Ground in Mesa, Arizona. Duntov figured he could go 160 mph on the pavement in Arizona. EX-87 did even better — it hit 163 mph.

Weather foiled the high-speed runs on the beach near Daytona in December 1955. When Duntov returned the following month, he drove a 1956 Corvette prototype with a 307-cid V-8 and a three-speed gearbox to a new record of 150.58 mph (two-way average) in the Flying Mile. He also broke the Standing Mile record at 91.69 mph.

These feats helped revive Chevrolet's "Corvette Masterpiece." In December 1955, Ed Cole announced that Chevrolet would give factory support to a private team of Corvettes at the Sebring 12-hour race in March.

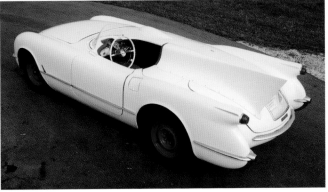

△ Vroooom! No delicate, screen-type headlight covers for this curve-straightening competition-style roadster. The smooth, sleek lens protectors aren't for looks.

◁ The racing-style windscreen, cockpit tonneau and extra tail fin contributed to the car's track manners and performance.

△ How would you like to be an automotive photographer? Then you could do "kamikaze" shoots of cars like the EX-87 — a true piece of American automotive history.

Kamikaze Shoot

One of the biggest problems photographing cars is location, especially for action. Another is getting historic cars out of storage, fired up and ready to and run on public roads. I needed EX-87 (a 1954 Corvette factory dream car) taken out for a photo shoot and it was buried in a storage building at Bob McDorman Chevrolet in Canal Winchester, Ohio.

I took the car's caretaker, Dave Landenburg, aside and asked for help. I was a little frustrated and told him, "People think that all a photographer has to do is show up and take pictures, but I need a mechanic who can get this car fired up and running or the picture just isn't going to happen."

Dave understood my dilemma. "Oh, you mean it's like when somebody brings their car into the dealership to get it fixed and they think that just because I'm the service manager, I can just twinkle my nose and their car will be ready in a few minutes?"

"Yes!" I screamed.

"O.K., well wait right here," Dave said.

In a matter of 10 minutes, there were a half dozen service people walking to the buildings behind Bob McDorman Chevrolet. They pushed cars out of the way and got EX-87 out into the light. Then they fired it up. The V-8 made a raucous sound. It was loud. The solid lifters were clattering. EX-87 is a *man's* ride.

"Can you drive it?" I asked Dave Landenburg.

Dave didn't even answer. He just asked me where I wanted it. I motored out on the tree-lined back roads of rural Canal Winchester.

To get "action" photos, I use a gyro that I screw into the bottom of my Nikon camera's body. I plug the gyro into a dry cell battery that I wrap around my neck or into a car's cigarette lighter socket. After five minutes, the gyro is up to 22,000 rpm. It feels like it's making its own gravity.

The function of the gyro is to stabilize the camera for slow shutter speeds. I can't use a tripod, because by that time I'll be

hanging from the "camera car" shooting the vintage Corvette that's off to our side or behind us.

This time, I wedged myself inside the trunk of my Chevy Cavalier rental car and held up the trunk lid with the size 14 boot on my left foot.

I figured that Corvettes — even dream car Corvettes — are *real* sports cars made to run high speeds. Since I didn't have a racetrack, I decided to use a winding country road. The trees by the side of the road showed good motion with a shutter speed of under 1/30th of a second.

My driver was one of the retired men who shuttle cars for McDorman Chevrolet. He did a good job staying ahead of EX-87. All we needed was a speed of 40 mph, which was the legal limit along some of the stretches we were driving on. In other spots, the limit was 55 mph.

I got some good shots with my camera and we pulled off the road. At this point, I jumped out of the trunk and into the front seat for the trip back to the dealership.

I got my shot, but it took a whole lot more than twinkling my nose.

Later, we took more static photography at the dealership, including shots from on top of a ladder that allowed me to show the car's special features. These included the fin behind the driver and the tonneau cover over the passenger compartment.

This type of picture taking is what automotive photographers call a "kamikaze" shoot.

I might have been a little more nervous shooting the '54 had I known its history. EX-87 played a major role in the revival of the Corvette.

It's a humbling experience to see a historic car in person and then photograph it. My thanks go out to Bob McDorman, who approved the shoot, Dave Landenburg and Nathan Sheets, who directed the shoot.

Full Service 'Vette Collection

▷ Lit-up Corvette and Socony Mobil Vacuum neon signs illuminate the Thomas' Corvette collection, but the overriding theme of the place is Texaco.

△ Doyle and his wife Karen sit in circa-1950 metal chairs near the pump islands outside the door of the service station office. The atmosphere is so relaxing that it's easy to drift back to happier days. Doyle's Fire-Chief gas pump is set on 22.9 cents per gallon.

Doyle Thomas actually built a replica of a Texaco service station to display his Corvettes in. It is located on some wooded acreage next to his house in Longview, Texas. His "private museum" is part of a trend towards collecting petroliana that's happening among car collectors across America.

People driving by stop and look through the black wrought iron gates. It's easy to see why. Doyle's classic-looking "gas station" is quite a sight.

"It's constructed of metal with pumps and islands out front," says Doyle. "The stripes on the front of the building are real; they were purchased off a real Texaco station. The trademark Texaco stars I bought at a swap meet were new in the box."

Doyle still has that box, which Texaco used to ship the bright red, 5-pointed stars to a dealer in Tennessee. He placed one star over each service bay door as a nostalgic reminder of the dedicated service station operators who worked for the Texas Company years ago. They wore uniforms with starched shirts, matching pants and captain's hats. They were ready to check a customer's oil, fix flats, sell batteries or install a set of tires. They even gave away dishes after a prescribed number of fill-ups.

At "Doyle's Texaco," the front room behind the pump island is an office with a desk, a phone and memorabilia galore. There's a functional service bay with a hydraulic lift that's great for minor repairs. The middle service door leads to a cavernous 60 x 100 metal building best described as a wonderland of classic 'Vettes and memorabilia.

We figured that Doyle Thomas built his Texaco station for car storage, then added the gas station memorabilia to help showcase the cars. Actually, the reverse is true.

"I grew up with five cousins — all girls," Thomas explained. "My uncle wouldn't let them go anywhere on the weekend unless I went with them. I saw them having fun running around in the 'American Graffiti' years. So I got hooked at an early age — collecting . . . saving things like microphones or pictures . . . buttons . . . glasses . . . radios . . . just anything old."

Thomas was born in 1950. He recalls that his uncle bought a new Corvette hardtop in 1963. Everywhere they went, the split-window coupe created a sensation. That got him "hooked" on Corvettes. He got his first 'Vette "right out of high school."

It wasn't Doyle's original intention to collect Corvettes. "I'd just buy them one at a time, get them paid for and find me another one. I'd hang onto everything."

"Doyle's Texaco" doubles as a hot rod and rock 'n roll-style diner venue for parties and get-togethers. A bar, a couple of booths and some tables and chairs sit near the front of the "filling station." You can play pinball or punch in "My Blue Heaven" (a vintage Fats Domino song) on an old jukebox. Of course, you can also mill about among the 'Vettes and talk cars. While you're conversing, there's enough memorabilia to keep your eyes busy for days.

We noticed Corvette Grand Sport body parts on a wall. Doyle launched into an explanation of the "two front flares and hood." A man named Chuck — a full-time employee who

△ Doyle's Texaco looks like a place that Buzz and Tod might have stopped while touring across the country on the Route 66 television series. But all of the cars seen here actually belong to Doyle and Karen Thomas.

▷ A 35th anniversary Corvette in front of part of the mural.

▽ Most of the cars in Doyle's collection are 'Vettes, but he has almost as many street rods and customs. He has a "1955 Nomad" that is really a 1990 Corvette.

△ Seen from another angle, the '57 'Vette is backdropped by another wall of memorabilia.

works on Doyle's cars — explained that they came from Dana Mecum's Grand Sport vintage racing car. Doyle bought them from a mechanic who wrenched on Mecum's racing team. He stored the exotic 'Vette panels in his attic for over 25 years.

Every car has a tale to tell. Doyle's favorite is the '63 split-window coupe. It is black with a red interior and has only 21,000 miles. And it isn't the only low-mileage car in the collection. There's also a '57 'Vette with 10,000 original miles. Finished in red with a white cove, the convertible made a stunning sight parked in front of a movie theater recreation. "Now Showing, American Graffiti," says the marquee. The coming attractions are Walt Disney's "Old Yeller" and "The Seven Year Itch" starring Marilyn Monroe and Tom Ewell.

Doyle Thomas is very interested in the history of his Corvettes. He has a '67 that's a 390-horse roadster. Doyle has records of all six owners of the car. They all lived around St. Louis, Missouri. Then, he brought the car to Texas.

Another low-mileage example is an '82 Collector's Edition. Doyle bought this one when it was six months old. He says he drove it "sparingly" for about six months. When it had only 3,100 miles on the odometer, he just "set it up" because it was so nice and he liked it.

A '73 'Vette is the one Doyle has owned the longest. He's had it since 1975. Then there's the Polo White '54, which is a numbers-matching, three-owner car. The '55 was a project car. Chuck earned his college money putting it together.

A mural painted across two intersecting walls is the work of Pat Anderson, of Roanoke, Texas. "Mel's Diner" is the central theme. "I've always been infatuated with Mel's," Doyle explained, referring to the diner made famous on the old "Happy Days" television show.

Other elements of the mural include a picture of Marilyn Monroe talking in a telephone booth behind the Texaco station. There's a Route 66 drive-in restaurant and lots more stuff to see.

"It makes it fun," says Thomas. "You can enjoy a collector car more when you've got it displayed nicely with memorabilia all around it. It just all ties together." What better way can you think of to show off a "Corvette Masterpiece?"

Cascade Green '56 Dual Quad

The most striking feature of Dick Mills' 1956 Corvette is, without a doubt, the color. It's a 265-cid 225-hp dual four barrel and has literally every checkable option for a '56 Corvette, except for a high-lift cam (not offered with Powerglide automatic transmission) and power windows (which were hydraulically-operated in 1956). Its Cascade Green color is what makes this convertible with a power-operated folding top stand out in a crowd of solid-rear-axle (called "straight-axle") Corvettes.

Strangely enough, Cascade Green — though considered desirable now — was the least popular color in 1956. Back

△ Cascade Green was not a popular color for Corvettes back in 1956. This makes cars painted in the very '50-ish hue rarer and more desired today.

◁ Although the distinctive color gives the 'Vette a "Boulevard Cruiser" appearance, the dual-quad V-8 up front makes it a performer.

△ Two optional 265-cid V-8s were offered in 1956. The "Turbo-Fire" 225 featured solid valve lifters, two Carter four-barrel carbs and dual-exhausts. It was good for 225 hp at 5200 rpm. The Turbo-Fire 240 option added a high-lift camshaft to get up to 240 hp. A close-ratio three-speed manual all-synchromesh transmission with floor-mounted gear shifter was standard equipment. The two-speed Powerglide automatic transmission was a $175 option.

then, Venetian Red (used on 1,043 cars) was the favorite. It was followed by Onyx Black (810 cars), Polo White (532 cars), Aztec Copper (402 cars), Arctic Blue (390 cars) and Cascade Green (290 cars). Of the Cascade Green cars, exactly 147 had the optional two-tone paint combination option that featured a Shoreline Beige cove. Mills' car is one of them.

When Dick found his '56 Corvette, he didn't even know the original color. After all, he was not looking for a car of a certain color. He had owned a '54, a '60 and a '62 and the next Corvette he wanted was a 1956-1957 model with the single headlights and clean styling lines.

Treasure hunting turned up a real "Duesie" of a Corvette — a '56 that had been in storage for 18 years and hadn't been started in 16 years. The '56 was Dick's "ticket" to a full restoration job. He had owned a total of six Corvettes and still hadn't done his first body-off-frame, concours-type restoration.

While stripping the Metallic Blue body finish, Dick realized that the car had been re-painted. He was elated when he uncovered the original paint. It was a striking color and certainly didn't match the customized interior.

The interior had a typical early 1960s cosmetic "do-over," with incorrect black-pleated seat covers, a painted black dash and black carpeting. (A beige interior would have been the standard stock interior for a Cascade Green '56 'Vette).

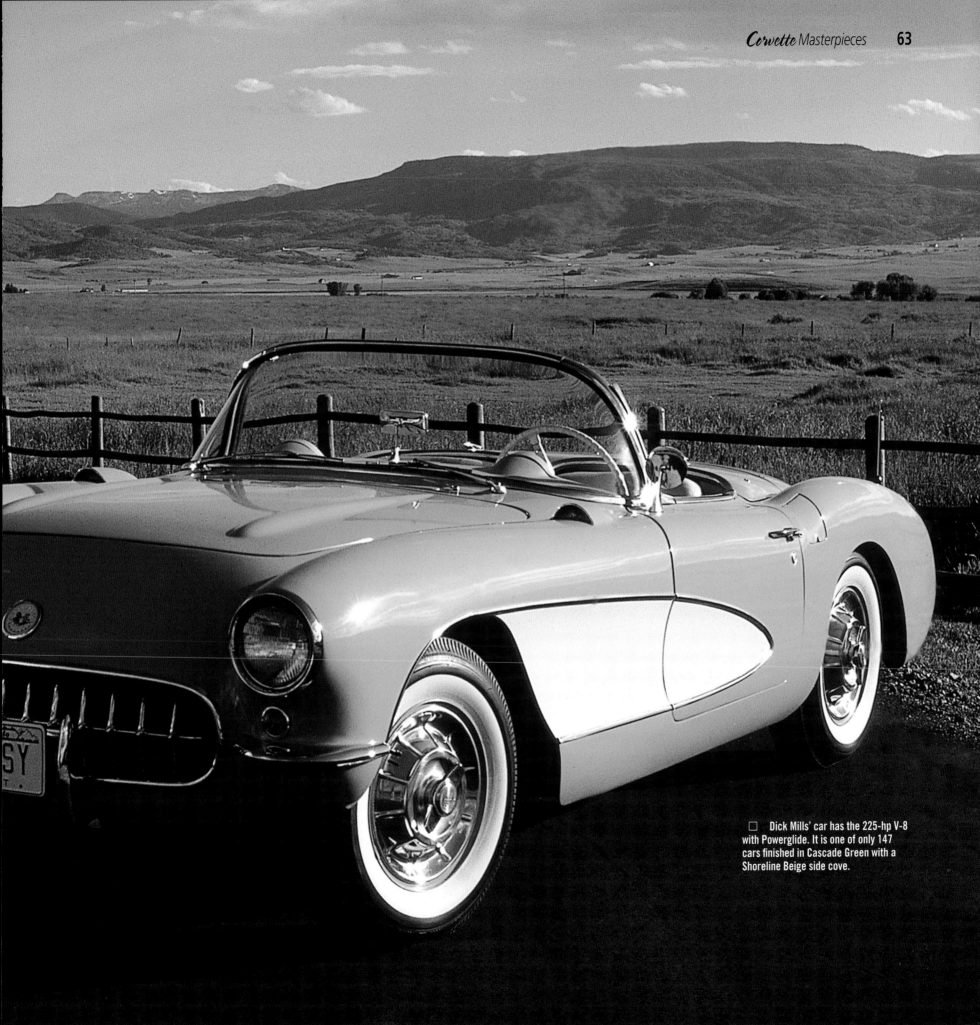

☐ Dick Mills' car has the 225-hp V-8 with Powerglide. It is one of only 147 cars finished in Cascade Green with a Shoreline Beige side cove.

▷ The dashboard layout was themed the same as in 1953-1955 models. A new rearview mirror, located at the center of the top of the dash, was adjusted by using a thumbscrew.

▽ The Corvette hit its stride as America's "real McCoy" sports car in 1956.

▽ New Mercedes-inspired forward-thrusting front fenders housed the uncovered chrome-rimmed headlights.

Except for these cosmetic mismatches, Dick's classic 'Vette was complete and original down to its stock engine block and cylinder heads. It had its original dual four-barrel Carter carburetors, factory air cleaners, Delco generator, factory-installed 3.55:1 axle and literally every little part and piece it left the assembly line with. Even the 1956 windshield-washer bag was still intact under the hood.

The signal-seeking radio has a "Wonder Bar" inscription that is generally considered a new-for-1957 detail. It takes an expert to know that very-late-production '56 'Vettes could be ordered with an optional radio bearing the Wonder Bar script. Dick's '56 was built on September 14, 1956, about two weeks before 1957 model-year production began on October 1st. Dick suspects his car probably shares other erudite details with '57 models.

Dick did about 25 percent of the painting and body work on the car, plus a great deal of the mechanical restoration. His cousin Ron Straut gets credit for the other 75 percent of the ground-up restoration. He even dip-finished the frame and suspension pieces so that the undercarriage matches the beauty, if not the spectacular paint color, of the top side of the car.

Although this '56 'Vette was displayed on the show grounds of the National Corvette Restorers Society (NCRS) national convention in Steamboat Springs, Colorado, it was not eligible for concours judging because it hadn't competed in a regional NCRS show. Dick lives in Steamboat Springs and drove the car out for display. It was one of the favorite vehicles in a field of nice Corvettes.

Cascade Green is a popular color today. "You wouldn't believe how many people at car shows say my '56 is the prettiest 'Corvette Masterpiece' in the whole show," he beamed.

1956 Corvette LS1 Resto-Mod

△ **A former Corvette designer picked this Resto-Mod 'Vette for an award.**

I n our automotive love affairs, the bond between man and machine is intimate. It's more so when the car in question is a Corvette and even more so when a man resurrects a 'Vette from ashes.

We photographed Larry Cleveland's '56 one afternoon and never really stripped away the layers of intimacy. Later, we "visited" Larry on the phone for more details. In the end the walls came down.

We figured former C4 Corvette designer Jerry Palmer had a secret reason he liked Cleveland's '56 Corvette. Of all the cars at a big Labor Day weekend show at the National Cor-vette Museum, he had picked this '56 for his "celebrity choice" award. We first saw the car parked on the grounds, with people milling around it. Then Palmer walked up and engaged Larry Cleveland — and his wife Sandy — in conversation.

"I'm Jerry Palmer," the designer said, enthusiastically, while extending his hand in greeting. Cleveland was flabber-gasted. After talking for five minutes, Larry and Jerry sat in the car, smiling. They looked like two kids in a new Christmas toy getting ready to take a ride. Larry was the proud "parent" sitting behind the small, grippy, non-stock steering wheel in his Resto-Mod.

◁ Jerry Palmer (right) picked Larry Cleveland's '56 'Vette for a "Celebrity Choice" award at the National Corvette Museum's giant Labor Day weekend car show.

△ The front view of the Resto-Mod retains the classic lines and styling of the factory version.

▷ The neat-looking interior features a small steering wheel with a chrome tach attached to it.

"What'd Palmer have to say?" we all wanted to know. The designer could have chosen a C4 of his own design. He could have picked any 'Vette. The '56 Resto-Mod was his preference.

Not until several months later did we find out the gist of that conversation. "A Resto-Mod is my style," he said. "But if I make a hot rod out of a car, I like to give it a lot of respect for what attracted me to the car in the first place."

So, wrapped up in the need for speed and the cool looks of Larry's restored-and-modified 'Vette was an intangible element called respect.

Viewing a machine as a person is not a new concept. As a kid, we all gave names to our inanimate playthings. Thus named, those toys took on a certain persona.

Larry Cleveland's hot rod roots went back to the early-'60s when — prior to the draft-eligible age of 18 — he had a number of cars.

In early 1963, Larry bought a '40 Ford coupe. That summer he installed a fuel-injected 327-cid, 375-hp V-8 in the Ford. "I've never been a brand-oriented guy," Larry admitted. By the summer of '65, Cleveland was working as a line mechanic at a Ford dealership in Hastings, Nebraska, and lusting after a Weber-injected 289 Cobra roadster. Another car he almost bought then — he calls it a "close call" — was a '56 'Vette priced at $1,100.

His current 'Vette is no $1,100 purchase. "Seventeen-five ($17,500) was the asking price for a real basket case. Larry

was all set to turn the car down until his wife suggested that he was capable of bringing it back. "Oh come on, you can do it," Sandy said. "I know you can."

When a counter offer of $13,500 was accepted, Larry acquiesced. "The next thing I knew, we were loading it up and bringing it home," he recalls.

Larry had sold his business and had eight hours a day to spend bringing the '56 back to life. His respect for the car was the key to getting the job done right and it was that respect that we later learned came through Larry's conversations with Jerry Palmer.

"Many guys put independent rear ends in the straight-axle cars, so why did you leave yours alone?" the designer had asked the car builder. "To give respect for the car," Larry

had answered. "It's a solid-axle car (and) that's what it is. If I change the rear end, it's not really a solid-axle car anymore."

Corvette chief engineer Zora-Arkus Duntov was also included in Larry's verbalization of his respect for the '56 Corvette. He knew that Zora was always interested in getting more power from an engine, so the '98 LS1 V-8 was something that Larry felt Zora would have loved. Ditto for the four-wheel disc brakes and higher-tech rack-and-pinion steering.

Palmer had questioned why Larry Cleveland inserted back-up lights in the exhaust openings and Larry had explained that he felt this change had the Duntov "signature." He had experienced difficulty fitting the larger 2-1/2-inch exhaust pipes through the holes. He thought he might open them up and give Duntov more respect if he ever did another car.

△ **The car has the slammed-to-the-ground look that's popular amongst Resto-Mod builders. Its overall appearance is a tad cleaner than the "stock" look.**

▷ The LS1 V-8 tucked under the hood gives the just-over-2,500-pounds car some snappy acceleration.

▷ The designer could hardly believe this car had been raced.

Palmer was impressed with the car's torque. The LS1 V-8 really turns this 2,697-pound "ride" into more of what the '56 was actually envisioned as — a high-performance car of its era.

As the two men drove from the show and over Kentucky back roads, Larry Cleveland dropped a "bomb" on Jerry Palmer.

"I raced this car in Nebraska," Cleveland said. "In the Sandhills Open Road Challenge."

"I can't believe you did that," replied Palmer.

"I had a speed limit of 110 mph," Cleveland continued.

"And you came out unscathed?" asked Palmer.

"Yeah — and I won the race!" was Cleveland's reply.

Now, that's how Larry Cleveland and his '56 Resto-Mod "Corvette Masterpiece" won the respect of Jerry Palmer.

'57 Corvette "Air Box" Fuelie

M ilton Robson is one of the premier muscle car collectors in the world. His estate is located north of Atlanta, Georgia, just a short drive from Road Atlanta. It holds one of the finest private collections of American sports and muscle cars in the world.

When Robson buys a muscle car or performance car, he likes to get the highest engine option offered for that model. When he bought a '57 Corvette, he chose a car with the fuel-injected 283-cid V-8.

There were actually four different option numbers for the so-called "fuelie" Corvette in 1957. Options 579A and 579C were both rated at 250 hp. Options 579B and 579E were both

△ The "Air Box" 'Vette has a purposeful look with its body-color wheels and "doggie dish" hubcaps.

◁ The car's "monotone" appearance speaks of competition use.

☐ The "Airbox" Georgia vanity plate hints at the special character of this racy roadster.

rated at 283 hp. For the latter two, that was one horsepower per cubic inch, a milestone achievement that Chevrolet publicized very highly.

Of the two 283-hp options, the 579E package has tremendous bragging rights in the realm of performance. Basically, this option was the way to go if you wanted to race.

In the mid-'50s, Chevrolet considered the Corvette to be a good basis for amateur racing efforts. That's what "sports car" meant in those days. No sports car aficionado worried about air conditioning, power steering or other creature comforts.

Anyone really interested in racing ordered a Corvette that was street legal, but could be raced at the track on the weekends with a few modifications. This was the "sports" aspect of owning a sports car.

With Regular Production Option 579E, buyers got more than "just" the 283-cid 283-hp V-8. In addition, they got a fresh-air intake and a mechanical tachometer that was mounted on the steering column, where it was hard to miss.

The special intake — which picked up the nickname "Fresh Air Box" — rammed air from the car's radiator grille area to

△ **The Fresh Air Box on this car's fuel-injected V-8 is technically a special type of intake manifold.**

△ This Corvette is one of just 43 units that carried the Air Box option.

▷ The interior has a manual gear-shifter and the full array of GM gauges.

the fuel-injection system's air inlet. A less-known, but still important part of the 579E package was a right-hand-mounted generator. On the right side of the engine, the generator fan belt had a firmer grip on the water pump pulley. This was very important with a high-rpm engine.

With only 43 produced, the 579E package is extremely rare and this greatly increases its desirability. In comparison, the Corvette factory in St. Louis, Missouri, built 713 of the 283-hp 283s with option code 579B.

Milt Robson considers color a big deal. He feels that it is hard to beat Venetian Red as the best color of 1957. Cars with Venetian red exterior finish could be ordered with red or beige interior trim. Milt's '57 is red inside.

Robson is a fan of the manual transmission and prefers a stick shift instead of an automatic transmission in a high-performance car. A four-speed manual transmission finally joined the Corvette options list on May 1, 1957. Milt's car has this very desirable transmission. The car has everything Milt Robson wants in a '57 'Vette. It's the cream of the crop — a real "Corvette Masterpiece."

1957 SRIII 'Vette Resto-Mod: It's Downright Evil

Cass Casmire's '57 Corvette still looks vintage, but the body is lowered and widened. Painted black and wearing wider-than-stock C5 wheels, it looks downright evil. The custom round-tube frame and chassis accept Corvette C5 front and rear suspensions, as well as the highest-performing engine in the General's GM arsenal — the 405-hp LS6 V-8 from the awesome Z06 Corvette.

Dropping a C1 body onto what is essentially a C5 chassis is not for the weak of heart or thin of wallet. If it were, everybody would be doing it.

Cass Casmire got professional help from SRIII Motorsports in New Lenox, Illinois. This custom shop builds and sells a

△ Lowering and widening the classic '57 Corvette body gives this Resto-Mod roadster a unique image.

◁ The SRIII blends the nostalgic lines of the Gen I Corvette body with the modern technology of a C5 chassis and a 405-hp LS6 V-8.

△ Details like the large 5-spoke rims and the brake-cooling air scoops added ahead of the rear wheel wells reflect the design skills of SRIII Motorsports.

▷ Under the hood lies the throbbing hi-po V-8 from a current Z06 supercar.

full-tube frame that fits 1953-1962 C1 Corvettes so that the later C4 suspension setups can be mounted.

Cassmire wanted to step up the SRIII Motorsports specifications by one Corvette generation and build a custom chassis for a C1 Corvette that would accept the even later C5 front and rear suspensions.

The C5 chassis arrangement is quite different from those that went before it, because it has the transmission mounted behind the driver. This gives it tread width measurements far wider than those of a stock '57 Corvette. To adopt the earlier body to the later chassis, it must be modified to fit the C5's wider track and bigger wheels.

Instead of incorporating bigger wheel wells and destroying the '57 'Vette's vintage looks, Casmire asked the crew at SRIII to widen the whole body to fit the custom chassis. The result is a '57 body that looks vintage stock, but is actually several inches wider than a factory-stock '57.

Fitting the rockers in front of the rear tires with a set of

scoops made sense. These are provided with stainless steel mesh. The current high-performance Z06 Corvette utilizes such scoops to channel air to the rear brakes.

The dashboard inside Casmire's '57 is slightly customized to hold a JVC sound system. Air conditioning, which wasn't optional in 1957, was added to the car with a VintageAir system. SRIII Motorsports even went with dash vents to channel in cool air. The seats in the car are from a C5 Corvette, but they have been modified to fit the widened '57 body and stitched up in black-and-red leather.

Casmire's '57 is a genuine "Corvette Masterpiece." It has classic looks with a high-tech, high-performance attitude. One look tells you this lower-than-low car with its big wheels and tires is just wicked.

△ **The dashboard is slightly updated to accommodate a JVC sound system, a VintageAir A/C system and upgraded instrumentation. The C5 seats look great.**

Casting a Spell: Hypnotic '57 Fuelie has Original Paint, 18,653 Miles

△ Car collectors — especially the Corvette variety — consider well-kept original cars, like this '57 "fuelie," to be the peak of perfection.

Original cars have a historical aura about them. Peering into the original silver acrylic lacquer on Al Maynard's 283-cid 283-hp fuel-injected '57 'Vette transports a Corvette person back in time.

Al admitted the fiberglass body has been "wheeled out a few times" and the paint is getting thin. There are some blotches, but amazingly the lacquer hasn't gotten checked through shrinkage caused by hot and cold weather and time. There is no "spider web" crazing in the paint. The surface of the finish is smooth.

Amazingly, people back in 1957 looked at the same paint . . . people who enjoyed Elvis Presley, Hoola-Hoops and the futuristic magic of Rochester fuel injection. Girls who wore itsy-bitsy-teenie-weenie polka-dot bikinis beheld their reflections in the same paint.

Al Maynard walked around the car and rattled off its history like a combination museum-tour-guide-and-used-car salesman.

"Yeah, right down to the carpeting, everything in the car is original," Al explains. "The bumpers have never been re-

chromed; the glass is perfect; the hardtop is perfect. The only thing we did was take the body off the frame to clean up the chassis. We put a NOS exhaust system on it. It's got NOS — not reproduction — tires. We just went through the brakes and the linings. Just cleaned it up is all we did.

"The motor only had about 7,000 miles on it," Al continues. The original owner — a man named Clark Irwin — had taken the factory-installed motor out of the car and put in a built-up 283-cid V-8. He actually raced the car. The original motor was just set aside and kept in perfect condition. "We

took it apart to check it out . . . to put in new rings and bearings," says Al. "But it didn't need anything."

Irwin was a GM engineer. He and a buddy both ordered '57 Corvettes to be delivered with the 1-hp-per-cube 283 "fuelie" V-8. They got a surprise when they raced side by side, because Clark's car was always slower.

"We couldn't figure out what the heck was going on," Irwin told Al Maynard. "We did some investigating. The dealer had ordered the wrong motor. That first car had the hydraulic-lifter camshaft."

△ Year-of-Manufacture (YOM) Michigan tags are the crowning touch on this pretty presentation of pristine preservation.

The dealer re-ordered a 283/283 and Irwin took delivery of this car in August 1957. That explains why it has a very late-in-the-year vehicle identification number: 6050.

According to Al Maynard, Irwin was a fanatic about originality. "He didn't lose one nut or bolt from this car," says Al. "He had the original pig, the original four-speed transmission — I mean everything in that car was just the way he got it." A pig refers to the rear axle. The car came with a 3.70:1 ratio "open" rear axle.

Irwin took the 'Vette on his honeymoon. He drove the car on the street. Finally, he went racing. But, to preserve the

originality, he used a built-up small block and installed a posi-traction rear axle with 5.13:1 gearing. When he added a tach on top of the steering column, he used "rubber bumpers and grommets," refusing to drill holes or permanently alter the car in any way. To keep the carpet like new, he installed more carpeting on top of it. Irwin even added an aluminum hood without altering the body.

Al Maynard lives in Clinton Township, Michigan, not far from the GM Tech Center in Warren. He heard about the low-mileage, original '57 Corvette. The car was the type of American performance car Al craved: low production number, origi-

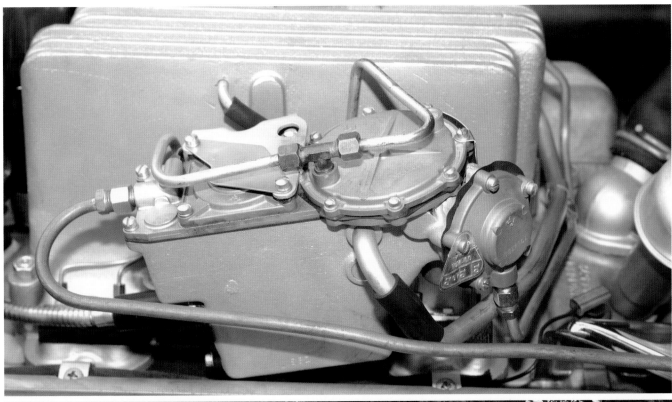

◁ If you want to know how the original fuel-injection setup looked on your car, when it left the Corvette factory, you can just look under the hood of Al's car to see the correct way to fit things together.

◁ With everything on the car conforming to exact factory specifications, this 'Vette could put enthusiasts of the Corvette nameplate into a trance.

▽ The inside is as original as the outside.

nal paint, high horsepower.

Al has never put his '57 'Vette in a competitive show, but he agreed to put it on display in the Bloomington Gold special collection.

"Jim Purvis asked me to bring the car," he explained. "Bloomington had a collection of first-generation Corvettes — straight-axle models — and my car freaked a lot of people out. People took pictures because of the car's original fasteners and its late-in-the-year VIN. They were checking this and that out and they couldn't believe the car was so original."

We agreed it must have been the original 1957 paint working its hypnotic spell on the Corvette enthusiasts. "Look into my eyes . . . look deep into my paint . . . you are now under the spell of a 'Corvette Masterpiece.'"

Custom '58 Vette Rod

△ The factory tried to give the '58 Corvette a "customized" look, but Mike Walker outdid the GM designers by coming up with this nifty '58-based Resto-Mod roadster.

To most observers, this black-and-red convertible is a classic Corvette. After all, it looks like a 'Vette and goes like a 'Vette, so the viewer must consider the possibility that it is a 'Vette. However, technically, this vehicle isn't even a Chevrolet. It's a kit car of a very special nature.

Street Rods Only, of Macon, Georgia, used its 25 years of experience in custom-fabricating vehicles to build this "Corvette Masterpiece."

The story of this car actually begins in the early-1990s, in Mexico, where two brothers named Mastretta became enthusiastic about first-generation Corvettes. They used high-tech computer programs to create three-dimensional drawings of 1958-1960 Corvette bodies.

The Mastretta brothers began manufacturing their reproduction Corvette bodies. Then, they got even more enthusiastic and built entire cars. They used a custom chassis of their own manufacture under their bodies. The interior components for these cars were all custom parts, too.

Producing cars from the ground up proved to be an expensive operation. After 20 complete cars left the Mastretta brothers' factory, they stopped making them and went into other ventures.

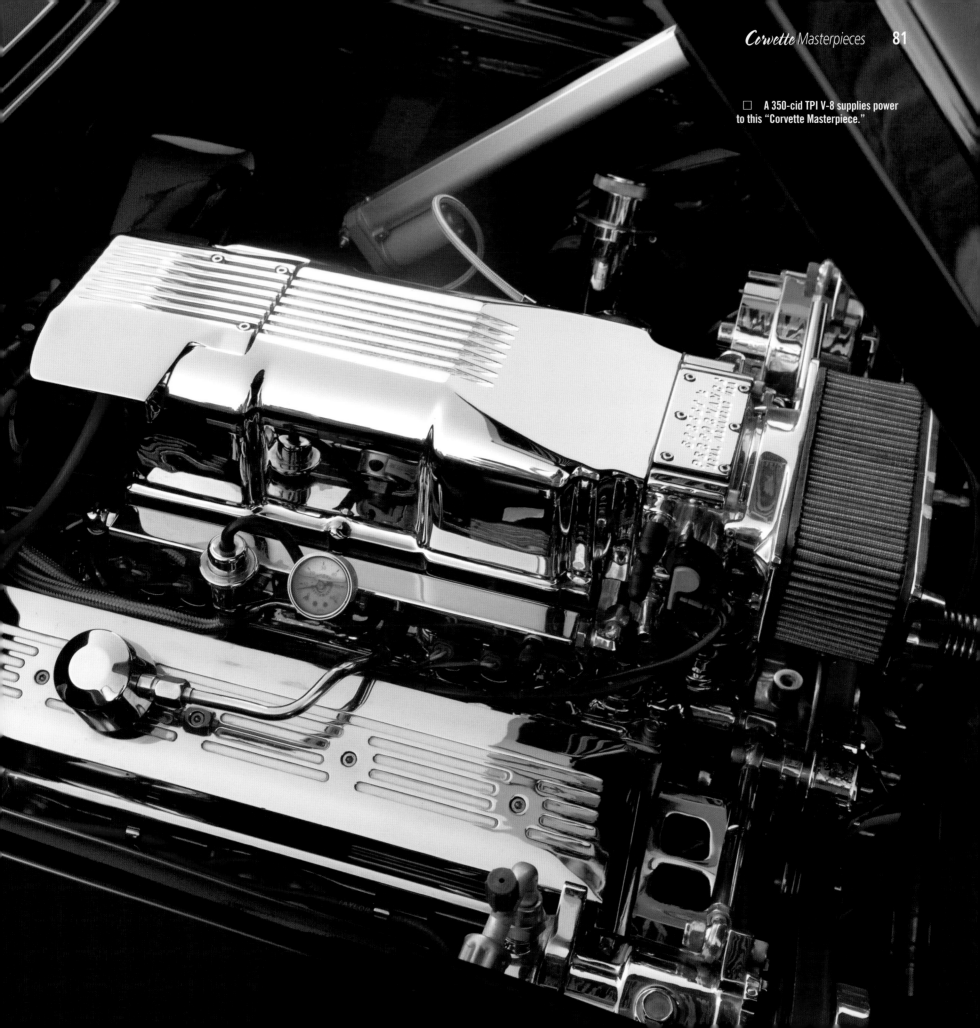

A 350-cid TPI V-8 supplies power to this "Corvette Masterpiece."

△ Builder Mike Walker put his personal stamp on this black beauty.

▷ A stock 'Vette interior was inserted in the modified '58 body and topped off with a custom steering wheel and individualized touches.

In the meantime, Mike Walker, owner of Street Rods Only, decided he wanted to start building vintage Corvettes. He flew to Mexico about the time the Mastretta brothers decided to sell off their bodies, chassis and parts inventory.

Walker built one of the Mastretta's Corvette kits. Then, he got a bit more creative and built this replica of the '58 Corvette. He modified the car's layout to make it more of a street rod.

Mike used an independent Dana rear end instead of the more rigid Chevrolet 10-bolt rear. The Mastrettas had used a Mustang II front suspension, which seemed unacceptable for Corvette enthusiasts. After all, Chevys and Fords are big rivals.

Walker modified the Mastretta frame's 4 x 2-inch boxed steel tubing to accept Corvette C4 components front and rear. He beefed up the chassis with Aldan adjustable coil-over shock absorbers at all four corners.

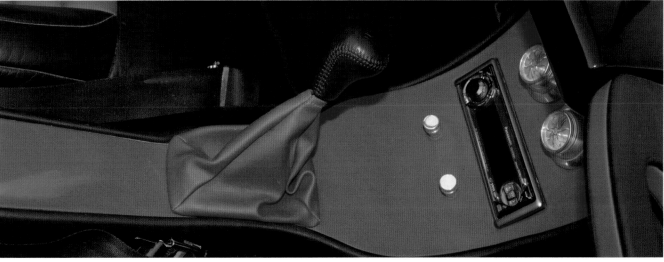

△ Like most Resto-Mod 'Vettes, this one "assumes the position" with fat, low-profile tires that make it hug the earth.

◁ The 350 up front is hooked to a Tremac 6-speed gearbox that gets stirred into proper gear with a console-mounted short-throw shifter.

The Mastretta bodies had a full-custom dash and interior. Mike modified the '58 body to accept a stock Corvette interior, including door panels, seats, dash pad, console and instrument cluster.

The engine bay can hold just about any V-8. Mike chose a reliable 350-cid V-8 with a polished Tuned Port Injection unit for this build. Behind the 350 is a Tremac six-speed manual transmission that spins a set of 3.08:1 gears in a Dana 36 rear axle. The gears are well-suited to highway cruising

Unlike original '58 Corvettes, this hot rod accommodates massive 18 x 10 inch Big Weld rims up front. In the back are 20 x 10 rims from the same manufacturer. Other popular street rod features on this car included a PRC custom aluminum radiator that's cooled by dual fans and a Flaming River steering column.

Many kit cars are replicas of the most popular older vehicles, but Mike Walker's "Corvette Masterpiece" honors a glitzy-looking Chevrolet sports car that wasn't all that popular until relatively recent years — the '58.

Joie Chitwood Thrill Show 1958 Corvette

△   Stunt driver Joie Chitwood used this '58 'Vette as part of his traveling auto-thrill show 50 years ago. Today, Chitwood's grandson is President and Chief Operating Officer of Indianapolis Motor Speedway.

Anybody who grew up in the '50s and '60s remembers the Joie Chitwood Thrill Shows. In fact, the Internet says the legendary thrill show driver's family carries on the tradition today. They operate the "Joie Chitwood Thunder Show." Joie Chitwood III, the stunt driver's grandson, is also President and Chief Operating Officer for Indianapolis Motor Speedway.

Jim Beecham, the owner of Vette Customs, a Lansing, Michigan, restoration shop, brought this Joie Chitwood stunt car to the Bloomington Gold Corvette show. Though he doesn't own the vehicle himself, he learned much about the history of this car while painting it. Beecham found out that Joie Chitwood had used the '58 Corvette in his show for one year.

Chitwood got the Corvette from Hooper Motor Company, a Chevy dealer in Warnersville, Pennsylvania. Beecham believes Chevrolet loaned him the Corvette for publicity value. It was part of Joie's act for just a single year, which makes it seem as if some kind of agreement had been made.

Beecham has seen a photo showing the sports car parked beside a '58 Impala and both cars have the Chitwood logo on them. This makes him wonder if someone has the auto-thrill-show Impala. The thrill-show Corvette came with a hardtop, but no fabric top. It also had no radio.

☐ The car has a hot 1-horse-per-cube "fuelie" V-8 linked to a four-speed manual gearbox.

☐ One could imagine the car's doors flying open like this when it landed after leaping off a ramp, but in this case the motivation for the open hatches is to show off the special door lettering.

△ George Rice Chitwood was born in Denison, Texas of Cherokee Indian heritage and a racetrack promoter gave him his "stage name." He was the first driver to wear a seat belt in the Indy 500 race.

Under the Corvette's hood is 1958's hottest engine, the 283-cid fuel-injected V-8. The motor is linked to a four-speed manual transmission and a 4.11:1 rear axle to help produce jackrabbit starts. It also has sturdy 15-inch wheel rims. With equipment like this, there's no doubt Joie could hit the ramps fast.

Apparently, the stock Corvette suspension was tough enough for some thrilling jumps. Jim said the car always hit the ramp on the down slope. The Corvette's jumps were nothing like the river-spanning leaps that the "General Lee" Dodge Charger made on the "Dukes of Hazard" television show.

Those Chargers all but "exploded" on impact, but after pieces came flying off, the cameras would show another, similarly-painted Charger, driving away as if nothing happened. In Chitwood's real-life show, the crowds got to see Joie's Corvette accelerate, drive up a ramp, jump across an open area to the other ramp and then drive away. There were no "camera tricks" in his show!

Jim Beecham said that ownership of the Corvette was transferred to one of Joie's Lansing buddies in 1959. This man operated a flying service. When he died, his wife gave the car to Skip and Marianne Strong, also of Lansing.

Skip and Marianne had the car completely restored before deciding to have Jim Beecham try to sell it for them at the Bloomington Gold Corvette show. Jim received an offer of $145,000 for the car. He thought that was pretty good, but wasn't sure. He wanted to get the very best price for the historic Corvette and people were telling him the car was worth more.

The following Labor Day, the car sold for $120,000 at the Kruse International auction in Auburn, Indiana. The following January it showed up at the highly-televised Barrett-Jackson Collector Car auction in Scottsdale, Arizona, where the "high-rollers" gather.

"This is a three-owner car with only 18,700 actual miles and includes the original 1958 registration signed by Joie Chitwood," the auction program stated. "What an opportunity to own an absolutely beautiful, one-of-a-kind, documented automobile of such historical significance."

Without showy banners all over it, this Corvette would have looked like any other one, but it did have low mileage and the rare 290-hp fuel-injection package. Its Snowcrest White paint and a red interior made it a real head-turner, too. The car was also in really nice condition, since it had been

☐ The powerful Chevrolet fuel-injection option gave the car the extra acceleration needed to pull off some amazing stunts.

hidden away for over 45 years. Everyone wanted to see what it would bring.

The question was how its history as part of the Joie Chitwood thrill shows would affect the price someone was willing to pay for it at the highly-publicized Arizona auction. Would there be someone in the audience who remembered the Joie Chitwood Thrill Show and found the car a sight for sore eyes?

All cars are consigned at no reserve at Barrett-Jackson, so everyone knew the car was going to sell to the highest bidder. When the dust cleared and the shouting was over, the winning bid for the '58 'Vette was $154,000, including a 10 percent bidder's fee.

As we left the auction, we couldn't help thinking that if we owned this "Corvette Masterpiece" we'd have the same problem we'd have with a baseball that Joe DiMaggio autographed . . . wanting to play catch with "Joltin' Joe's" signature on the ball. In the same manner, we'd want to sell tickets and jump "Joltin' Joie Chitwood's" Corvette over a set of those old thrill-show ramps. What fun that would be to fire up the "fuelie," throw the stick into first gear and fly through the air!

☐ The car has been completely refurbished to its thrill show format.

Investigating the Resto-Mod . . . by Driving 3 Examples

△ **Resto-Mod Corvettes blend the best of the old with the best of the new inside, as well as outside.**

I remember when my friend Mike McComas finished his '57 Corvette. We couldn't wait to fire it up. The car's looks were "to die for." Everybody loves the lines of a "Straight-Axle" 'Vette. But, when we actually drove the car we were disappointed. It rode like a buckboard.

That's why so many people build hybrid Resto-Mods. They want the handling of a late-model Corvette with the classic looks of a 1953-1962 C1 edition.

Resto-Mods are a big step up from an "Ol' Skol" modified car. Beefing up the suspension and increasing the horsepower fall under the Ol' Skol car-building techniques. There may be upgrades to the suspension like stiffer shocks, stabilizer bars and firmer coil springs, but the frame and chassis designs remain vintage.

To really build-in the handling of a late-model Corvette, the pro builders start with a new frame and attach a late-model suspension. Billy Dawson is one of those builders who started out as a Corvette enthusiast simply wanting his own Resto-Mod. Then, he started selling new frames and whole chassis with suspensions attached. Before too long, he was completely rebuilding whole cars.

When I visited Billy Dawson's Corvette Corrections I

asked him why he got started. He turned and pointed at a '58 Corvette wearing a set of 15 x 7.5-inch C4 wheels. The C-4 Corvette, of course, was a ZR1 look-alike.

"I built that car," Billy explained. "I'd drive it to a show and people would say, 'Hey, nice '58.' Then they would start to get suspicious. Lots of people add bigger wheels to older Corvettes, but enthusiasts really think something is going on when they see four-wheel disc brakes."

Billy's '58 is not your normal C1, of course. In fact, not a whole lot of anything is normal around Billy's shop, which is located in Seguin. That's in the rolling hill country of South Texas, about 14 miles east of New Braunfels. The shop is about a 35-minute drive north of San Antonio. Dawson lives on some acreage there. His large shop is behind the house. Prior to building Corvette frames, Dawson built airplanes there.

"I built four of those things," he said. This time there was no need to point. The Hatz biplane stood large in the shop like a contraption that the Red Baron flew in World War I. Billy built one Hatz for a friend. He then got so interested in the planes, he developed a kit for other builders.

△ **To understand the motivation for building a Resto-Mod 'Vette, you really have to go out for a ride in one . . . or two . . . or three.**

△ **Billy Dawson stands beside the custom frame he designed for the C1 Corvette. The Chevrolet engine cradle has already been installed in this frame.**

▷ **Here's a Corvette "rolling chassis" with the engine, transmission and rear end installed.**

The shop looks like an old airplane hangar. Against one wall, behind a biplane suspended on a rotisserie, there was a red '57 Corvette awaiting a new chassis.

Billy didn't originally intend to get into the Corvette business. People just started requesting chassis, bare frames and even whole cars. During my visit, Billy had three C1s completed and ready to sample.

I started by taking a look at the various frames and chassis sitting around the shop. One frame was a "roller" with the rear end installed. Billy's son-in-law, John, helped us push this black roller into the sunlight. There I could see things that didn't catch my attention first. For example, the frame had no X-member.

"I grew up in the machine shop next door," Billy advised. "My dad was a fabricator. I was drag racing at the age of 13. I built almost everything I ever had. So, I figured I'd just build my own Corvette frame, starting from scratch." Without any real plan, he laid box tubing out on the floor and started assembling his C1 chassis.

"I had the front and rear suspensions out of an '87 Corvette, so I just went at it," Dawson recalled. The old X-frame in his '58 Corvette was rusty and no good, but Billy wouldn't have used it anyway. He knew from the start that the vintage frame was a liability when it came to installing modern engines, transmissions and rear ends.

◁ If you enjoyed building model cars when you were a kid, you'll love building Resto-Mod 'Vettes. The bodies — like the one seen here — give the cars their "Resto" character. The drive train, wheels, tires, sound system and seats supply the "Mod" elements.

▽ Billy cuts back the "wings" on the cover of the Dana axle. These normally go completely across the back end. After they are cut, the exhausts pipes can fit through the opening.

△ The original A-arms on C1 Corvettes are of pressed-steel construction. They are primitive compared to the forged-aluminum A-arms of the C4 Corvette. Also, notice the C4-style mono-leaf springs that mount to the stock C4 cradle.

"With the original frame, the transmission has to sit on top of the X-member. By eliminating the X-member and going to a double H-frame, I get the engine/transmission down about 2.5 inches lower, which also drops the CG (center of gravity). Now, you can install a Ram-Jet 350 or a tall fuel-injection system with no hood clearance problems."

Designing an exhaust system to fit the fabricated chassis was another issue. The pipes had to run through the X-frame. Billy moved to the back of a rolling chassis and held a piece of exhaust pipe on top of the frame on one side of the Dana 44 rear axle cover.

"I cut the cover — the arms or the wings, that is — off the cover. Then, I re-formed them to allow the exhaust system to be mounted to our chassis." This way, the exhausts fit the chassis with no clearance issues.

While I was looking at the back of the chassis, Billy pointed out, "The way we mount the rear end in there is a lot different from the way they were originally mounted. You can see where the rear end pumpkin is sandwiched between the lower frame rails and the upper frame rails. There was no mount there; instead there was a ladder bar that came forward and mounted to the transmission. There was no mount on the rear end at all. It hung on these two bushings and a ladder bar. I can show you a ladder bar if you want."

I was learning that frame-and-chassis building can get pretty complicated. The fact that a fabricator built this one on the concrete floor of his shop with no plan was mind-boggling. Experience definitely is the greatest teacher.

Where did the strength come from if the X-member was gone? Dawson pointed to "H-rails" he had fabricated to run along the length of the frame. At the front of the car, the frame rails on either side split and divide into two rails. "With a single-rail frame, you don't have much torsional strength," Dawson said. "It will twist on you, but on this car, if you jack up one corner, it's going to take the whole car up with it. The frame doesn't flex from side to side."

"Where did you get this idea?" I asked him. "Did it come from another frame or is it your own design?" Billy didn't want to take credit, but he had to. "No, it just happened. It is more luck than brains."

Dawson's frames accept both front end and rear end C4 suspension components. The rear axles used are either the Dana 36 or Dana 44, which are also used on C4 Corvettes. Car builders can utilize just about any GM V-8 they want . . . small block or big block . . . even the six-liter Cadillac Escalade engine. The engine choice dictates the type of transmission. With the LS1 V-8 the Camaro/Firebird six-speed manual is used. That's because the '97 and up LS1 Corvettes came with a transaxle.

△ **The dark blue '59 'Vette is fitted with a 330-hp LT1 V-8.**

Three C1/C4 Corvette Drives

Chassis fabricator Billy Dawson gave me the chance to sample three of his Resto-Mod 'Vettes. The plan was for me to drive one car while Billy and son-in-law John drove the others on an excursion into the rolling hill country. Then, we'd stop and keep trading cars until I had a crack at all three.

I started with the dark blue '59 powered by a 1995 Corvette 330-hp LT1 V-8 linked to a 4L60E automatic transmission.

The second — and hottest ride — was the light blue '59 Corvette with a wild Reher-Morrison 383-cid 440-hp engine hooked to a six-speed transmission.

The third Resto-Mod 'Vette was a '58, which was the first car Dawson built; the car that got him into business. It had an L98 tuned-port-injected V-8 with a 700R4 automatic transmission. This car was sprung with the softest-riding mono-leaf springs ever built for a C4.

Sliding into the front seat of the dark blue '59 was an awakening. I had wondered about fitting my 6-foot 3-inch, 190-pound frame into the cockpit of any C1 'Vette. Long ago, I had just been enthralled by the acceleration of the warmed-over 283 in the first C1 I ever drove. It was a red '60 model and I remember that I could get rubber in all four gears. However, my shoulders were so close to the steering wheel that my arms got tangled up on turns.

On Billy's '59, he modified the seat tracks so they went farther back than normal. My shoulders had plenty of room against the steering wheel. I even had plenty of room to maneuver my long legs.

▷ With automatic transmission, this Resto-Mod 'Vette drives more like a C4.

△ Multi-talented fabricator Billy Dawson is seen here in his shop with one of his chassis, and a Hatz biplane in the background.

◁ After some modifications to the seat tracks on the C1 Corvette, the seats can be made to move back further than in a stock-condition car. This provides more driver legroom.

I had heard about C4-hung C1s driving like a C4, which is logical, because the suspension comes from a C4. Essentially, you're in a C1 body with complete C4 mechanicals, so the ride one would surmise, would be just like the ride of a C4. By the time the car moved 20 feet merely rolling in the driveway, I knew that it did not feel like a C1. However, once we got underway, I realized that the car didn't feel like a C4 either. I put the trans in D3 (not D4) to allow the 4L60E automatic transmission to shift no higher than third gear.

I chirped my rear tires and got up to 55 mph in traffic as the three of us cruised. Billy chirped the rear tires in the Reher-Morrison-powered car ahead of me. John was behind us in the green '58. I eased my hands off the wheel of the '59 and the car continued to track straight. It felt good on the road.

Traffic thinned out to nothing on the back roads and Billy nailed the throttle on the Reher-Morrison '59. The exhausts

bellowed. I stayed back a good eighth of a mile for acceleration jumps, but there was no opportunity to test top speed.

The steering wheel blocked my line of sight to the digital read-out speedometer. (A tilt wheel would have been a big plus.) The original speedometer needle was not active with the digital read-out, but it was still there for effect. I could see the tach. The car's acceleration was quick enough to pull back the muscles in my face.

As we wound through curve after curve in the rolling hills, the Resto-Modded '59 bore little resemblance to the buckboard springing of an original car. The suspension felt rough, but not as rough as in a stock '59 — at least in my judgment. Also, the roughness was much more controlled than back in the '50s.

An original '59 'Vette would be much scarier to drive through a curve at speed, as it would experience pronounced body lean. An original car would have drifted into the outside

△ Here's how the 5-spoke rims look when the car is standing still.

▷ Billy Dawson's light blue 1959 Corvette depends on a 383-cid 440-hp Reher-Morrison-built engine for motivation.

lane at a high rate of speed or, worse yet, into a field alongside the rural roadway. Dawson's stout frame and stiff springing keep the '59 body much flatter around corners. Still, the feel of the car is not purely C4, either.

A decreasing-radius turn on a downhill off-ramp showed just how good the car did handle. The large-diameter steering wheel required lifting my hands once to grab more wheel for the tight turn. A smaller-diameter C4 wheel would not have re-quired me to lift my hands. There was no opportunity to push the car into the corner until it slid. Even without the luxury of sliding, the car obviously is vastly improved over a stock C1 in handling. It was a great ride.

Next, I hopped in the six-speed '59 'Vette with the hotter engine and we lit out for parts unknown. There was zero traffic and the sun was warm. It was October. I was beginning to really like this assignment.

The road ahead was as straight as a string. I got my car in front of our "parade" this time. After a mile or two, the Corvettes being driven by Billy and John were no longer in my rearview mirror.

The suspension on the '59 Resto-Mod felt pretty much the same as the one in the first '59. The main difference in the cars was the second one had a lot more oomph. The 440-hp Reher-Morrison 383 developed one horsepower for every 6.4 pounds, which is getting beyond muscle-car territory and into the 427 Cobra realm. What a ride this one was.

On the way back, we stopped at a gas station for fuel and I got my chance to switch to the green '58. I almost decided to stay in the six-speed car because it was so much fun to drive it, but I'm glad I decided to get in the '58. In this 'Vette I finally got to experience a C1 that felt like a C4. The soft C4 springs made this car feel much more civilized.

△ Here's the light blue '59 'Vette going through its paces.

▷ The '58 from Texas went
on the 2003 Power Tour.

It was at this point that I realized the C4 modifications to the two '59 'Vettes did not mask their stouter springs and higher-performance engines. All the cars were lighter than stock C1s and all had a four-inch longer wheelbase than a stock '58-'59 model, so they all had a somewhat unique feel. However, in terms of suspension upgrades, the '58 was in a class of its own.

Billy Dawson confessed that he was still "experimenting" with spring rates. If I had one of these Resto-Mods built, I would go for the 383-cid small-block V-8 and the six-speed manual transmission, but I would also order the softer suspension. I think this combination would make for a real "Corvette Masterpiece."

Corvette Racing History: '59 Purple People Eater

△ The "Purple People Eater" was first ordered and prepared by Nickey Chevrolet of Chicago. Tom Stephani, the son of the dealership's original owner, is still active in vintage racing and fondly remembers this car from the old days.

For six weeks in 1958, "Purple People Eater" was the number one-selling record on the pop charts in America. The words, about a "one-eyed, one-horned, flying Purple People Eater" would be perfect to blare over the radio of this '59 Corvette SCCA racing car that uses that name.

Then again, a silly song may not fit the car's all-business character. In fact, it has no radio or other amenities. Power steering wasn't available in '59 and there's not even a heater in the car.

From day one, the famous Nickey Chevrolet dealership, of Chicago, Illinois, ordered this 'Vette as the starting point for a racing car.

Lance Miller pulled this colorful 'Vette out of the Miller family collection to be photographed. Lance's dad Chip was a big-time Corvette collector before he passed away from a rare disease in 2004. Now, Lance takes care of the car collection, which includes the "Flying Purple People Eater."

Lance told me that Chip actually found this 'Vette at the first Carlisle swap meet in 1974. Chip was one of the promoters

☐ The "Purple People Eater" was a real racing machine and captured the 1959 SCCA National Championship in the 'B' Production Class.

PURPLE PEOPLE EATER

△ After successfully racing for a few years, the car was taken off the road.

▽ According to lance Miller, his father Chip Miller and Ken Heckert bought the car, verified its racing history and had Kevin Mackay of Corvette Repair restore it.

of that event, which is different than the related Corvettes @ Carlisle venue.

Chip Miller and Ken Heckert purchased the '59 racing car, which was in rough condition, for $800. In the '50s and '60s, a racing history wasn't really a plus when selling a 'Vette. Prospective buyers often felt that racing cars had been abused. So, this car's racing history was actually covered up to make it "more valuable" for its body and chassis parts. Racing hardly factored into the 1974 deal.

However, by 1974, forward-looking collectors like Chip Miller were getting tuned into vintage race cars. Still, it wasn't until 1985 that Chip and Ken decided to get serious about giving the car a restoration.

Hecker noticed the Purple People Eater on page 93 of Karl Ludvigsen's book *Corvette: America's Star Spangled Sports Car*. It shared some racing features with the 'Vette that Chip and he had purchased, including the number 33 painted on the side.

A driver named Bob Spooner was behind the wheel in the photo in the book. The car's latest owners tracked him down and Spooner verified the car's special features. What he told them was sufficient to document its racing heritage.

Spooner knew that "Gentleman" Jim Jeffords was the first driver of the car in 1959. Jeffords drove many of the outstanding racing cars of that era, including a Scarab and a "Birdcage"

□ Jim Jeffords originally campaigned the car in SCCA events.

△ The backwards-K on the door graphics derives from the famous Nickey Chevrolet logo, which also shows the fourth letter in the name backwards.

▷ Many of the 283-cid/283-hp '59 fuelies saw racing action.

Maserati. Chip Miller contacted Jeffords and more of the car's history began to unfold. Jeffords even explained that the Purple People Eater name — originally based on the record — eventually stuck when he told people he only had one good eye.

Jeffords probably could see much better than he wanted other drivers to know, because he won the SCCA B-production championship in 1958. He did a repeat performance in 1959, with help from Ronnie Kaplan and a crew headed by Lionel "Lindy" Lindheimier.

Also known as the Mark III, the purple '59 racing car wore the number 1, indicating the driver was the current national champion. Nickey Chevrolet and Jim Jeffords also won the 1959 B-production SCCA championship and continued to make Corvette racing history with the flying Purple People Eater.

Chip Miller and Ken Heckert restored the '59 'Vette to its original racing configuration and presented it at Corvettes @ Carlisle in 1998. Both Jeffords and Spooner were there to celebrate the occasion and autograph the car. Sadly, Spooner passed away in 2000.

Chip Miller purchased Ken Heckert's share of the Purple People Eater. He toured in this famous "Corvette Masterpiece" in 2003, to celebrate the Corvette's 50th birthday.

Chip Miller's 1960 Briggs Cunningham Corvette LeMans Racecar

△ Sportsman Briggs Cunningham — best known as an America's Cup winner — was the original owner of this car.

◁ The late Chip Miller in the cockpit.

This Corvette, once owned by Briggs Cunningham, won its class at the French Grand prix at Le Mans in 1960. Such big-time racing cars don't usually drop out of thin air. However, every once in a while, they do.

Ask Kevin Mackay, a talented Corvette restorer who focuses on cars that raced at Sebring and LeMans. Or ask Dave Reisner, a Corvette enthusiast who worked with Mackay to track down this car by its VIN, through connections the two men made at LeMans.

△ The car has been restored to look as it did when raced.

▽ Details are important when restoring a famous racing car.

Chevrolet Motor Division pulled the plug on factory-financed racing in 1957 to adhere to the American Manufacturer's Association (AMA) ban on factory participation in the sport. In following this mandate, General Motors put the kibosh on Zora Arkus-Duntov's dream of having a Corvette win the Le Mans race.

With GM out, sportsman Briggs Cunningham stepped up and fielded a trio of 'Vettes for the 24-hour endurance race in 1960. The late Chip Miller, who eventually came to own this car, knew the story well.

"Two of Briggs' cars ran at Sebring," Chip once told me. "Mine was the No. 1 car in 1960. Briggs actually drove the first part of the race until the car developed a noise in the rear end. He didn't know what caused this and brought the car into the pits. The mechanics looked things over, then (driver) John Fitch went out and the rear axle snapped. That caused Fitch to flip."

The Corvette took a DNF (did not finish) at Sebring, but it was fixed up for Le Mans. The other entry from Sebring also ran in France, along with a third Cunningham-backed Corvette.

Unlike the purpose-built CR-5 Corvette racing cars of today — which tend to become instantly collectible — Cunningham's 1960s racing cars started out as production-line Corvettes and had no collectors waiting to buy them when the race was finally over.

☐ Special competition lighting was required.

▷ **Knock-off wheels made for faster pit stops.**

△ **The car's race-ready image goes along with its role as a famous Corvette racing machine.**

The St. Louis resident who owned the Corvette had no idea what it was in terms of racing history. Over seven years, Mackay developed a telephone relationship with the man, who finally decided to sell the car because his wife wanted a new Navigator.

"I told Chip (Miller) that if I ever got the car, it was his," Mackay recalls today. Miller told Mackay to "call anytime" if he got the car. When he finally called Chip at 1:15 a.m. and woke him up, Miller knew right away what the call was about. Within a day he did a wire transfer and started arrangements to have the car shipped to Carlisle. Then he went to Kevin's shop in Valley Stream, N.Y. to see it.

Miller recalled his initial inspection. First, he popped the hood and checked the VIN, which matched. Then, he noticed other details like the windshield wiper transmission being relocated on the cowl. You even could see the outline of where the body was filled in and where the quick-fill gas cap had been added. Mackay peeled back the layers of paint and uncovered other unique features. In addition, the VIN was stamped on the frame, proving the car was original.

"That car was the most difficult restoration we completed in 20 years of doing such work," says Kevin Mackay. "It had so many hand-made parts and we wound up with 3,750 man-hours in the job." The people involved with the car, who could document restoration details, were mostly in their 80s and 90s. "Still, we had two of the original drivers come to Valley Stream," Mackay pointed out.

Chip Miller was the perfect owner for this Corvette. He and his partner Bill Miller founded the Corvettes @ Carlisle show. The restored car debuted during a 14-day tour that started August 1, 2002. It was put on a truck and shipped directly to the Meadow Brook Concours d'Elegance in Michigan where it earned a Best in Class award. Then it went to the NCRS Convention, a Straight-Axle Corvette event, Pebble Beach and the Chevrolet display at the Monterey Historic Races at Laguna Seca.

Only 17 months later, Chip Miller passed away. Miller had always been a very serious Corvette collector and was particularly fond of 1960 models. His roots in the straight-axle Corvette segment also went way, way back.

"I graduated from high school in 1960," he told me when I took these pictures. "It was during college that I really discovered 1958-1960 Corvettes. I liked them. They were the Corvettes of my youth. I bought a '60 Corvette in 1962 when I graduated from college. It was my first Corvette."

Chip happened to be at the Monterey Historic Races in California, in 1987, when Mike Pillsbury unveiled the No. 2 car from the Cunningham Le Mans team. It was the car that Dick Thompson — the racing dentist — had driven.

"It came on a trailer into the Doubletree Hotel parking lot

That's why some unknown party, at some time in the '60s, converted this Le Mans-winning Corvette back to stock street format. Chip Miller's educated guess was that this happened in the 1963-1964 time frame. After that, it seemed like the Corvette racing car had vanished into thin air.

It was decades later when Reisner helped Mackay track down the long lost LeMans winner. After getting the car's serial number, they had contacts in the law enforcement field who were able to find the car in St. Louis, Missouri. This was before the privacy act prevented state DMV's from giving out names and addresses of past owners.

△ **The removable fiberglass hardtop improved the car's on-track aerodynamics.**

and I just about fainted when I saw it," Miller said of this near twin to his car. "It was so cool. It had Halibrand wheels . . . the quick-fill (gas cap) . . . the notch in the back window. I'd never in my life seen a cooler car. I love Grand Sports. I love a lot of Corvettes. But I have to say that, for me, having graduated high school in 1960, this car held a particular mystique."

Miller felt enough enthusiasm to invest a large sum of money to restore his car the right way. He also put in thousands of hours of his own time as he said, "just in research, locating parts, documentation and making sure that everything is right on the car."

His best source for information was the '60 Corvette that Pillsbury, also deceased now, had restored. That car later went to the Bruce Meyer Collection in Beverly Hills.

Pillsbury had gotten quite lucky when he gave a seminar, in Boston, about the '60 Le Mans entry. Alfred Momo, a Jaguar dealer who was the head of Cunningham's race team, still lived in Long Island at that time. He attended the seminar and

sat listening in the audience. Moved by Pillsbury's talk, he approached Mike and asked if he would like some original pieces for the old racing car.

Apparently, Briggs Cunningham made extras of everything, like the exotic seats. They were aircraft jump seats of World War II vintage covered in velour. When Chip Miller's car was being restored, Bruce Meyer graciously allowed the seats to be pulled from the Dick Thompson car so Mackay could accurately recreate them.

Essentially, the two cars are alike, as they were built to the same specifications. Pillsbury had also lucked out by getting the fabricated dash plate for the gauges, the hood louvers and Halibrand "kidney" style wheels. Such parts allowed Mackay to get things right when doing Miller's car over.

When you total the costs involved in designing and machining the hood pins, it shows they were especially time-consuming and expensive to reproduce. "By the time I was done with those two little hood hold downs," Miller pointed out,

△ **The car's restored "race car" look is totally authentic.**

△ **The crossed-flags emblem is truly apropos.**

"You're talking, modestly, $4,500-$5,000. I had to have a Ferrari restorer out in Northern California design, machine and assemble them."

The result was as authentic a re-creation of the original Cunningham Corvette as Chip could ever dream of. No detail was omitted and no expense was spared. As the exhaustive restoration proceeded, it almost seemed like fate was on Chip's side. He had found a set of five Cunningham wheels advertised in the National Corvette Restorers Society's *Driveline* magazine.

"They were bare wheels — no spinners, hubs or anything," he revealed. "They were just bare wheels, but they were absolutely 100 percent Cunningham wheels."

Actually, Chip had called too late on the ad. The wheels had been sold. But, he got the owner's name and ended up buying the wheels from him. Amazingly, they were precisely the wheels Cunningham used; they were painted blue to seal the pores in the magnesium. Chip believes some of these *very* wheels were used on his car at Le Mans.

Mackay says that Miller dreamed showing the finished car at LeMans in 2010 — the 50th anniversary of Cunningham's effort to win event. "I want to get one of the original drivers in the car," Chip told Kevin.

Driver Bob Grossman was gone, but driver John Fitch is still alive and in good health. He'll be 93 or 94 years old in 2010. "God willing, both he and I will drive that car on the course," said Miller. "I've got a lot of goals and that's a real one. It will be absolutely monumental and almost unheard of, but I've got this thing in me that's telling me it should happen. I'll make it happen if there's any way."

Sadly, that dream died in 2004 when Miller — a man who meant so much to the Corvette hobby — passed away on March 24. Chip loved the car you see here. You have to be a car person to understand the link between man and machine. This car was his "Corvette Masterpiece."

1961 LS7 Corvette:
20th Century Meets 21st Century

From any angle, this Corvette looks like a '61 model. However, it is a highly-modified '61. Under the hood, the change is obvious. The engine is an LS7, the 427-cid 505-hp V-8 that first appeared in the 2006 Corvette Z06.

Larry Allman, of Bremerton, Washington, was watching and waiting when Chevrolet unleashed the fury of the Z06 on the streets. What got him excited was the crate engine program that debuted along with the new high-performance model. The LS7 engine was going to be available from GM Performance Parts.

"I said that engine just has to go in an early Corvette," Allman recalls. "That was just a must. So, that's when I got the idea to do my car."

Through "a lot of finagling" Larry got one of the early engines. He deposited money in four or five different Chevy dealerships, trying to get one of the first LS7s. He ended up getting the second one offered to the public.

Larry had already determined that dropping a 505-hp engine into his Corvette would overpower the stock 1961 chassis. In addition, the updated six-speed manual transmission that he wanted to use would not fit inside the ancient X-frame.

△ **Out for a drive in what may be the world's quickest '61 'Vette.**

△ Larry did not want to cut into the interior of the convertible top well in order to mount modern tires, so he fabricated hand-made rear fenders that were exact replicas of the stock fenders. He then moved the fenders an inch and a half out on each side so some fat "rubber" could fit inside. The result is a car that goes down the road like a modern 'Vette.

Larry first replaced the 1961 X-frame with a tube chassis from SRIII Motorsports, of New Lenox, Illinois. To this frame, he attached the front suspension of a C5 Corvette and the independent rear suspension from a C4 model.

Like every 1997-up Corvette, the high-performance Z06 uses a transaxle. In the factory setup, GM moved the transmission all the way to the rear of the vehicle. A torque tube bolts onto the back of the engine and runs back to the transaxle. Larry couldn't use this arrangement without very drastic alterations to the car's interior to make room for the transaxle between the seats. His solution was to go with a Camaro six-speed transmission that bolts to the back of the engine. This worked with the independent rear suspension from a pre-1997 C4 Corvette.

Basically, Larry had to engineer his "1961 LS7" from the ground up. This shows up in the wide tires, which are an absolute necessity for handling the big-time horsepower the LS7 generates.

"I wanted at least 10.5-inch tires on the back, but you can't fit those inside the wheel wells of a stock '61 body," Larry explained. "A lot of guys chop into the interior of the convertible top well and lose the top. I didn't want to do that, so we handmade fenders that were exact replicas of the stock fenders. I moved them an inch and a half out on each side. Then, I could get the wide tires under there, still have a stock look and not lose the convertible top."

Larry wound up with his own style of "Corvette Masterpiece." It's an LS7-powered '61 model that looks like a Gen I Corvette. However, when you punch the accelerator, you unleash power on a level with that of a late-model Z06.

☐ Larry Allman felt that the LS7 engine "just has to go in an early Corvette." He carried out his thinking in a fine fashion.

Plain & Simple: A C5 Resto-Mod 'Vette That Looks Like a '62

▷ Basically, this red '62 Corvette Resto-Mod is a modern C5 model in every way except the retro look of the body. Ben says he has turned down $180,000 for his creation.

Ben McMurray's '62 Corvette is more than a Resto-Mod. Underneath and inside, it's actually a 1997-2004 C5 model. Ben owns Corvette Country, a specialty Corvette shop in Fayetteville, Georgia. He buys and sells and concentrates mostly on service, paint and bodywork. He began in 1985.

In 1994, McMurray purchased a '62 Corvette body. His plan was to put the classic body on a C4 platform. Unfortunately, there was too much difference between the first-generation (C1) 'Vette and the later fourth-generation (C4) car.

"I waited until they came out with a longer-wheelbase Corvette," said Ben. "When they did this with the C5 (fifth-generation) Corvette, they also put the gas door on the left-hand side of the car. This worked out perfectly with the '62."

With years of experience and a shop behind him, McMurray went where no one else had gone before. He put the '62 body onto a C5 chassis, complete with the C5 interior.

Now, you may have seen a C5 customized to look like an older Corvette. One popular conversion resembles the original '53 Corvette. What makes Ben's C5 a little different is that it's topped with a *real* '62 body.

The conversion was a tall order. "I had to cut out the '62 floorboard and firewall," Ben explained. "Then, I had to do a lot of cutting in the trunk area to make everything fit. The outside door latches, the inside door latches, the mechanisms that make the door work are all from a C5 Corvette. I had to do a lot of modifying to the door jamb and the door itself."

The appearance of a '62 cockpit fitted with a C5 dash and seats is very striking, to say the least. "I only had to trim the pad," Ben advised. "Then I had to put a little dash cap on it cause it didn't fit all the way up."

Having built a couple of Grand Sports using a C4 chassis, McMurray had experienced with "Resto-Modding" a Corvette. "I did them all basically the same way, with all the modern

△ The plan for this car was to put the '62 body on a C4 platform, but it wound up riding a C5 in the end.

◁ Boy does the modernized interior in this open-air 'Vette look cool.

▷ Back in the '60s the automakers didn't "style" engines like they do today. There is not mistaking the distinctive Corvette V-8.

▽ The car advertises its builder — Corvette Country of Fayetteville, Georgia.

conveniences," he said. "Everything that was on the newer car is on these cars and everything works. That includes the power mirrors, power door locks and cruise control."

Fire up this Resto-Mod 'Vette and you're basically driving a C5. You have running lights, back-up lights and even '68 Corvette side marker lights. Ben noted, "Everything is from a Corvette, except the Buick LeSabre side mirrors. But they are fully electrically operated." The exhaust pipes exit in back like they do on a C5, but the bezels come off a '72 Corvette.

"It took us 2-1/2 years to build the car," McMurray pointed out. "It took a lot of fitting and re-engineering. It's not something you just do." Ben didn't have a kit to help him. He built this "Corvette Masterpiece" all by himself.

Concept Corvettes At GM Design

△ **And they call this "work." The author had to fly to Detroit to take pictures of the historical Mako Shark dream Corvette.**

The assignment: to photograph one of GM's factory dream cars — the Mako Shark Corvette — for the box cover of an Ertl toy.

There is only one Mako Shark. It is garaged at the GM Design Center on Mound Road in Warren, Michigan. I called and got in touch with Dale Jacobson, Project Coordinator for Design Properties and Vehicle Management. We set a time and date to do photography.

In talking, I discovered that there were three other interesting concept cars at the GM Design Center: Bill Mitchell's 1959 Sting Ray racer, the Manta Ray (first been called the Mako Shark II) and the Aerovette (which started as the 4-Rotor).

Dale Jacobson and Mike Eradodi work in a garage at the Design Center. Both are car enthusiasts who really like Corvettes. I asked them why the exotic Corvettes were there. "This is where they were built and this is their home," said Dale.

△ There's something fishy here. The badge says "Corvette Shark."

▷ Would you believe woodgrain trim on a Corvette dashboard?

△ The car really seems to have a genuine "shark nose" when seen in profile view.

▷ The "Mako Shark" name appears just above the side-exit exhaust pipes.

I asked if it would be a problem to photograph the other Corvette concept cars. Dale said that would be OK. He felt the test track at the nearby GM Tech Center would be the perfect place. I got really excited when I saw the high-banked oval track. It made a great background for all of these cars — especially the '59 Sting Ray racer.

Dale started at GM in 1968 (March 5th was the exact date, he recalled). He was hired as Bill Mitchell's chauffeur. Mitchell designed the original Sting Ray. "I was his 27th private chauffeur," Dale said. "All the guys were taking bets on how long I'd last, but I was the guy who won the blue ribbon." He kept the job for years.

Naturally, I asked Dale what his secret was. "Mitchell didn't like people talking," he said. "He liked to *do* the talking. In the early stages, I was questioned by all kinds of management about where Bill was. I always kept my mouth shut and said nothing. I'd say, "If you want to know where Bill is, ask him, don't ask me; I'm just the chauffeur.""

Dale learned that the track would be in use the next day and there was no guarantee of availability the day after. Dale said we could go anyway, since no one would be there early in the morning. Dale and Mike were probably veterans of photo shoots, because they told me to meet them at the track at 5:30 a.m. They'd have the cars there before the sun came up. We'd use the magic light of morning to get our

pictures and get out.

I asked Dale if there was more than one Mako Shark. Factory pictures seemed to show multiple versions. In reality, the same Mako Shark went through numerous changes. The engine currently in the car is the legendary, 1969 ZL1 — an all-aluminum 427. Dale said the car had gone through many engine changes. "I think I personally put four or five engines in that thing," he claimed.

The Mako Shark saw numerous design changes, too. "It had a bubble top on it at one time," Dale recalled. "It was a twin bubble top and got lost somewhere along the line. It was like a double clear Plexiglas see-through roof."

What a privilege to see these 'Vettes lined up for pictures.

△ **The present experimental engine is a 427 Chevy V-8 with a single, low-profile, four-barrel carburetor. It produces upward of 425 hp. The Mako Shark is built on a slightly-modified production-type Corvette chassis.**

△ The rear of the '59 Sting Ray racer illustrates the long, flowing shapes that car designers embraced in that era.

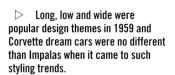

▷ Long, low and wide were popular design themes in 1959 and Corvette dream cars were no different than Impalas when it came to such styling trends.

In factory photos they look mythical in form and shape, yet they fire up, run and make noise like any 'Vette.

The Mako Shark was photographed first, because it was needed for the cover art. Next came the most exotic of the cars: the '59 Sting Ray racer. This was a car that Bill Mitchell designed and raced on his own dime; the first 'Vette to use the Sting Ray name.

It all began in 1957, when Corvette chief engineer Zora-Arkus Duntov created the Corvette SS. This was a pure racing car with a tube frame and an exotic De Dion rear end. It now resides in the Indianapolis Motor Speedway "Hall of Fame" museum.

Mitchell managed to get a second Corvette SS chassis. He wanted to make a Corvette that looked much more like a sports car.

☐ Like most Corvette experimental models, the '59 Sting Ray racer was fuel injected.

☐ The Manta Ray had bite-you-in-the-butt styling mean-looking enough to scare away the competition.

▷ A gussied-up ZL-1 V-8 powered the Manta Ray.

◁ In contrast to the car's outer skin, the interior was clean, stark and angular.

△ Sting Ray style roof and trade-mark round taillights clarified the dream machine's Corvette roots.

◁ If a shark inspired the Mako Shark's designer, a hammerhead shark must have sparked the Manta Ray's rear-end styling.

"His car was known as the 'mule,'" Jacobson elaborated. "They tried different engines, different suspensions and other different things on this car. When Mitchell got hold of it in '59, he actually put a body on the car that resembled what it looks like today." This vehicle became the Sting Ray racer. It was the first Sting Ray and became the basis for the production Sting Ray in '63.

The Manta Ray (a.k.a. Mako Shark II) was the third car. It looked as exotic as the other two. This car's original name led some people to call the Mako Shark the "Mako Shark I." Dale stressed that there was really only one Mako Shark — the '61 version. To make sure there was no need for the Mako Shark I name; the factory simply renamed the Mako Shark II and called it the "Manta Ray."

About the time the car's name was changed, some of its features were also redesigned. Stylists replaced the rear win-dow louvers with a tunnel-type backlite. The car also got a very pointed front end with a chin spoiler.

Dale recalled these design revisions like a real Mitchell afi-cionado. His description of the high-peaked fins on the fenders dipping into the low hood was great. He spoke of the high rise hood with perpendicular lines across the front of the hood as if he were giving a course in car art appreciation. Mitchell would have been proud of his ex-chauffeur who became a corporate executive.

The Mako Shark II/Manta Ray design was picked up for the '68 C3 'Vette, but the show car must have gone through numerous other design changes and engine swaps. The current engine in it is an all-aluminum ZL2. The car is truly exotic in a "Rube Goldberg" way with gadgets like flip-out rear turn signal indicators, a clamshell hood and two banks of three quartz-halogen headlights.

△ "Op-Art" was all the rage in the '60s and the Manta Ray's wheels would have pleased any followers of that school.

☐ The Aerovette was originally tagged XP-882 and a few folks might have thought that such a wild creation could do 882 mph!

△ Later, the car became the Four-Rotor Corvette.

▷ The Aerovette has carried a number of different engines over the years. The original was a 400-cube V-8. It also had a Wankel engine at one time.

When the third car — the Aerovette — finally hit the track, I had a "concept car disconnect" due to the fact that the Aerovette and most of its innovative features never made it to production. Maybe it was too wild.

This car started out as an experimental vehicle called XP-882. It was first powered by a 400-cid V-8 mounted amidship and connected to an Oldsmobile Toronado transaxle.

Jacobson remembered that the car appeared at the 1973 Paris auto show with another engine — a 4-Rotor Wankel power plant. It became known as the four-rotor Corvette. Bill Mitchell later replaced the Wankel engine with a small-block V-8 and re-named it the Aerovette.

The car was originally supposed to be the 1980 production-type Corvette with an all-new mid-engined chassis and a transversely-mounted engine. With its futuristic image, it looks more like a spacecraft, than a sports car. "Bi-fold" gull-wing doors add to its strangeness. One feature that did make it to production was its *deformable* plastic nose and tail section, both finished in body color.

Mike Eradodi opened the doors, the trunk deck lid and the engine cover. Everywhere I looked, the Aerovette was absolutely wild. Like the other vintage show cars at the GM Design Center, it's a real "Corvette Masterpiece."

◁ **The front view of the dream car shows off its aerodynamic lines very well.**

△ **The car has bi-fold gull-wing doors and a number of access hatches.**

△ **Originally, this design was viewed as a production possibility for model-year 1980.**

The Sting Ray Story

The Sting Ray was designed and built by William L. Mitchell, vice president of GM Design Staff in 1959. Mr. Mitchell purchased a chassis from Chevrolet Engineering. At his own expense, he designed a unique thin-shelled fiberglass body for minimum weight. It had an advanced multi-tubular chassis with a De Dion rear suspension and inboard rear brakes.

Powered by a fuel-injected, high performance engine, this car was driven by Dr. Richard Thompson as an independent racing car on the sports car club circuit in 1959 and 1960.

Although this car never won a major race, it usually placed high enough that the car was considered to be very successful. It was raced at Laguna Seca, Elkhart Lake, Cumberland, Lime Rock, Bahamas and at many other sport car meets.

After the 1960 racing seasons, the car was retired. The origin of the design theme for the 1963 production Sting Ray Corvette can be seen in this earlier model.

☐ The first Sting Ray had fuel-injected power.

☐ Though it was retired in 1960, the Sting Ray racer has been preserved by General Motors.

1963 Grand Sport 001 Roadster Raced in 1966

△ **The well-waxed racing car beads up the moisture from a rainy day photo shoot.**

Corvette racing sleuth and restorer Kevin Mackay, of Valley Stream, New York, hooked me up with this Grand Sport roadster and the L88 coupe featured in the next chapter of this book. Both cars raced side-by-side in the 12 hours of Sebring in 1966. Harry Yeaggy, of Cincinnati, Ohio owns the roadster. It wore the number 10 at Sebring and was the first Grand Sport Corvette built.

Most Corvette enthusiasts think about Grand Sports like religious fanatics fantasize about the Holy Grail. Both are unattainable, but their followers have fun dreaming about changing that reality. Chevrolet only built five of the exotic Grand Sport racing cars and anyone seeking one will wind up making excuses such as, "Well, even 'Indiana Jones' didn't wind up with the Holy Grail."

Racing drives innovation and some of the highest-performing Corvettes ever made evolved from racing. Such is the case with the illustrious 1963 Grand Sports. The reason for their existence was the adage "win on Sunday, sell on Monday," which suggested that a checkered flag in weekend racing would send customers to new-car showrooms.

In 1963, Chevrolet Motor Division's competition involvement was still restricted by the ban on racing involvement that the American Automobile Manufacturer's Association adopted in 1957. Therefore, the Grand Sport Corvettes had to be produced on an "underground" basis, although the project still unfolded inside the walls of the Chevrolet factory.

Corvette chief engineer Zora Arkus-Duntov supposedly said, "The handwriting is on the wall," when he saw Carroll

☐ The Grand Sport could have been dubbed the "Grand Snort" and the name would have fit it well.

☐ With its hefty competition belts and special instrumentation, it's clear that this car was built with going fast in mind.

△ Two big, round dials tell the pilot what's going on.

△ Gauges are basic but accurate.

Shelby's lightweight Cobra roadster zoom past a Corvette Z06 on a racetrack late in 1962.

Imagine you're in the same boat Zora was then: you have this gorgeous new-for-1963 Corvette with all the "goodies" for the sports car crowd. For nearly a decade, your beloved Corvette has cultivated a heritage of winning road races, but now your company says, "No racing." At the same time, your crosstown rival, Ford Motor Company, is making racing headlines with its lightweight Cobra sports car.

The Cobra — an ancient AC Ace with a small Ford V-8 — featured an aluminum-body-and-tube-frame combination that weighed scarcely 2,000 pounds. The Corvette, on the other hand, weighed 3,100 pounds in racing trim. Sure, the Corvette had big-block V-8s that gave it the potential to win (as well as a superior suspension), but the Cobra won races mainly because it was a super light machine.

So Zora Arkus-Duntov decided to bend the GM Corporate rules and secretly build a Corvette that could rival the Cobra on the racetrack. His goal was to subtract about 1,100 pounds from the Sting Ray to make it competitive.

Duntov started with a new tube frame. It was stronger than the stock Corvette platform that used square section beams. It also made the car lighter by 94 pounds. Elsewhere, the Chevy engineers took pounds off their new "lightweight" sports car.

This Corvette-on-a-diet was officially named the Grand Sport. It had many weight-saving modifications.

Traco Engineering prepped the motor. Vrooom! Vrooom!

Unique nameplate spotlighted the G.S.

Heavy-duty wheels suited racing chores.

Instead of using cast steel upper and lower control arms, the engineers fabricated sheet metal replacements. They drilled out the rear control arms to remove metal and cut more weight. They even fitted the differential into an aluminum housing. A pound was saved here and a pound was saved there and the savings added up.

Even the window divider used on "split-window" coupe versions was deleted. Plexiglas windows were used. The flip-up headlights were replaced with fixed-position units of a more aerodynamic design. They had Plexiglas covers. Over several years of racing, the roadster took on the configuration you see on these pages.

Chevrolet planned to homologate the Grand Sport, which means to make it eligible for racing. To achieve that, a production run of 125 units was envisioned. Duntov felt amateur racers would buy these lightweight Corvettes to have a chance against the Cobra on racetracks.

Under the hood, a 327-cid small-block V-8 with lightweight aluminum cylinder heads and exhaust manifolds was planned. In this format, the Grand Sport coupes weighed a race-ready 2,283 pounds.

Bunkie Knudsen, a racing fan and the boss over at Chevrolet had approved the Grand Sport plan. Then, word leaked out to the executives on the 14th floor of the GM Building. Company chairman Frederic G. Donner cancelled the production program.

By this time, enough parts had been made to build five Grand Sports. This allowed Duntov to get a few of the cars into the hands of professional racers. Chevrolet loaned a third car — No. 003 — to Dick Doane, a Chevrolet dealer from Dundee, Illinois. Grady Davis, of Gulf Oil Company, got the No. 004 car that was raced by the famous "Flying Dentist," Dr. Dick Thompson.

The No. 1 car (the one seen here) and the No. 002 car, remained in the hands of Chevrolet Motor Division, which kept them hidden. Some enthusiasts say the cars were supposed to have been scrapped. At some point in their corporate hibernation, they were converted to roadsters.

Since Grand Sports weren't going to be sold to the public, the racing cars were assigned to the Sports Car Club of America's C-modified class. They made their racing debut on April 7, 1963 in the SCCA's opening race at Marlboro Motor Raceway, in Upper Marlboro, Maryland. According to the book, *Corvette*

Grand Sport, a faulty fuel injector left the No. 004 Grand Sport on the starting grid that day.

Ed Lowther drove No. 004 at Danville, Virginia on April 28, finishing fourth overall and third in class. That was not bad. There was one first place finish that year, too. But, the Grand Sports did not rack up an enviable season record overall.

Aerodynamics — or the lack thereof — was a big problem with the cars. Dr. Thompson actually went airborne in one race, immediately after cresting a hill.

Duntov and other 'Vette enthusiasts in Chevrolet Motor Division did not like standing on the sidelines while factory-backed Cobras tore the Grand Sports up in '63.

The Cobras got their come-uppance at the Nassau Speed Weeks in November 1963. In that venue, Grand Sports No. 003, 004 and 005 "ran away" from their rivals in each of three races.

Apparently, the Grand Sport racing program wasn't in any way approved. There's a legend about Chevrolet sending its engineers on "vacation" during the Nassau races, though, in reality, they were there as a racing support crew. The engineers helped solve rear differential overheating problems by installing external differential oil coolers on the rear deck, just below the windows.

This underlines the fact that as the Grand Sports raced, their specifications and looks were changed. For example, Chevrolet swapped the original iron-block 327-cid V-8s for full-race, aluminum-block 377-cid V-8s with four 58mm DCOE Weber carburetors atop a cross-ram intake. Appearance-wise, the cars' wheel wells had to be flared to accommodate bigger wheels and tires.

The Grand Sport pictured here is No. 001. Drivers Dick Guldstrand and Dick Thompson shared the driving of this "Corvette Masterpiece."

△ "Bunkie" approved the car and "Rocket Roger" backed the racing efforts through his Chevy dealership. Gulstrand and the "Doc" shared driving chores.

△ Beefy racing suspension goodies helped on track.

1966 Penske L88 Racer

△ **Bad A__! Pardon the French, but there's only one way to describe the rear view of a full-bore midyear Sting Ray racer.**

The No. 001 Grand Sport roadster in the previous chapter and the 1966 coupe you see here are a pair of "mid-year" Corvette racing cars that produce some sentimental feelings.

The Sting Ray fastback — sometimes called the "Developmental Coupe" — is also known as the "Mystery Motor Coupe." While often mistaken for one, it is not a Grand Sport. However, it does have a unique history and a rare L88 V-8.

The Grand Sport roadsters raced in a prototype class against mid-engine cars like the Ford GT, Ferrari Dino, Chapparal and Porsche 903. The L88 developmental coupe raced in GT class against other front-engined production cars.

Design-wise, the Grand Sport was old school by '66, when mid-engined cars dominated in sports car racing. However, No. 001 (racing No. 10) could easily outrun its competition in a straight line. A.J. Foyt drove a Ford GT Mark II at the 12 Hours of Sebring that year and was surprised when No. 001 flew by him on the straightaways. Corvette driver Dr. Dick Thompson recalled Foyt asking, "What's in that damn dinosaur? It went by me like I was stopped."

What was in the "prehistoric" Grand Sport was a brand new just-for-racing engine that Chevrolet had whipped up. They called it the L88. In 1967, this hot big-block V-8 would become an ultra-limited-production engine used in 20 cars.

At Sebring, the Grand Sport ran off course on lap 65, after running into a Morgan. There were houses along the track back then and the car scrapped a concrete driveway. Thompson limped it into the pits, but the damage could not be fixed.

Although it looked like a Grand Sport, the developmental coupe was different. It came out of the St. Louis, Missouri Corvette assembly plant, rather than an experimental shop in Flint, Michigan. It was not a tube-frame prototype car.

The developmental coupe did have an L88. In fact, that engine had helped it cinch a class win at Daytona. A victory at Sebring gave it two GT Class victories in a row. The car was a good example of how Chevrolet was willing to help amateur racers on an under-the-counter basis.

The L88-option is usually considered a 1967 option. It was in that model year that Chevrolet installed 20 of them in production type Corvettes. To find out why the developmental coupe had this engine, Corvette racing expert Kevin Mackay did some special research.

According to Mackay, it was in October 1965 that racing legend Roger Penske received a call from Zora Arkus-Duntov.

The Corvette chief engineer told Penske that a competition version of a new 427-cid big-block V-8 — known as the "Mark IV" engine — was going to be made available to select racing teams. This was the now-fabled L88.

Penske called Elmer Bradley, vice president of marketing for Sun Oil, to persuade him to sponsor a special Corvette in the 1966 Daytona 24-hour race. The oil company's 103-octane Sunoco 260 gasoline, which was going to be specified for L88 engines, was a natural product to promote through racing.

Sunoco then air-freighted two 55-gallon drums of Sunoco 260 to the GM Desert Proving Ground, in Mesa, Arizona, for use in a car nicknamed the "Sunoco Special."

GM issued a "Service Kit" that Chevrolet tested in the field. This meant that cars like the Sunoco Special had discreet backing from people inside Chevrolet. Chevrolet installed L88 engines in what Mackay calls "test cars used at Mesa." He learned that the developmental coupe was not tested at Mesa, however.

Mackay's research shows that GM Engineering sent one L88 V-8 to the St. Louis assembly plant, where Corvettes were assembled in those days. He says they then sent a second such engine to Traco Engineering Company of Culver City,

△ **Strap yourself in and let's go for a real ride.**

▽ **High-octane racing fuel was required.**

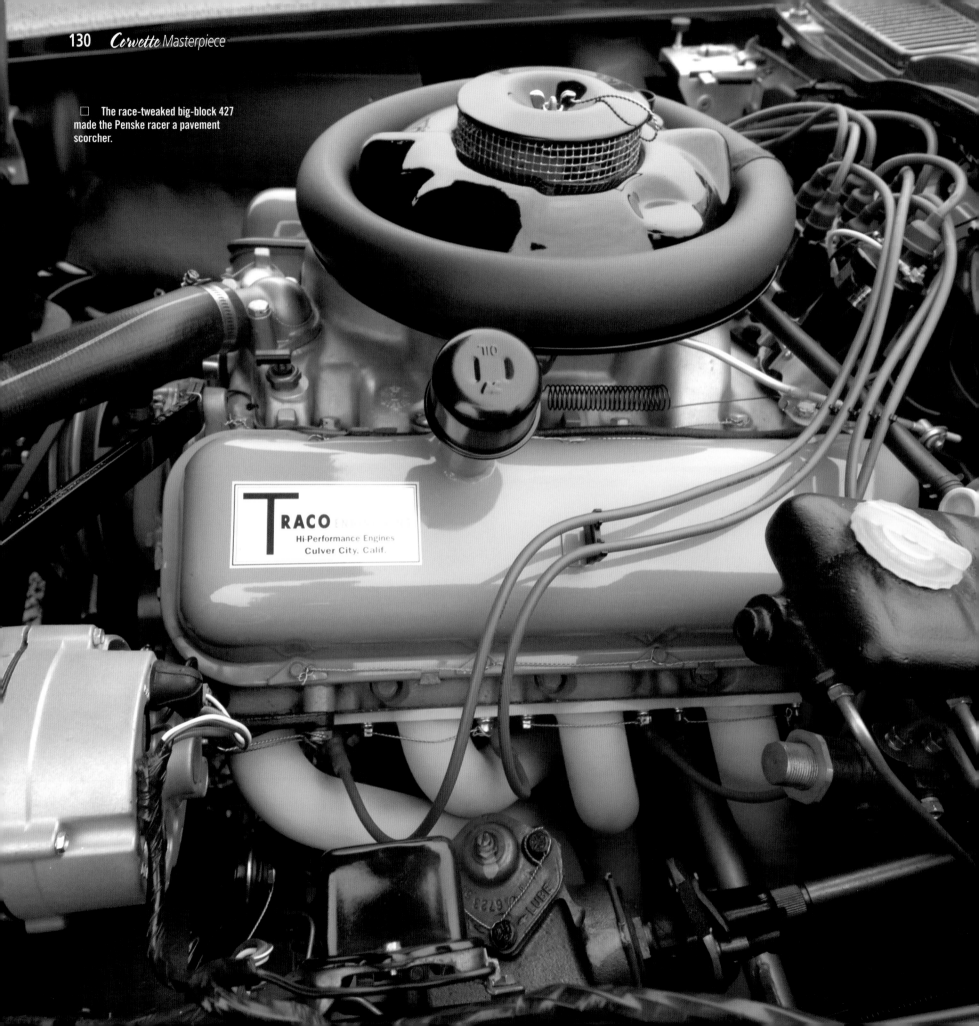

☐ The race-tweaked big-block 427 made the Penske racer a pavement scorcher.

T RACO ENGINES
Hi-Performance Engines
Culver City, Calif.

△ **The headlights were encased in protective covers.**

California. Mackay also learned that Chevrolet's Engineering Center sent a special prototype cowl-induction hood to the St. Louis factory.

Mackay cites a document that describes a January 10, 1966 meeting between Chevrolet and Sunoco representatives. It identifies the developmental coupe as "a 1966 Corvette fitted with an L88, 427-cubic-inch high-performance engine."

The car's other specifications included an M22 heavy duty four-speed transmission, J56 heavy duty brakes, an NO3 36-gallon fuel tank, an F41 heavy-duty suspension, a prototype 2.73:1 positraction rear axle, the prototype cowl-induction hood, a transistorized ignition, a 1965-style front grille assem-

bly (which was lighter in weight than a 1966 grille), a standard black interior and Rally Red paint. Both a radio and heater were "factory delete" items.

According to Mackay, racing driver Dick Guldstrand picked up the red big-block coupe at the St. Louis factory on January 14, 1966. The engine would not fire and run because the carburetor lacked a choke mechanism. Autoworkers pushed the car to the side and handed Guldstrand the keys. Apparently, he poured fuel down the throat of the carburetor to make the L88 fire and flames shot out the exhaust pipes.

Mackay understands that since the coupe had no heater, the assembly line workers offered Guldstrand a blanket to keep

△ **The headlights were encased in protective covers.**

☐ Big, fat pipes running down the side of the car were required to empty the engine of spent gases.

△ **The restored car is blood boiling.**

him warm on the drive to Penske's race shop in Philadelphia. Penske's crew then prepared the car for Daytona.

Mackay learned that the tech inspectors at Daytona made the crew remove some large aluminum fender flares from the coupe so it could qualify as a "stock-production" vehicle. Apparently, many other racing features got by the inspectors.

An important engine swap, for example, went unnoticed. The night before qualifying races, somebody flew in the special race-prepared L88 that Traco built in California. Then, Penske bent the rules even further by having his crew replace the tires on the car with wider "cheater" tires during the first pit stop. The wide tires were pulled off during the last pit stop, when it was apparent the coupe would win in GT class.

Kevin Mackay first saw the developmental coupe at a Malcolm Konner Corvette show, in Paramus, New Jersey, in 1983 At that time it was painted Nassau Blue and had a tri-power set-up. The original exterior and interior trim were still there. The owner knew the car's history and was asking $135,000 for the car at that time in 1983.

An enthusiast named Gene Shiavone bought the coupe in 1987. Mackay says Shiavone paid "a lot more" (than $100,000) for the car. The new owner shipped the car to Dick Guldstrand to have its heritage validated. He then restored the car to its 1966 Sebring appearance. Schiavone campaigned the car in vintage races. Eventually, he also purchased the No. 001 Grand Sport.

Mackay had the opportunity to buy the developmental coupe in 2001. He says, "I am blessed to have such a piece of history."Corvette Repair, Inc. — Mackay's Valley Stream, New York restoration shop — restored the car to concours condition. It was painted the same blue color it was when raced at Sebring with a No. 9 on its doors.

Kevin's research found that records from both the Corvette factory in St. Louis and the Chevrolet Tonawanda engine plant in New York confirm no L88 engines were put in Corvettes that were sold to the public in 1966. That makes Kevin Mackay's one-of-a-kind "Corvette Masterpiece" a COPO (Central Office Production Order) car authorized by the Chevrolet Central Office.

Grand Sport Replica
One Flying Go-kart

Masterpieces are always copied, whether they are paintings, sculptures or Corvettes. In the case of this copycat Corvette, the copy is a copy, but it is not a "fake." When Zora Arkus-Duntov and his crew created racing cars, they actually wanted Chevy customers to copy what they had done.

Modern copies of Corvette racing cars — like this one owned by Dennis Manire — are intended for car shows, rather than races. Manire is a "midyear" Corvette fanatic from Florida who lives and breathes Corvettes. He loves showing his cars.

One of Dennis' favorite Corvettes is a replica of the first Grand Sport. The famous Grand Sport was built as a coupe. Racing car builder and owner/driver Roger Penske later turned it into a roadster. Dennis Manire's car pays tribute to the roadster.

Manire and his wife Cindy, of Titusville, Florida, bought the replica after it was finished. Manire said the son of the car's first owner worked at D & D, the Akron, Ohio company that sold the car as a kit and built it. D & D is no longer in business.

△ **Replication is the sincerest form of flattery.**

▷ "63 UFO" reads the rear license plate.

▷ The ZZ3-type 350 V-8 motivates this monster.

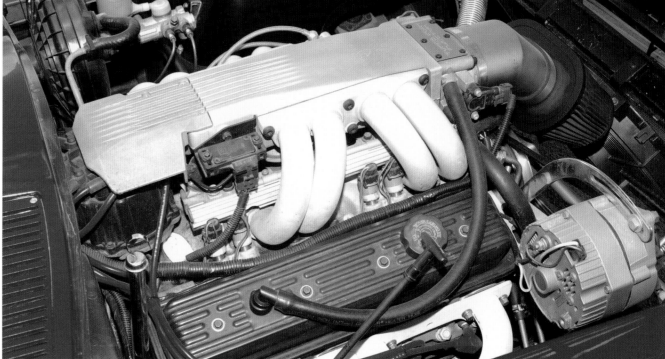

▽ Dennis Manire built the beast.

The Grand Sport replica was built on a tube frame. "A lot of people get concerned that a Corvette was ruined," Manire explained. "Our car was constructed in a way that avoided destroying a real Corvette."

The five original Grand Sports were also built on tube frames. Dennis feels his replica is built as well as the originals and is "actually somewhat better" as far as handling is concerned, since it has a high-tech C4 Corvette suspension.

"I saw it in a magazine five years ago and just loved its looks. I wanted something that was different and unique from what everybody else had," Dennis recalled. He bought the car to exhibit it at shows.

Because it looks true to the original, the Grand Sport replica turns heads. Other replicas do exist, but these replicas are not something you see at every car show.

"We've had a '67 'Vette for 22 years," said Dennis. "It is a ball to drive and gets attention wherever it goes, but the Grand Sport is, like, 25 times better. It becomes a show car when you get gas or stop somewhere to eat. You're a one-car car show."

△ The hot looks of the replica racer are back with a warmed-over drive train, but it's the scoops, power blisters and side pipes the folks see first.

◁ Corvette enthusiasts love getting their cars autographed by personalities.

The replica's hot looks are backed up by hot performance. Dennis said, "It's like a big go-kart."

Dennis and Cindy have friends in the RV business. They have a scale that you can drive each wheel up on. The replica weighed in at 2,200 pounds. The Grand Sport's rival — Carroll Shelby's 289-powered Cobra street car — also had a tube frame and a weight of 2,200 pounds.

The light weight of Dennis' car is related to the equipment features it doesn't have. He has a sign listing non-available items that he brings to car shows.

"My sign always gets people to smile," he pointed out. The sign explains that the car has no top, no windshield wipers, no heater, no air conditioner, no side windows, no door locks, no spare tire, no jack, no emergency brake, no hood release and no defroster. "Just to be cute, I put down that it doesn't have cup holders," Dennis noted.

The car has a 350-cid GM Performance Parts ZZ3 crate motor, Appletone rack-and-pinion steering and wide BF Goodrich tires, so it is really one "flying go-kart." And though it is hard to believe, this "Corvette Masterpiece" is licensed for street use.

☐ In 1964, the sight of a 'Vette on the street was like spotting a spaceship.

'63 Corvette Z06 Package Made for Racing

◁ **The Z06 was built for driving and made to go fast.**

Today, there is a brand new Corvette Z06 model that is a special high-performance car. However, the first Corvette Z06 package was a made-for-racing option offered in 1963.

The 1963 Corvette Sting Ray featured a brand new design. For the first time ever, the Corvette car-line offered a real coupe. It was a fastback with a split rear window. The car you see on these pages is a low-mileage '63 Z06 coupe.

As mentioned earlier in this book, Chevrolet had officially dropped all official factory support of racing by 1963. However, it still offered certain features and options that clearly had racing applications.

Some were standard equipment. For example, all '63 Corvettes had a new independent rear suspension that was a big plus on racetracks.

The Z06 package was an extra that included a 327-cid 360-hp fuel-injected V-8, the N30 "big tank" option (an extra-large gas tank needed to reduce the number of fuel stops during races), a heavy-duty suspension and heavy-duty brakes. A handful of cars with the Z06 option even left the factory with knock-off-style racing wheels.

The first two batches of Z06 Corvettes, built in October of 1962, went directly to well-known racers. A.J. Foyt got one of those cars. Nickey Chevrolet of Chicago got another. A third

This Raven Black Z06 coupe is the only '63 Corvette that's been documented to have left the factory with knock-off wheels.

△ These knock-off-style racing wheels feature these rare two-bar spinners. It came from the factory with a three-bar style.

▷ A fuel-injected 327-cid small-block Chevy V-8 was a part of the Z06 option.

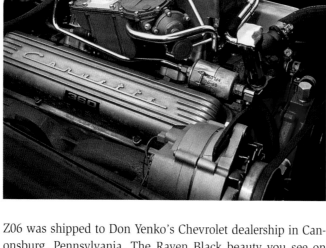

Unfortunately, the Corvette knock-off wheels were prone to porosity problems and poor sealing around the rims. These problems often resulted in air leaks. Because of this, only 12 cars got the option before it was cancelled.

The great-looking wheels, with the rare two-bar spinners, went with a '63 "split-window" coupe like a pair of silk stockings go with a *Playboy* centerfold. Too bad they were so rare. This black coupe is the only car sold with the original knock-off wheel option that's known to exist today.

The car also has the N03 option. The big fuel tank has enough space to hold 36.5-gallons of gas baffled between its upper and lower halves. The tank is contoured to fit the coupe like a sweet pea fits a pea pod. It integrates a jack and storage space behind the seats. The tank's special location and position were designed to minimize the effects of having 200 pounds of fuel sloshing back and forth at the rear of a racing car.

The racing package on this coupe also included enlarged wheel wells, which allowed oversized tires to be mounted for racing use. It is actually the inner wheel housings that were changed to accommodate up to 7.65 x 15 tires mounted on the six-inch wide knock-off rims.

Z06 was shipped to Don Yenko's Chevrolet dealership in Canonsburg, Pennsylvania. The Raven Black beauty you see on these pages was another in the group. It was purchased by independent racer Edward Schlampp, Jr.

Schlampp picked his car up at the Corvette factory in St. Louis, Missouri, on February 27, 1963. He campaigned it in Sports Car Club of America A-production road racing.

The Corvette knock-off wheels were something that Corvette racers needed in 1963. Their strongest rivals drove Ford-powered Shelby Cobras with knock-off-style wire wheels.

◁ The neat 3-spoke steering wheel had a sophisticated look.

◁ Detailing added to the Corvette's appeal inside and out.

△ Only 12 cars got these great-looking wheels.

The 1963 Z06 cars like this one also featured a dual-circuit master cylinder for power-assisted drum brakes with sintered metallic linings. These brakes do not work well until they heat up. Then, they really stop the 3,200-pound Corvette very well. They are only practical for racing.

Rubber brake-cooling scoops — known as "elephant ears" — were supplied loose in the car, rather than installed. They were designed to ram fresh outside air to the sintered metallic brake shoes. This option was available only on '63 'Vettes with the Z06 package. This heavy-duty brake system (which became the legendary J56 option in 1964) included vented rear plates and cooling fans that spun with the hub.

The Z06-only heavy-duty suspension option was also engineered strictly for racing. It included springs with seven extra-thick leaves in place of the 9-leaf springs used on stock Corvettes.

From its knock-off wheels and fat tires to its big gas tank and fuel-injected 327, this Z06 "Corvette Masterpiece" looks exactly like it did when it left the factory to go road racing.

Custom 1965 Corvette

△ It's hard to change the basic shape of a midyear "Vette, but customizing is all in the details.

▷ "Wicked" plate says it all as far as looks go.

When Ron Champe retired, one of the things he wanted to do was build the "midyear" Corvette of his dreams. He would build the car, from the ground up, in his own way. Time was no object, but he wanted to keep the original look. Modifications to the car would not cross over a certain line.

For instance, Ron decided to use a custom aluminum billet grille built by Alumicraft. He felt this grille's design would not spoil the car's vintage looks. By eliminating the door handles, Ron felt that he accentuated the flow of the "factory" body lines. The front bumpers and antenna were pulled off to clean up the original styling.

☐ **The underhood treatment stresses the clean look.**

▷ **The customizing extends into the interior.**

▽ **Although it's a retirement project, the coupe is anything but "retiring" in character.**

Few people notice the custom-made inner fender panels designed to conceal the open inner fender vents, wiring harness and Vintage Air coolant lines. The firewall was smoothed out and the door jambs were filled in, but otherwise the body remained the way it left the assembly plant in 1965.

Ron started his "retirement project" in January 2003. By August 2004, the body was ready to be refinished. Ron farmed out the actual "squirting" of the paint.

Ken Zikelli, of Zeke's Street Machines in Enron Valley, Pennsylvania, applied the base coat/clear coat Twilight Blue Pearl color. The shadow striping down the center of the body is subtle and hard to see.

Ron's project took 2,300 hours. He finished building his "Corvette Masterpiece" in just 30 months. The car made its debut in June 2005.

Curbside Service – Corvette Style

It was Wednesday in St. Charles, Illinois and the Bloomington Gold Corvette show didn't start there until the next day. A few Corvettes were coming in off Route 64 and pulling into the Pheasant Run hotel and resort where one of the biggest Corvette venues in the country takes place. Some of the vintage Corvettes were being driven and some were traveling on trailers.

The author was in a Wal-Mart parking lot a few blocks from the hotel. He had spotted a beautiful '65 Corvette coupe that looked like a "Corvette Masterpiece." Guessing the owners would be back soon, he decided to wait and talk with them about their car. The Corvette's silver paint, knock-off wheels and gold-line tires looked great. Having this car in *Corvette Masterpieces* would certainly be worth a short wait.

△ The author spotted the beautiful '65 Corvette coupe in a Wal-Mart parking lot and thought it looked like a "Corvette Masterpiece." Lee Lasher was the car's owner and his buddy Mike Hofmann came along to have fun — and change oil.

◁ The handy-dandy oil change kit consisted of an oil filter wrench, a plastic oil pan, a filler spout and a 5-qt. jug of oil.

▷ The engine was fitted with fuel injection and turned out to be a 327-cid 375-hp V-8.

▷ The Floridians explained they had gone to a quick-change lube center and heard there was a two-hour wait, so they decided to take things into their own hands.

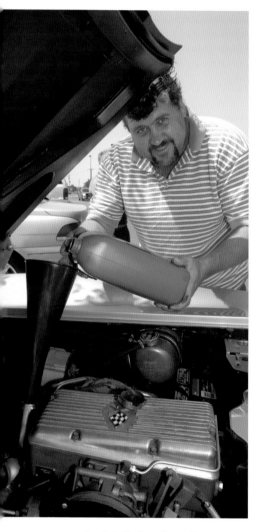

△ Into the funnel goes the "black gold."

▷ The owner of this 'Vette wanted to know what it was worth without buying an *Old Cars Price Guide*.

Finally, two men approached the car. One was about stocky and around 50 years old. He had on shorts and a dark blue, sleeveless muscle shirt. His blonde hair was thinning and he had a "vacation tan." Around his neck was a bright gold chain. The man glowed. His legs kicked side to side as he walked in a self-assured manner. He wore a pair of gold-rimmed sunglasses with amber-colored lenses.

"Just drive it up on the curb," the man instructed his friend, in what sounded like a thick New Jersey accent.

"Let's move it over there. Get it out of the way." His friend, a taller fellow, said something. He also sounded like he was from New Jersey — or maybe the Bronx.

"Nice 'Vette," said the author. "What's under the hood?"

This was a ploy to get a look at the engine before asking if we could shoot pictures of the car for the book. The Corvette's body looked to be in show condition and the interior was pretty sharp, too, but sometimes the engines in beautiful cars are not detailed for show.

"Can I see the engine?" the author asked.

"Sure" was the answer and the man in the muscle shirt popped the hood open.

Corvette people are friendly enough to do things like that, especially when you show interest in their "ride." The V-8 engine under the hood was fitted with fuel injection, just like the fender badges indicated.

"It's the 375 horse 327," the man advised.

☐ The '65 Corvette fuelie's silver paint, knock-off wheels and gold-line tires looked great.

The engine was not show detailed. It looked pretty good, but the author wasn't certain it was "Masterpiece" quality. Then, the two men pulled out oil-change equipment and provided him with a "human-interest" angle for a story. Believe it or not, they were going to change oil on a fuelie 'Vette right there in a Wal-Mart parking lot!

The man with the gold chain took a scrap of wood and made a ramp to raise the car up from the asphalt to curb level. In other words, he was going to drive his 3,0000-lb., $100,000 Corvette up a flimsy board and change his own oil in the street.

The author began snapping pictures as the men spread their handy-dandy oil change kit out on the hot pavement. It consisted of an oil filter wrench, a plastic oil pan, a filler spout and a 5-qt. jug of oil.

"What are you doing?" the men asked.

"Taking a picture," said the author.

"I don't know if I like you taking a picture of us changing oil here," the man replied. So the author introduced himself and explained that he wanted to do a human-interest story. Gold-chain-wearing Lee Lasher said he was the car's owner. His buddy Mike Hofmann was playing oil changer. Both men were from the Ft. Meyers, Florida area. Mike was getting more of a kick out of the media exposure than Lee was.

"Well, we like people who drive their Corvettes," said the author. "And we like people who work on their own cars, especially in a Wal-Mart parking lots."

The Floridians explained that they had gone to a quick-change lube center and were told that there was a two-hour wait to get an oil change. "We said we'd do it ourselves," said Lee. "That's what we like about Corvettes, the owners can work on them."

What's this car worth? " Lee asked the author. Then he

△ The car's interior got a little hot sitting in the sun.

☐ The car had been shipped from Florida to Illinois for the Dana Mecum Auction at Bloomington Gold.

△   How many of these did they make in silver?

held up his index finger to indicate his opinion on price.

"One digit," he explained. "That means $100,000 — minimum. It's a 375-horse fuelie. They only made, what, 771 of them? How many of those were silver?"

Lee did his homework. His thinking about his Corvette's value agreed with the *Old Cars Price Guide* when you add up all the options on the car. Lee said that the previous owner had traded the Corvette in on a BMW at a "Bimmer" dealership.

"Like that one," Lee noted, as he pointed at a 745 series BMW parked nearby that was also silver.

Mike Hofmann drove the Corvette up on the crude wooden ramp. The thin board creaked and groaned and cracked in half.

"Higher," said Lee. "You need to get on top of the curb."

Mike revved the 327 and let the clutch out another couple inches until. Soon, the Corvette's tire was perched on top of the curb. Lee reached down with his hand and with an easy push broke off the bottom half of the splintered board.

"Block the rear tire," the author advised, as he picked up a chunk of wood and stuck it behind the tire. The three men, who were total strangers two minutes earlier, were now partners in an oil change. That's what you call "Corvette bonding."

Mike Hofmann crawled under the car and pulled the oil drain plug. Changing oil was no big deal for him. He owned a repair shop and had a crew that worked on cars every day. He said he owned over 20 cars himself. His business card read, "Southern Hot Rod & Classic Restoration."

Lee Lasher was a car guy, too. His collection included hot muscle cars and Corvettes. Both men had come to the Midwest for Bloomington Gold. They had shipped the '65 Corvette up for the Mecum Corvette Auction that is part of Bloomington Gold. And even though they were selling the car, they were determined to give it an oil change — even if they had to do the job themselves!

Corn-Fed Big Block

△ The small front / big rear tire combo makes the car look like a cat ready to leap.

◁ This is a big block with an "attitude."

This 1966 Sting Ray coupe stood out from the rest of the "midyear" Corvettes parked around it at Bob Mc-Dorman's annual car show on September 13, 2004.

The car proves that it sometimes takes only a few exterior modifications to make a Corvette look *really hot*. If you go too far with modifications, you can ruin the looks. The owner of this car — Randy Leibrock — seems to have hit the nail on the head with his updates to a classic design.

First of all, Randy stuck with the stock Tuxedo Black paint. Black is hard to beat for a performance car that you want to

△ The inside is definitely as cool-looking as the exterior.

△ Moroso valve covers hint at the car's go-power.

give a sinister look. Tuxedo Black really helps to set off chrome pieces like the Centerline wheels, the factory side-pipes, the thin chrome bumpers, the trim around the windshield and the brightwork decorating the bulge on the big-block-style hood.

Leibrock fired up the engine and we headed down the interstate highway until we found the perfect setting. This corn-fed "Corvette Masterpiece," with its "Darth Vader" appearance and subtle modifications, looked just great on a smooth road with corn fields running down either side of it.

☐ Obviously, this was a big-block V-8 car. All you had to do was look at the raised hood.

Behind the 8-Ball

△ **The car was restored to the format it was in when it went to Daytona International Speedway for the American Road Race of Champions wearing this same black-with-yellow trim finish.**

To understand this saga about an old racing car, you have to do what Captain Renault suggested in "Casa Blanca" and "round up the usual suspects." The central character in our tale is Corvette enthusiast Doug Bergen. Doug had the idea to go racing. Then, he found Bob Johnson, a 40-year-old beginner in racing and struck pay dirt. Bob lived in Bergen's hometown of Marietta, Ohio, and had real driving talent.

Corvette racing authority Kevin Mackay knew the names Johnson and Bergen very well. In the early '90s, Kevin had been reading older car magazines and searching for stories about interesting Corvette racing cars. He had noticed the names of Bob Johnson and Doug Bergen showing up a lot.

Bob Johnson successfully raced three Corvettes that Doug Bergen built. The first car was the black-and-yellow 1966 coupe that you see in this section. The others were 1968 and 1969 Corvette L88s. Both of the other cars are "another story for another time."

The featured Corvette has a known history. It was driven by Johnson at racecourses like Sebring, Le Mans, Watkins Glen and Mid-Ohio. It was also Bob Johnson's first conveyance to super-stardom as a driver.

Doug Bergen (l.) and former race driver Bob Johnson pose with the Tuxedo Black "8-ball" big-block road racing Corvette that Johnson campaigned years ago.

Corvette Racer Bob Johnson Started with a Spitfire

Before driving Corvette racing cars, Bob Johnson, of Marietta, Ohio, raced a Triumph Spitfire in Sports Car Club of America (SCCA) G-production class. The year was 1966 and Johnson was 40 years old.

The same year, in the same city, a successful businessman named Doug Bergen got the idea to go racing with a new Corvette. Bergen ordered a 1966 Sting Ray coupe with the 427/425 V-8, an M21 four-speed manual gearbox and a posi-traction rear axle. The car was sold with the radio delete option and was originally Tuxedo Black with a Saddle interior, the rarest trim combinations.

SCCA rules were amazingly easy to follow back then. You were allowed to run tires a little bit wider than stock, but you were not allowed to modify the fenders. You could change brake pads, but you had to keep stock calipers.

Bergen was on a tight budget and didn't swap the gas tank for a fuel cell, since fuel cells were not required. A roll bar was mandatory, of course.

Bergen modified the hood by replacing the latch with one hood pin and pulling the "gills." He also installed a racing seat and two Raydot racing mirrors on the fenders. He pulled the bumpers off the car to save weight.

Bergen called on Marietta resident Bob Johnson to drive the Corvette. Bob racked up first place finishes in the national races at Cumberland Airport in May, at Mid-Ohio the Johnny Appleseed 150 in August and Marlboro, Maryland in September. He also took second in the IRP National in October.

For the 1967 season, Johnson drove the '66 coupe again. He finished third in the Central Division and went to the SCCA Runoffs, also called the American Road Race of Champions. He was among the leaders there when a head gasket blew. That pushed him back to a 7th-place finish.

Johnson started racing and winning with a stock 425-hp engine. He had it slightly race-tuned with a

modified Holley four-barrel carburetor. In the second race, the 427 spun a bearing. Bergen had to call Yenko Sportscars, in Canonsburg, Pennsylvania, to buy a new big-block V-8. The new 427 pretty much got an L88 build, which was the coming thing for Chevrolet racers.

By that time, the team of Johnson/Bergen had gained attention and won support from Chevrolet. The company provided parts to them on an out-the-back-door basis. When Bergen's 1968 L88 Corvette arrived, he returned the '66 coupe to near-stock condition and sold it. He kept the Yenko L88 style motor and the car's roll cage.

The second owner held the car until 1975. A third owner kept the '66 until MacKay picked it up for Marc Mehl. Then the car was restored to the format it was in when it went to Daytona for the American Road Race Of Champions. The color scheme is the same black with yellow trim. It wears No. 8 on its side. Bergen called the Tuxedo Black '66 the "8-ball." The name fit because so many racers fall behind the 8-ball out on the track.

◁ The car turned up only 100 miles from the original owner's home.

▽ It's no mystery why it's called the "8-Ball" car.

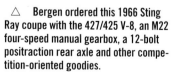

△ Bergen ordered this 1966 Sting Ray coupe with the 427/425 V-8, an M22 four-speed manual gearbox, a 12-bolt positraction rear axle and other competition-oriented goodies.

Kevin Mackay learned that both Johnson and Bergen were from Marietta. He quickly tracked down Bergen's phone number and phoned him. "It was tough at the beginning", Kevin explained. "He thought I was a tire kicker."

It turned out that Bergen no longer had the '66 'Vette. In 1968, he had returned the competition-prepped coupe back to as near stock condition as possible and sold it. He had a brand new Corvette — the '68 L88 — to make race ready. Lucky for Mackay, Bergen had kept his original owner's card for the '66. This gave him the vehicle identification number (VIN), which he passed on to Mackay. Kevin got Corvette super sleuth Dave Reisner involved. Reisner tracked the car down. It was only 100 miles from Bergen's home.

"The car was a regular knock around *driver*, with custom wheels and a custom interior," Kevin Mackay recalled. Kevin knew that the owner wasn't aware of what he had. However, he'd owned the Corvette since 1975 and didn't want to sell it. He said he had "grown attached to the car as if it were part of my family."

While it did not have its original engine or paperwork (except Bergen's paperwork), the VIN proved the Corvette was Bob Johnson's old racing car. Eventually, Marc Mehl, a well-known collector from New York, bought the vehicle.

☐ Rockin', rollin' and racin' were what the '60s were all about.

Kevin Mackay saw the car in Ohio. Then a transporter picked it up and took it to Mackay's shop in Valley Stream, New York. About a month later Doug Bergen saw the car in Valley Stream.

The car's owner had a landscaping business. He had customized the vehicle and painted the body "Lawn Green." He didn't know the car's racing background and he may not have cared.

Doug Bergen couldn't identify the car immediately. Then he spotted something familiar. "See that little plate there," he said. "I put that little aluminum plate in to support the cracking floor."

Bergen and Johnson ran into the coupe again during an event at the National Corvette Museum in Bowling Green, Kentucky. They talked about the car and about the racing experiences they had in the "Corvette Masterpiece."

△ In 1966, vinyl interior options for Corvettes included: Black, Red, Brigh Blue, Dark Blue, Saddle, Silver an Black, Green, White and Black and White and Blue.

△ Details "make" the restoration pop — even on a racing car.

1967 435-hp Convertible; Those Were The Days

△ **Milt Robson's red '67 Sting Ray ragtop carries the 427-cid 435-hp V-8.**

Those were the days — going to Milt Robson's place to shoot pictures of muscle Corvettes. One of them was this awesome, red, 1967 Sting Ray convertible. It has the 427-cid 435-hp V-8 with a four-speed manual transmission and all the bells and whistles.

Back then, Milt's friend Jake was alive. Milt and Jake had gone to high school together. Milt had the luck and the cars, but there wasn't a nicer guy in all of Georgia than Jake.

One week, we were there shooting cars. Tuesday was "picking night." Milt and the boys had a band and played once a week. I spied some slot machines and went over to play.

After awhile, Jake came by and watched me popping in nickels. "Don't use your own money!" he said. Jake pulled open the back of the slot machine and had me rake up a big pile of nickels. "Use these," he said.

Jake used to get cars out and position them for taking pictures. Milt's estate had plenty of great settings with roads and trees and brick surfaces galore. When Jake wasn't there, Milt gave me the okay to just pick whatever cars I wanted and drive them out on the estate and set them up for photos. Somehow the pictures never came out as good as when Jake was along.

☐ Four-speed gearbox is linked to the big "Rat" engine.

◁　This "Corvette Masterpiece" carries triple two-barrel carbs.

▽　The powerful Corvette brings back memories of the past.

☐　You could call this beautiful car a "Georgia Peach" because of the photo backdrop.

Today, Milt has a bigger estate with a bigger building to house his new-and-improved car collection. But we still love his old place and think about how great it was to put his '67 Corvette on the brick drive and have such a beautiful Georgia backdrop for a photo.

The '67 Corvette is the classic L71 Tri-Power finished in red on red. Jake drove it right on the spot it's parked. There's probably no flashier, higher-optioned, better-looking Tri-Power '67 Corvette convertible than this one. It's truly a "Corvette Masterpiece."

△　What a great car to photograph.

△ Possibly the purest expression of 'Vette art.

△ The coupe was cool, too!

1967 Corvette 427

Some consider the 1967 the best looking of the early Sting Rays. Its styling, although basically the same as in 1966, was a bit cleaner. The same egg-crate style grille with Argent Silver finish was carried over. The same smooth hood seen in 1966 was re-used. The crossed flags badge on the nose of the 1967 Corvette had a widened "V" at its top. On the sides of the front fenders were five vertical and functional louvers that slanted towards the front of the car.

Minor changes were made to the interior. Most noticeable was the relocation of the parking brake from under the dash to the center console. The new headliner was cushioned with foam and fiber material. Four-way flashers, directional signals with a lane-change function, larger interior vent ports and folding seat-back latches were all new. At the rear there were now dual round taillights on each side (instead of a taillight and optional back-up light). The twin back-up lights were now mounted in the center of the rear panel, above the license plate.

Standard equipment included a new dual-chamber brake master cylinder, six-inch wide slotted rally wheels with trim rings, an odometer, a clock, carpeting and a tachometer. The optional finned aluminum wheels were changed in design and had a one-year-only, non-knock-off center. Ten lacquer exterior finishes were offered:

Tuxedo Black, Ermine White, Elkhart Blue, Lyndale Blue, Marina Blue, Goodwood Green, Rally Red, Silver Pearl, Sunfire Yellow and Marlboro Maroon. All convertibles came with a choice of a Black, White or Teal Blue soft top. The all-vinyl foam-cushioned bucket seats came in Black, Red, Bright Blue, Saddle, White and Blue, White and Black, Teal Blue and Green.

The Corvette "427," with its own funnel-shaped, power bulge on the hood, had been introduced in 1966. Its big-block V-8 was related to Chevrolet's 427-cid NASCAR "mystery" racing engine and the production-type Turbo-Jet 396. A 427-cid 435-hp 1967 Corvette convertible carried only 7.7 lbs. per horsepower. It could hit 60 mph in 5.5 seconds and do the quarter mile in 13.8 seconds. Three four-speed manual gearboxes — wide-ratio, close-ratio and heavy-duty close-ratio — were optional. A desirable extra was side-mounted exhaust pipes.

Cars with 427s got a different power bulge hood and more top horsepower (435) when fitted with three two-barrel carburetors. The special hood had a large, forward-facing air scoop, usually with engine call-outs on both sides.

There were four versions of the 427 in 1967. The regular L36 was nearly unchanged from mid-1965. Next came the L68, with 400 hp. The Tri-Power L71 (as used in Milt Robson's car) delivered 435 hp. Extremely rare — and off in a class by itself — was the aluminum-head L88. Only 20 were built. This powerhouse was officially rated at only 430 hp, but really developed nearly 600 hp!

Deuces wild!

Talk about a winning hand! Three deuces to a full-house 427, the Turbo-Jet V8's got it, cold. And that's precisely what Corvette offers, among other things, in the new '67 Sting Ray. In fact, you can order it two ways: 400 horsepower with hydraulic lifters or 435 horses with solid lifters and a real special-performance camshaft.

On the other hand, you traditionalists can still get the 427 V8 with a big four-barrel on top, putting out 390 horses. The whole works comes with that well-known Corvette independent rear suspension, 11¾-inch disc brakes all around, new 1967 styling touches and comforts galore. And it has safety features like the GM-developed energy-absorbing steering column and seat belts with pushbutton buckles, standard.

Take the base 300-horsepower Turbo-Fire 327 V8 or order any of the other four engines available. Decide on the extras, like AM-FM radio, you can add. Choose the standard three-speed or Powerglide or the four-speed gearbox you can order. Shuffle up the equipment the way you want it, and deal yourself a Sting Ray.

'67 Corvette

◁ **Three dueces was a wild setup for a small, lightweight Corvette.**

Wolf in wolf's clothing.

Some cars tell you all about themselves at first glance. A big soft family sedan. (Ho hum) An utterly practical station wagon. (Ehhh) A plodding sort of economy car. (Wheee) Or a Corvette. A tough, wide-tired, bulge-hooded "let's go driving" Corvette.

A Sting Ray with the 427-cubic-inch 435-horsepower three-deuces V8 you can specify. It *is* what it looks like.

'67 Corvette

CHEVROLET GM

△ **This ad promoted the "big-block" 'Vette as "a wolf in sheep's clothing."**

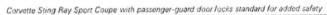
Corvette Sting Ray Sport Coupe with passenger-guard door locks standard for added safety

GM

CHEVROLET

The Black Knight: 1967 L88 Convertible Racing Car

△ **Another masterpiece of automotive styling.**

For the '67 model year, Chevrolet succeeded in keeping the L88 engine option (essentially a race-tuned 427) pretty much hush, hush and pretty much a mystery except to racing buffs. This made Zora Arkus-Duntov very happy, because the L88 gave his team a Corvette that could be raced competitively.

Chevrolet (the company) acted like a feudal Baron carrying out the will of the King (General Motors) to stay clear of racing. Racing driver Tony DeLorenzo was the "Black Knight" in the King's court. He even campaigned this black L88 racing ragtop.

DeLorenzo was "raised in the palace." His father was a Chevrolet executive. It was his pleasure to use his high-born training in service to the advantage of his sovereign, who carried the honorable Bow Tie shield.

DeLorenzo was a zealous competitor on the field of battle. He "charged hard" in Sports Car Club of America amateur road racing events.

No ordinary "knight in shining armor" could accomplish the same thing because the Baron would not permit jousting (on the racetracks). GM was more concerned about selling cars and making money.

Zora Arkus-Duntov and his team did a good job of making the Corvette an attractive street-performance car. But they also needed ways to disguise a racing car as a street car so they could slip it out of the castle to the Black Knight.

This is where the powerful L88 engine option came in. To disguise it, Zora rated the engine at 5 hp less than the L71 Tri-Power version. The L71 carried a 435-hp factory output rating, so that meant the L88 was a 430-hp engine "on paper." Duntov forgot to tell the horsepower police at GM that the 430-hp number showed up at just 5,200 rpm. Above 6,000 rpm, the L88's output peaked at an estimated 530 hp. In fact, some sources have pegged it as high as 620 hp! Now, that was a big lance for the Black Knight to take into battle against Carroll Shelby's 427 Cobras.

DeLorenzo ordered a black car with a blue "stinger" hood stripe. It had the L88 V-8 and all the L88 high-performance features that enthusiasts want today: the No. 3904351 block, the No. 1111240 distributor with no vacuum advance, the dark reddish-brown plug steel core wires with no braiding or ground straps, the filter element mounted with a specially molded duct in the hood, the open aluminum plenum intake, the No. 3904387 aluminum heads and the M22 four-speed.

△ The first owner had the inside track to put a really special package together.

△ **This was the only L88 with power window switches on the console.**

As if the car were secretly built for a knight in Lord Zora's special detachment, the car had one power option that no other Corvette with the L88 engine was allowed: electrically-operated power windows.

If this luxury extra smacked of elitism, so be it. DeLorenzo's car was scheduled to do battle flying the Bow Tie colors that Zora and other enthusiasts inside Chevrolet were unable to fly.

Unfortunately, DeLorenzo still couldn't slay the Cobra. With 1,000 fewer pounds of weight to carry, the 427 Cobra proved to have the edge on the racetrack. However, the Black Knight was a worthy competitor.

After his "commission" expired, DeLorenzo sold the racing car. It continued to be campaigned until 1982. It was re-fitted with a small-block Chevy V-8 to run in D-Sports races and won the GT championship.

By 1982, the Black Knight had been racing for 15 years. Since people say one year on a racetrack is equal to 10 on the street, the ancient road warrior was really showing its wear. "Had you seen it in '83, in the shop, you would have laughed," said current owner Steve Hendrickson.

Looking at the car with its concours restoration, it is hard to imagine how worn out it had become by 1982. "The body

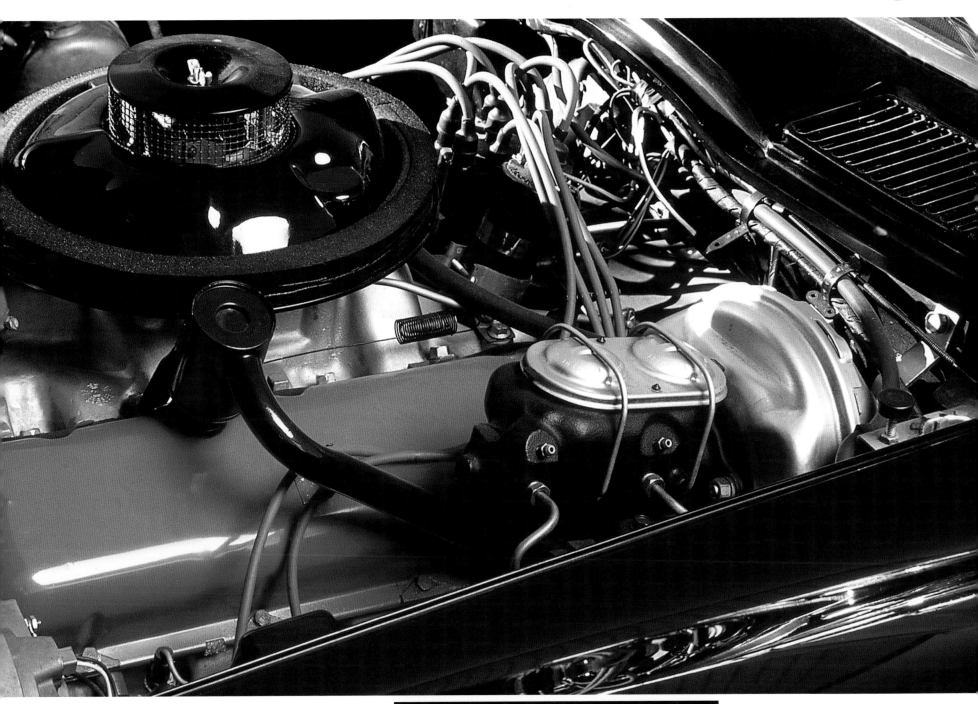

was orange and white and many other colors," Hendrickson revealed. "The windshield posts were sawed off and the interior was gutted. It had rear flares and a 1965-nose. It just looked absolutely horrible."

Despite its battle scars, the old Black Knight seemed like a treasure to John Simonsen, a Canadian who deals in old race cars. He found the car in Canada in 1983. It still had the original Protect-O-Plate, which documented the rare L88 engine option. Paper work from the original title was in the name of Troy Promotions. (It has not been changed to this day).

Simonsen sold the car to Wayne Walker, owner of Zip

△ Though equal in cubes, the "Rat" motor failed to slay the Cobra.

◁ The once battle-scarred ragtop looks pristine today.

△ **Only two black 'Vettes carried the L88 option.**

Products and a well-known Corvette collector. Walker sent the car to Ken and Gary Nabors, of Houston, Texas for a full restoration. In 1984, the Black Knight was ready for exhibition at the big Bloomington Gold Corvette show, where it won a Gold Award and attracted the attention of Steve Hendrickson.

When Wayne Walker put the car up for sale in 1985, Steve was ready to purchase it. The price was steep, but the two finally made a deal for $85,000. At that time, it was a world's record price for an L88-optioned Corvette. Today, such a car could bring over $1 million.

Of the 20 Corvettes built with L88 engines in 1967, only 12 have turned up that are fully-documented cars. Steve's '67 model is one of two black cars with the L88 option. The other black car is a coupe with a red hood stripe.

The Black Knight was restored to look the way it did when it left the assembly line. Steve Hendrickson calls it a miracle, because so much of the car was missing when it was pulled off the racing circuit. And the Black Knight still looks as good as the day the restoration work was finished. Hendrickson has displayed his "Corvette Masterpiece" several times in the Special Collection at Bloomington Gold.

Z06 '67 Stingray:
Having Your Cake And Eating It, Too

S tyling-wise, Ron Johnson's Corvette looks like a '67, but the 18 x 9.5 wheels are bigger than stock and hint that something has been changed. At a low angle, from the back, the suspension arms seem to have a 5-link setup, instead of the stock "trailing arm" design.

When you pop open the hood, the gig is up. There's an LS6 engine below. In case that doesn't ring a bell, it's the designation for the awesome 405-hp V-8 used in modern, high-performance, Z06 Corvettes.

For years, the '67 Corvette with a big-block V-8 was considered one of the most desirable Corvettes of all time. Today,

△ **The big wheels on Ron Johnson's car are a clear hint that it has changes from stock specs.**

◁ **The power blister indicates underhood goodies.**

△ **This interior might aptly be called "Varooom with a view!"**

the Z06 is right up there with the '67. It is a rocketship as far as performance goes and it has superior handling.

So which is better . . . the L88 or the Z06? How about combining the two? What if you put together a car with the features of the '67 big-block mated with Z06 technology?

This is exactly the type of car that Ron Johnson made. He pulled the engine from his 2001 Corvette Z06 and dropped it into a '67 convertible. The result is like having your cake and eating it, too.

In the old days, engine swaps were easy. You might have needed custom motor mounts to put a newer engine in an older car. Today, it's a lot harder.

Ron Johnson called on a man names Paul Newman — no, he's not the actor — to fabricate a complete custom chassis. This is the way things are done today. "Hybrid" cars are designed by mixing parts from different-generation Corvettes with custom-made parts like Newman's chassis.

Ron's C2 (second-generation) Corvette has a C4 (fourth generation Corvette) suspension. It came from a 1986 Corvette. Newman's "Car Creation" shop in Templeton, California built the modified C2 frame that accepts a C4 suspension. This makes the car handle as well as a late-model Corvette.

It would have been easiest to use a C4 engine, but Ron insisted on using LS6 (which is fifth generation). There's a major drive train difference between C4 and C5 cars: in a C4 the

△ LS6 under the fiberglass hood packs a whallop.

◁ Ron likes it with both top and pedal down.

△ **The sun glints off of the gorgeous paint on a car that represents the best of old and new rolled into one package.**

transmission goes behind the engine; in a C5, the transmission goes in the rear of the car to improve weight distribution.

Ron obtained a TKO 600 Tremac five-speed transmission. It included one of the first engine bell housings that could be used to mate an LS6 engine with a four-bolt style Corvette transmission case.

"To run the new hydraulic clutch that comes with new Corvettes, we either had to go to a six-speed transmission and hack up the interior console or find a five-speed designed like the TKO 600," Ron explained. "We got a transmission from one of the first production runs. We mounted it behind the

LS6. It fits right in the hole, so we were able to keep the stock interior."

Not having to modify the stock interior to make room for the larger original transmission was a big plus in making the car easier and cheaper to put together. Except for C4 high-back bucket seats, a Grant steering wheel and carbon-fiber-backed custom gauges, the interior is completely stock.

Ron says his updated '67 "Corvette Masterpiece" handles like a C4 and has the acceleration of a Gen V Z06. This type of car is really the dream of many Corvette fans today. They can have the best of old and new in one package.

The See-Through 1969 L88 Corvette Corvette From The Outside

According to Kevin Mackay, "It's likely that 50 percent of the workmanship that goes into a restoration is covered by the (car's) body panels." Since Mackay is the owner of Corvette Repair, Inc. — a restoration shop in Valley Stream, New York — he should know.

"We just kind of pushed the envelope a little further to show what it takes to restore a Corvette," was Mackay's explanation for the car you see on these pages. He calls it the "See-Through" car.

With the body panels removed, enthusiasts can view the hidden parts of a Corvette. Mackay refers to the metal structure that many different parts are attached to as the "birdcage." Like Corvette factory workers did in production, modern restorers must bond the fiberglass body panels to the birdcage. The birdcage is like the car's skeleton.

Parts attached to the birdcage include the windshield, door hinges, doors and nose. The birdcage is painted with a dull-green, rust-inhibiting paint. Later, the birdcage is bolted to the chassis. The chassis consists of the frame and the suspension components.

The See-Through Corvette has its body panels removed, so many other parts are visible. For example, Mackay pulled

△ **What happens when Kevin drives the car in public or to shows? "Oh, people go nuts," he says.**

Kevin Mackay has been in the Corvette restoration business for over 20 years. In building this car, he wanted to show people the kind of work his shop does. He figured a "See-Through" Corvette was the best way of explaining what the shop does. It lets the work speak for itself.

▷ "I wanted to do something that no one has ever done before," Kevin Mackay says. He succeeded in doing so.

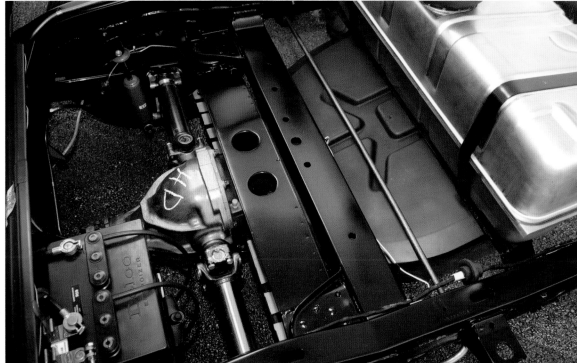

the fiberglass door skins to reveal the inner workings of the manual window's rollers. These move the glass up and down via the crank handle.

△ The "See-Through" L88 Corvette has been a big hit in the Corvette hobby.

The See-Through Corvette's engine is fully exposed, since its fiberglass hood is missing. The inner fender wells and side fenders are visible, as are the gas tank and differential. When seated in the driver's seat, a person realizes how close the Corvette driver is to the spinning driveshaft. Mackay's shop even gave the car see-through floors.

The car that Mackay modified for the public's "viewing pleasure" is actually a rare Corvette. It is one of 116 ultra-high-performance L88 models built in model-year 1969.

The car's emblems appear to be floating. They are in the same locations they would be in if the fiberglass panels were in place.

△ Mackay peeled the fiberglass outer skin off to reveal what's inside the doors.

"We've done a lot of crazy things, like the drivable chassis," Mackay pointed out. "Once, we did a suspended body exhibit for the Bloomington Gold Corvette show's "Special Collection." Another time, we cut a Corvette in half. That was the 'Cut-Away Corvette.' You could sit in it and drive it, too."

Mackay says his See-Through Corvette takes things "one step further." The car has proven a big hit everywhere it goes. Kevin displays the unique car at 'Vette shows and occasionally drives it on the street. People often stare at it in disbelief. They can't believe that the L88 is 100 percent street legal.

"Everything is operational," Mackay noted. "The wipers, the headlights (low beams and high beams) the turn signals, the horn. Everything works."

In order to pass a New York safety inspection, Mackay had to make a few compromises. At the rear of the car, he installed an new-old-stock rear body panel (a part that is almost impossible to find) to mount the back-up and brake lights and the license plate holder to. Front and rear bumpers were also required. He could have left off emblems — such as the crossed-flags on the front nose and the Stingray script on the sides of the front fenders — but he decided to use them. The way they are screwed in place, the emblems appear to be floating in air.

"People gawk when they see the car on the street," says Mackay. "They wonder what it is." Kevin actually drives the car on occasion. He's never even been pulled over by police or state troopers. Some officers have even given him the thumbs-up sign.

At car shows, Kevin's L88 is usually surrounded by curious people. With prices on 1968 and 1969 L88 Corvettes nearing a half million dollars, Kevin eventually plans to install the car's body and create a restored L88.

According to Mackay, when it was a complete car, this Corvette was the only fully-documented black-on-black L88 with factory side-pipes and its original gas tank sticker.

'68 Yenko Sunray DX Racing Car
Never Titled, Never Registered

The Yenko name is synonymous with high-performance cars. Yenko Sportscars was a Canonsburg, Pennsylvania dealership that first became famous for its Yenko Stinger. Later, it turned out SYC Novas, Chevelles and Camaros.

Yenko started out by swapping "big-block" V-8 engines into customer cars at the dealership level. Then, Don Yenko and his father found a way they could order batches of cars with factory-installed big-block V-8s. They ordered the cars the same way police cars or taxicabs or other "fleet" cars were ordered, using GM's Central Office Production Order (COPO) system.

To high-performance buffs, "COPO" became synonymous with factory-427-powered Camaros. However, a fleet of taxicabs with special heavy-duty seats could also have been produced as COPO cars.

You could say Yenko's involvement with the Corvette was much "racier." In '68 Corvettes, a 427-cid V-8 was already available as a factory option. No COPO ordering was required. Many private racing teams ordered Corvettes with 427 engines.

Corporately, Chevrolet had been officially out of racing involvements since the Automobile Manufacturers' Association adopted a ban on its members promoting high performance. That was back in 1957.

△ This car — built under the Central Office Production Order system — is one of only 80 made in 1968 with the L88 big-block V-8.

△ **A barn-burning barn find, the car looks great in its No. 3 racing livery and definitely seems to have "attitude."**

△ **The huge side pipes were needed for racing.**

In 1963, Corvette chief engineer Zora Arkus-Duntov had gotten his fingers slapped by the upper brass at General Motors for building five Grand Sport racing cars. By 1968, any Chevrolet racing involvement was a very secretive, "underground" effort. However, Chevrolet still offered options for its showroom cars that racing drivers could use to great advantage.

Any buyer of a new 1968 Corvette with an extra $437.10 to spend could add an L71 427-cid V-8 with three two-barrel carburetors and 375 hp to the car. An additional $805.75 purchased the L89 option, which included a pair of very neat, heat-shedding aluminum cylinder heads.

These were high-performance engines, but they did not have the performance of another option coded the L88. This version of the 427-cid V-8 was pretty much off limits in "street" cars.

"You really had to know somebody to get an L88," our favorite Corvette authority Kevin Mackay said. "These engines were for off-road use. They required at least 103-octane fuel. None of the cars ever had radios. They tried to steer the public away from these cars."

Duntov and his group of racing enthusiasts inside Chevrolet steered the L88 engines to serious racers. One of their best conduits was Don Yenko.

There were 80 cars built in 1968 with L88 engines. One

was this Sunray DX racing car that Kevin Mackay's shop restored. Corvette Repair did the bodywork and paint and restored the car.

David Morgan and Hap Sharp drove the convertible to a first in class and sixth overall in that 12-hour endurance race. It wore racing No. 3 and a removable hardtop during the race. The car even made the cover of Chevrolet's own Corvette News.

Ralph Morrison, the director of Sunray DX's motorsports program placed a special order for the Polar White racing car using the "Buyer's Key Pass Program," which was available only to qualified Corvette racers.

There were actually three '68 model Sunray DX racers. The first two competed at Daytona in 1968. One of these cars was built from parts. It started out as a 435-hp Corvette that had been on the showroom floor at Yenko's dealership.

This Polar White car is the third Sunray DX racing car. It has a black interior, the M22 heavy-duty close-ratio 4-speed transmission, J56 heavy-duty brakes, the F41 special front and rear suspensions and a 4.56:1 positraction rear axle. The car was built at the Corvette plant in St. Louis.

Although federal law made a heater mandatory in 1968 (even in Corvettes with the L88 engine), this car still came through without a heater. A "delete" plate covers the dash

where the heater goes. It also came without a spare tire, since it was made strictly for off-road use.

For racing use, the interior trim and carpets were removed. A roll bar was installed. The suspension was beefed up with bronze upper and lower control arm bushings. A 40-gallon fuel cell was installed. Racing seat belts were required. Many bolts used in the car's construction were safety-wired so the nuts would not loosen. The L88 engine was left "fairly stock." The main upgrade was a set of "Special Le Mans-type headers."

In late '69, Sunoco bought out Sunray DX and sold the racing cars. The No. 3 Corvette went to the Quaker State Oil racing team, which raced it under the company's green and white colors in 1970-1973. Fred Kepler captured the N.E. Region A/P race at Watkins Glen. Privateer Joe Searies later campaigned the car, driving it until 1977.

Kevin Mackay became the car's fourth owner in August 1990. "We found it in a barn," said Kevin. "It still had all the original body panels, all the original interior."

△ The big 427 was specially tuned by Yenko Sportscars for racing and carried decals to attest to it.

◁ The stripped-down-for-racing interior has no trim items or floor carpeting.

In the racing tradition, this car was never titled, registered or street-driven. It's been a "track star" all of its life. That's a real testament to the character of "Corvette Masterpieces" that have the L88 engine.

1968 Corvette L88

△ **The L88 is a legendary Corvette option. To stay on the safe side, Chevy advertised 430 hp, but it was more.**

Carl and Kathy Hatcher own this 1968 Silverstone Silver Corvette coupe. It is a very neat car with a black leather interior and a lift-off hardtop. It came from the factory with the M22 close-ratio four speed, another nice option to have. Toss in the positraction rear axle, 3.56:1 gearing, J56 brakes and F41 heavy-duty suspension and you begin to realize this car has a lot of performance options. But the kicker is what lies under its hood — a legendary 'Vette engine option that goes by the RPO code L88.

With 1967 L88s, it was considered de rigueur to opt out of basics and the cars even came without a radio and heater. The delete plates used to cover the holes in the dash were signs that a car was intended for racing. Today, the weight-saving equipment deletes are a badge of honor to 'Vette collectors. Things changed in 1968, when Federal motor vehicle safety regulations required a defroster. As a result, a heater was mandatory and could not be deleted. The Hatchers' L88 has a heater — along with a radio delete plate.

Of course, radio or not, an L88-equipped car is a desirable Corvette to own. One reason for this is that Chevrolet tried hard to hide the option and that made it very rare. An automaker today could not fool the car-buying public like Chevrolet did in 1967-1969. Imagine keeping a huge number of buyers from knowing about your top Corvette performance option! Today, the news about the L88 would be all over the Internet.

As the '60s wound to a close, the L88 option was certainly not advertised. In fact, its existence was largely a secret among racing drivers and hardcore enthusiasts. Chevrolet even discouraged dealers from ordering the L88 for the general public. Instead, the option was targeted specifically for racetrack use.

At the heart of the L88 package was the 427-cid V-8 tuned for all-out racing. The option also included certain mandatory upgrades. The transmission had to be the M22 choice (nicknamed the "Rock Crusher") or a beefed-up M20 Hydra-Matic. Other L88 requirements included the RPO G81 positraction dif-

▽ **Here you see one very smooth-looking high-performance machine that's a true rarity to behold.**

△ **The L88 was a pretty plain car in an era of lick-'em-and-stick-'em muscle machines.**

△ **Call-outs told what was lurking under the hood.**

ferential, the power-assisted heavy-duty brakes and the heavy-duty suspension with stronger coil springs and dampers.

A distinguishing exterior feature of every L88 was an elevated cowl-induction hood adorned with 427 badges on either side of the reverse-facing air scoop. But, otherwise, L88s were devoid of gaudy stripes or muscle car graphics. There was nothing to suggest that L88-optioned cars might be the fastest, street-legal muscle cars of their era.

With a gargantuan 12.5:1 compression ratio, aluminum cylinder heads, an aluminum intake manifold and a Holley 850-cfm four-barrel carburetor, the L88 produced well in excess of its 430 advertised horsepower. How much more powerful it was is a matter of who you listen to. A frequently-published figure is 560 hp at 6400 rpm. Some sources believe that, with the exhausts removed and 103-octane racing fuel in the tank, the L88-optioned 'Vette would pump out 600 hp.

GM, of course, fudged the numbers, advertising the L88 at 430 horses. Notice that it was conveniently rated at five less power units than the 427-cid 435-hp Tri-Power option (RPO L71). It is said that Chevrolet did that purposely to push buyers away from the L88.

Chevrolet didn't fudge on the price. The L88 option cost an additional $947.90 in 1967 dollars and $1,032.15 in 1969 dollars. These prices may not seem so high today, but a '68 Corvette coupe cost just $4,663 then — a convertible was $4,320

Sales of the L88 option totaled 20 in 1967. They quadrupled to 80 units in 1968, the year that a big body style change occurred. In 1969, the last year of the 427-cid big-block V-8, production of L88 packages came to 116.

Carl and Kathy Hatcher know that their silver L88-equipped coupe is a real "Corvette Masterpiece." That's why they enjoy sharing it with other enthusiasts at car shows.

☐ Sticker on console spelled out octane requirements.

Orange Crush

△ Exactly 2,072 Corvettes came with the 400-hp Tri-Power carburetor set-up in 1969.

Most Corvettes, especially late models, are machines for compressing time and distance. Ken Smith's '69 coupe is very adept at getting from Point A to Point B in a short amount of time. Under the hood is a 427-cid 400-hp big-block topped with a set of three two-barrel carburetors. This engine option was popularly known as "Tri-Power."

Since the car was restored, Ken has put less than 250 miles on the odometer. Basically, his '69 has become "a piece of art."

The car's Monaco Orange paint is not hard on the eyes. Ken says orange has been his favorite color since he was a kid. When he coached his daughter's soccer team, they used the name "Orange Crush" and wore orange outfits.

Ken was first smitten with an orange 'Vette in 1977. That's when he spied a Monaco Orange '69 'Vette at the National Council of Corvette Clubs convention in Dallas, Texas. Back then, a show car was not in Ken's game plan.

◁ Ken Smith's '69 Corvette is a heavily optioned car with a four-speed manual transmission, power windows, power brakes, a rear window defroster, air conditioning and leather seats.

"My father was with me when we were looking at show cars in 1977," Ken said. "I raced Corvettes with the NCCC. I tore up my cars all the time. I kept saying I'd love to have one of those show cars cause they look brand new. My dad said I liked to drive my cars too much and that people that own show cars just clean them and trailer them around like museum pieces."

Ken admits his father was right . . . back then. However, in the last 30 years, Ken "grew up." And Ken never gave up his dream of owning a Monaco Orange '69.

"I looked and looked and looked for years," he said. "Then,

when I got married, I kind of quit looking for awhile."

Looking wasn't easy, because Monaco Orange 1969 'Vettes don't grow on trees. Corvette offered this unique color in 1969 only. About three percent of the cars had it.

Other years had different shades of orange. In 1970, the Corvette came in Ontario Orange. Ken says that was more of a burnt orange, like the University of Texas' color. This shade of orange just didn't please Ken.

Monaco Orange, which matched the very popular 1969 Camaro Hugger Orange color, was the specific color Ken wanted. He also wanted the 427-cid big-block V-8.

△ The name of a sea creature went back on the Corvette's front fender, but it was now spelled as one word — Stingray — rather than two.

◁ By showing his '69 Corvette, Ken Smith has won 12 Top Flight Awards and a Duntov Award in National Corvette Restorer's Society events. He also took two Bloomington Gold wins and a pair of Triple Crowns at the Chevy/Vette Fest in Chicago.

In 1997, Ken finally got his chance to buy a Monaco Orange 1969 Corvette with a 427-cid engine and factory Tri-Power. The car's restoration had just been completed. It had been driven only 20 miles since the restoration. The owner wanted to sell the '69 to help finance the restoration of a mid-year Corvette like the one he had owned in college.

After more than 30 years of Corvette ownership, including racing, attending shows and daily driving, Ken changed his habits. Now, he is having fun trailering around the Corvette of his dreams and exhibiting it in car shows.

Showing a car is an integral part of the hobby for many collectors. Getting to see a 1969 Corvette that looks just the way it rolled off the assembly line is a real treat for show goers.

For Ken Smith, his Monaco Orange '69 is his "Corvette Masterpiece." He says that owning such a perfect '69 is "like having a piece of art."

The Monaco Orange paint on Ken Smith's car exactly matches the Hugger Orange color used on 1969 Camaros.

1969 Baldwin-Motion Phase III GT

△ **This rare Baldwin-Motion Performance Corvette was only two years old when Michael Murphy purchased it in 1971. His brother owns it today.**

What makes our featured Baldwin-Motion Corvette more than just a modified car is the fact that Baldwin Chevrolet sold it with a new-car window sticker.

In contrast, Motion Corvettes were customer-owned cars that were brought to Joel Rosen's Motion Performance shop for body modifications, engine swaps, custom tuning, etc. They were different from Baldwin-Motion cars, which were new Corvettes that Baldwin Chevrolet brought to Rosen's shop for upgrades before selling them as new cars.

Michael Murphy bought this Baldwin-Motion Corvette in 1971. That was years before cars like the Phase III GT were collectible. By 1990, the car was starting to get attention. Murphy's brother John — the current owner — remembers Michael turning down offers of around $100,000 over 10 years ago.

The special Corvette became Michael Murphy's most prized possession. "The car was his baby," John recalls. "He drove it

like there wasn't ever going to be another one. He took really good care of it, he garaged it and he took it to local shows. But that was the extent of where he showed it — just locally." Michael had the car repainted in red and silver in 1994-1995.

When Michael passed away, his brother hooked up with George Rubistello, who returned the car to its gold color scheme. When Rubistello took the car apart, he discovered traces of the original paint under the door panels.

Only six Baldwin-Motion Corvettes built by Joel Rosen have been located, according to Martyn L. Schorr, of Sarasota, Florida, a well-known automotive writer who handled public relations for Joel Rosen back in the '60s.

"This '69 is apparently one of the (Baldwin-Motion) cars," said Schorr cautiously. Amazingly, only one owner enjoyed this car between 1971 and 1997. It has now been restored to look just like it did when Schorr tested it for *Cars* magazine almost 40 years ago.

◁ The car has been restored, inside and outside, to look like it did 40 years ago.

Schorr was the editor of *Cars* in the glory days of the "super car" or "muscle car" era. Joel Rosen's Motion Performance was located on Sunrise Highway in Baldwin, Long Island. Baldwin Chevrolet was located nearby, as was Mary Schorr's home and *Cars* magazine office. Old copies of *Cars* carry ads from Motion Performance and write-ups about cars that Rosen prepped.

Marty Schorr was involved in the Baldwin-Motion program between 1967 and 1974. He handled the company's catalogs, advertising, public relations and product promotions; he even named the cars and the options for them.

"I had a financial interest in the company," said Schorr. "Joel and I were business partners in other companies. Most of this was kept quiet for obvious reasons." Today, the cars that Rosen created are extremely collectible. "Now people will pay big bucks to have a real one," Schorr pointed out. "Joel documents them for people."

Schorr's involvement in Baldwin-Motion programs partly explains why West Coast enthusiast magazines such as *Popular Hot Rodding* and *Hot Rod* did not cover the Baldwin-Motion cars to any great extent. "The California books wouldn't write about them, because I had everything first," Schorr revealed. "Having involvements with Joel didn't sway me editorially," Schorr added. "The cars were legitimately fast and good."

Rosen even offered a *written* guarantee that his Phase III cars would run the quarter mile in the 11-second bracket. That guarantee applied to our featured Corvette, which is one of the 10 built over three model years, 1969-1971. Rosen also spoke of the "Fantastic Five" muscle cars, which were based on the Impala, Chevelle, Camaro, Nova and Corvette.

"All of these cars were built one at a time, to an owner's custom order and everything was delivered to a Chevrolet dealer," Schorr told us. "You could get L88s, you could get anything you wanted on your car."

Murphy's Phase III GT is a testament to just how wild Rosen could make the cars. Schorr recalls driving this Candy-apple Gold Corvette when it was brand new. He photographed it for *Cars*.

Joel Rosen documents the cars he built, according to vehicle identification numbers, but the original file for Murphy's car was missing. Therefore, the best Rosen could do was write a letter stating that, from all appearances and details, this is one of the cars he created.

"The reason we can tell the car is original is that there are a couple things that were done on only one of those cars and nobody in 1969-1970 would have cloned a car," said Marty Schorr. "The cars didn't have any (collector) value and who cared? This car was painted Candyapple Gold and had Shelby Mustang scoops in the sail panels. It was the only car Joel built like that."

△ The specially-tuned 427-cid 435-hp V-8 was guaranteed to do 11 second quarter miles.

▷ The striping treatments used on the Baldwin-Motion Corvettes was designed to get attention.

▷ The roots of those unusual-looking headlights are not familiar.

John Murphy was close enough to his brother to know the history of this car from its arrival at Emerich Chevrolet in Manchester, Pennsylvania, around 1970. "How it got there, we don't know," Murphy admitted. "We've been trying to find (that) out for years."

Mr. Emerich, the owner of the Chevy dealership, also built racing car frames. A young man named Greg Stephens traveled from Florida to see him and saw the Baldwin-Motion Corvette on the used-car lot at Emerich Chevrolet. He said he had to have the car and bought it. Stephens drag raced the car in Florida and had a great deal of success. However, the car was eventually repossesed and wound up back in Pennsylvania.

"The man who financed it really didn't want it either, so he traded it off to a guy named Lawrence Luckenbaugh," John Murphy explained. "Lawrence and my brother were good friends; they rode to work together and, somehow or other, Lawrence traded the car to my brother for another Corvette and money."

According to Murphy, Luckenbaugh had the car long enough to repaint it. He changed it from Candyapple Gold with black stripes to blue and white.

The car appears to be complete and original right down to its matching-numbers 427-cid 435-hp big-block V-8. Rosen has installed an Edelbrock aluminum intake with a big four-barrel Holley carb and a "fly's-eye" air cleaner in place of the factory tri-power set up. To make it capable of 11-second quarter-mile runs, the car's engine is tuned for extra power in the ballpark of 500 hp.

Schorr told us that cars like this one were built on custom order, one at a time. They were configured to the customer's tastes. The original buyer must have liked Shelby-style side air scoops. They were used only on this car. The front end styling is also radical. It features scoops and headlight buckets that might be from a Datsun 240Z, although even Schorr doesn't know their derivation for certain.

"Most of the cars came through without covered headlights, because DMV rules and regulations changed," Schorr explained. "So, only a few of early cars (like this one) came that way."

Apparently, the car's taillights are from a Firebird. A Le Mans style gas cap was used. Ansen supplied the wheels. The bumper and the grille are stock Corvette items. The side louvers are also stock, but they were flipped over. The hood on this "Corvette Masterpiece" is completely custom made and provides one more bold statement about the performance offered in the Baldwin-Motion Phase III cars.

Motion Corvette:
A 43,000-mile original

John Shaw was the owner of this 1969 Motion Corvette when these photos were taken at the Corvette Expo, in Knoxville, Tennessee in March 2004. John is a Corvette-loving car dealer who regularly buys and sells vehicles. His car was about to cross the block at a Dana Mecum auction. If you were in his shoes, would you be selling what might rate as an irreplaceable Corvette?

Before the auction started, Dana explained the pecking order of Motion and Baldwin-Motion Corvettes to us. He said the cars that get top prices are those that Joel Rosen upgraded for Baldwin Chevrolet — a factory-authorized dealer that sold them as new cars. The second tier cars include those modified by Motion Performance that weren't sold through Baldwin

Chevrolet. The third tier cars include those that had bolt-on items from a Motion Performance kit added to them.

Dana Mecum pointed out that true Baldwin-Motion Corvettes have been sold for six-figure prices. "We had one last November," said the Illinois auctioneer. "It was a 1974 Can-Am (racing) car. We had a bid of $110,000 for it and the fellow wouldn't sell. That's the most we've seen associated with one of those, but among the early-year cars, I know of a 1969 model that sold in the $160,000 range."

Shaw's reserve price at the auction was a secret to the bidders, but he confided to us that it was $55,000. He said he had tried to document the origins of his car, but that he had found little success doing it.

△ **Motion Performance built hot Corvettes in Baldwin, Long Island, during the '60s and '70s and makes the Baldwin-Motion Camaro Resto-Mod today.**

△ Under the car's special "clamshell" hood lurks a 435-hp big-block Chevy V-8 with triple Holleys.

△ **The chrome lever on the right-hand side of the console activates the Hone overdrive unit.**

"There's a guy from New York flying in to look at it who I have it *sold* to," said Shaw. "He wants to look at it first. It really doesn't matter to me if he buys it or not. I enjoy it and love it and think it's beautiful."

Shaw's Corvette features a "Mako Shark" body kit that Motion Performance made for Corvettes. This kit was inspired by GM's famous Mako Shark show car. There was also a Manta Ray body kit based on a second GM show car called the Manta Ray.

On Shaw's car, the hood opens "clamshell" style to fully expose the engine bay. Rosen — a drag racer who had established National Hot Rod Association records — thought that this type of hood was great for engine tuners.

The back of the car is customized, too. It features "Venetian blinds" slats over the back window. The car has Western brand wheels — the type Joel Rosen was known to use. A pop-open GT quick-fill gas cap was similar to those used on racing cars. Side-mounted exhausts decorated the car.

Shaw believed his unrestored, 43,499-mile Corvette had the full Motion Phase III package. The engine was originally a 427-cid 435-hp V-8. A Holley 3-barrel carb had been installed in place of the factory Tri Power set up. It had Phase III valve covers and other goodies from Rosen's speed shop. These included chrome-plated push-in breathers and a fly's-eye air cleaner. A chrome lever on the right-hand side of the console shifted the Hone overdrive unit.

Shaw's involvement with the car began a year earlier, when he typed "Motion Corvette" and "Mako Shark" into an Internet search engine. The Mako Shark kit was sold through

Rosen's speed shop on Sunrise highway in Baldwin, Long Island, New York.

Rosen installed the kits for some clients, but in other cases, the car owners handled the installs. A Motion Phase III Mako Shark Corvette that Baldwin Chevrolet sold as new would be quite a piece of history and very valuable.

Dana Mecum talked about "speed shop" muscle cars. He said they were part of an era. He made them sound really special and we wondered if John Shaw should rethink the idea of parting with a Baldwin-Motion Mako Shark Corvette that had an authentic 427 V-8 under its hood.

Later, Shaw seemed to be reconsidering the idea of keeping his Corvette. Right before the auction, he said, "I am going to send Joel Rosen some information and see if I can get the car documented."

Rosen offers a service to document authentic Baldwin-Motion cars. For a fee, he'll look up the original paperwork and document the car the best he can. Shaw was unsure of the price of the research, but said it wasn't cheap. Still, he had already tried to go to the original owner for information.

The car's original owner was Reggie Fountain, the owner of Fountain Power Boats who had ordered the car new. Shaw bought it from a man who worked for Fountain. John had tried to reach Fountain by phone, without luck. He also tried faxing four questions to him.

When the car crossed the auction block, it drew immediate attention. The price quickly soared above $40,000, then hit $45,000, then $47,000. It was getting close to Shaw's reserve — the price at which he was committed to sell it. The ring

men asked Shaw to lower his sell price. "I can put 47 in your pocket," said one of them. Shaw's response was, "Get me fifty in my pocket and I'll sell it."

The bidding went on. In confidence, John told us, "I don't care if I sell it. I don't think it's a Baldwin-Motion car, but I do believe that Motion built the car and that it's got to be worth at least $50,000."

The ring man asked again and Shaw, trying to be amiable, said, "Put 49 in my pocket and I'll do it."

Despite the "juice" for a sale, the money just wasn't there. We saw the tension in the face of the bidder, a gray-haired man who looked to be in his 50s. He shook his head no; he wouldn't go higher than $47,000, so the auction was over.

The Motion Corvette was marked a "no sale." John Shaw would have to trailer his muscular Corvette back home to Greenville, South Carolina.

Whether the car had been invoiced through Baldwin Chevrolet or not, the special looks were still there. And Shaw knew a lot more about the car than he had before.

The previous owner had told him only that Reggie Fountain "had it custom built." The story went that someone took the mirrors off to make the car more streamlined; the 40-gallon fuel cell, the Hone overdrive and the 4.56 gearing were supposedly installed so Fountain could drive this "Corvette Masterpiece" from his North Carolina boat foundry to Florida without worrying about refilling his tank.

△ One of two body kits that Motion Performance installed on the cars it modified was this "Phase III" version with styling based on the factory's Mako Shark show car. (The Mako Shark is featured earlier in this book).

Rebel L88 Racer

△ Bob Johnson with his old race car today.

▷ Today the historic racing Corvette is part of the collection kept in Mike Yager's "MY Garage" museum in Effingham, Illinois. Mr. Yager just penned his first book – called *Mike Yager's Corvette Bible* – for Krause Books, the publisher of *Corvette Masterpieces*.

Kevin Mackay, Corvette racing car authority said "This could be a very long story," when asked about the car you see in this chapter. Mackay found this car in a junkyard in 1991 and bought it for only $7,000. That's enough to raise goose bumps when you think about what a fully-documented L88 racing car must be worth today.

Mackay was at a swap meet and bought a magazine called Corvette Corner. It had an article about this car by a writer named Walt Thurn. He called the Rebel "Scrappy" because "everytime it raced a piece would be taken off the car."

Thurn's article got Mackay more and more intrigued about how this 'Vette was ordered as a "factory lightweight." The article indicated that Orlando Costanza of Tampa, Florida was the car's first owner.

"I called information and within two minutes I had Orlando Costanza on the phone," said Mackay. "He says, 'Oh yeah, I used to own that car. I sold it to a guy named Toye English.'"

Next, Mackay discovered that English sold the car to Alex Davison, a man who owned a dry-cleaning business in upstate New York. This turned into a dead end until Mackay found out that Davison sold his business and became a lawyer. He

also sold the 'Vette to "somebody in the Carolinas — a dentist named Charles who raced the car."

So, Mackay contacted Harry Handley, the archivist at the Sports Car Club of America, and he found the most likely owner in his files. That was Dr. Charles West of Greenwood, South Carolina who raced a '69 Corvette. Kevin looked up West in a phone book and called him.

"Did you buy a 1969 Corvette from a gentleman in New York?" he asked. The answer was "yes," but, better yet, Dr. West still owned the car. It was in his private junkyard.

Instead of trying to buy the car, Mackay asked if he could see it. West said the car wasn't for sale, but Mackay was more than welcome to come and have a look at it.

Due to scheduling problems, Mackay wound up meeting Dr. West when he and his wife were returning from a wedding. It was midnight and the dentist was in a tuxedo. The three of them took a ride to the junkyard. Dr. West changed into overalls at his wife's suggestion. Wielding a flashlight, he led Mackay towards a large object under an old tarp.

"There's the car, the one I bought from Alex Davison," West said. He knew nothing of the Rebel racing car's heritage.

The tarp crumbled as Kevin Mackay rolled it back. He noticed the name Alex Davison on the door of the car. The rear glass on the hardtop still had the 1972 LeMans race team sticker. Mackay noted the original panels, the steering wheel, the gauges, the shifter, the seats and more.

△ **The power plant is a lightweight L88 with "open-chambered" heads which were good for a horsepower upgrade of around 10 percent.**

Mackay knew he had found an incredible car; one of the most significant Corvette racing cars of its era. It was the No. 1 production race Corvette in the world in 1972. It won back-to-back races at Daytona and Sebring. It held the record for the highest finish ever for a Corvette at Sebring: fourth overall.

The story of the Rebel is enough to fill a book by itself. Race car builder and driver John Greenwood decorated his L88-powered-Corvettes with the American flag. They became known as the "Stars & Stripes" Corvettes. Toye English decided to use the Confederate flag on his car to draw attention to his rivalry with Greenwood. The John Greenwood 'Vettes tested tires for BF Goodrich. The Toye English "Rebel" 'Vette became the tire-test car for Goodyear Tire & Rubber Company.

According to Mackay, the Rebel was one of four lightweight L88-powered Corvettes built. The term "open-chambered" adds even more mystery to this car. Most of them had "closed-chamber" aluminum cylinder heads. By opening the heads up, the combustion chambers breathed better and produced more horsepower. Kevin Mackay estimates they had a 10 percent boost in horsepower.

This racing car was built in January 1969 and used prototype open-chambered heads. This option was finally offered to the public, but not until June of 1969.

Questioned more about the history of the lightweight racing cars, Mackay explained that another erudite option was called the "trunk option." L88s built strictly for racing came

△ Everyone at the '72 French Grand Prix knew that Johnson's Corvette was an American entry and a racing Rebel.

◁ The car was a tire test car for Goodyear.

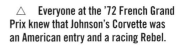

wheels. They were all ordered as hardtop convertibles and intended strictly for racing."

This particular L88 went to Costanzo, who wasn't the average "hot-shoe" driver. He had raced at Daytona and Sebring and had connections with Zora Arkus-Duntov and Gib Hufstaeder at Chevrolet. He ordered this L88 through Ferman Chevrolet in Tampa. It was earmarked for track duty. The original color that Costanzo chose was Daytona Yellow.

Mackay explained that the Rebel "pretty much won the Thoe English-John Greenwood rivalry." Greenwood had the fastest cars, but the Rebel was more durable.

Mackay's Corvette Repair, in Valley Stream, New York, ultimately restored the Rebel. Larry Bowman, a car collector from California, owns this "Corvette Masterpiece" today and is the designated "keeper of the flame."

with an oil cooler, headers and headlight covers (bubble clear covers that were also called "headlight kits") packaged in the luggage area. They were designed for owner installations.

Some Corvette historians believed that the lightweight cars had thinner fiberglass on their bodies. Mackay said, "I don't think they were made thinner, but the lightweight cars came without carpets. They also came with lightweight magnesium

1969 ZL1:
Supreme Bad Boy Muscle 'Vette

▷ Tipping the scales at 100 lbs. lighter than an L88, the ZL1 was a featherwieight version of the 427 built expressly for racing-car use.

△ John Maher had no idea his car would zoom to over $1 million in value. Basically, he was an enthusiast buying a hot Corvette in 1969. Maher belongs to the Corvette Club Of Western Pennsylvania.

John Maher holds a special place in Corvette history. In 1969, he ordered a brand new Corvette with the ZL1 engine option. This is the most legendary Corvette muscle car engine ever made. Maher has owned the Supreme Bad Boy Muscle 'Vette for nearly 40 years. To date, it's the only 1969 Corvette documented to have its original ZL1 V-8.

Before telling the story of Maher's Corvette, let's review how the ZL1 engine evolved. Back in the late 1960s, horsepower sold cars. Detroit automakers often competed over which manufacturer had the hottest and fastest new model. The sporty Corvette was often the car with the most horsepower.

Corvette entered the '60s offering only small-block V-8 engines. Chevrolet had a big-block V-8, but made it available only in full-size cars and trucks. At that time, the Corvette was still viewed as a sports car and was one of few cars of that genre available with a V-8. A small V-8 seemed like all that was needed in that market niche.

As the horsepower race took off in the mid-'60s, General Motors still adhered to the Auto Manufacturers Association ban on the advertising of horsepower and racing wins that had been adopted in 1957. In fact, the corporation had rules against direct factory involvement in motorsports.

△ Racing stickers decorating the 'Vette include one from early sponsor Gulf Oil, which helped to get the car ordered. Not everyone could buy a ZL1.

◁ Three of the '69 ZL1 Corvettes are known to exist and this one is the best one inside and out.

One of GM's strictures prevented the use of big-block V-8s in the smaller compact and mid-size cars that were getting popular at that time. In mid-1964, Pontiac found a way to circumvent this rule by releasing the mid-sized Le Mans with a GTO option that included a 389-cid V-8.

This opened the door to other GM divisions. Chevrolet had been working on a 396-cid big-block V-8 that became known as the "Mystery Engine." In 1965, Chevy decided to make this motor available by offering it in a SS 396 version of the mid-size Chevelle. Since it made little sense not to add the same engine option to Corvette offerings, that's exactly what Chevy did. The Corvette version of the big V-8 was tuned to produce 425 hp and made the Corvette more of a muscle car than a sports car for the first time.

In 1966, Chevrolet replaced the Corvette's 396-cid engine option with a 427-cid engine option. They also surprised the competition by adding a "Tri-Power" version of the 427-cid V-8 in 1967. Tri-Power was Chevy's term for three two-barrel carburetors.

It was also in 1966 that Chevrolet snuck a real racing engine, called the L88, into their option list. This happened because Corvette chief engineer Zora Arkus-Duntov and his crew wanted to help private teams racing Corvettes. The high-revving L88 was a powerful big-block V-8 that was primarily funneled to select racing car builders. Sales of this engine to the general public were discouraged.

The L88 earned an enviable reputation in racing, so work on the ZL1 — an even more powerful big-block racing engine got underway. The ZL1 was also a 427-cid purpose-built racing engine, but it was 100 pounds lighter than an L88 and said to be more durable. The weight savings came from the use of an aluminum engine block and cylinder heads.

The fact that the ZL1 Corvette engine became legendary has a lot to do with its *extreme* rarity. Most historians believe that only two or three Corvettes (and 69 Camaros) with this engine option were made. Timing also came into play. By 1969, the horsepower race and the muscle car era were nearly over. With the premature deaths of both, the ZL1 wound up becoming among the hottest of the hot big-block V-8s ever built.

Chevrolet built a limited number of Camaros with the ZL1 engine, to homologate (car speak for certify) the exotic 427 for National Hot Rod Association drag racing. One of these Camaros has sold, at auction, for over $1 million.

At least three 1969 Corvettes with the ZL1 V-8 have turned up. The car on these pages is the most authentic one with full documentation.

The car's owner, John Maher, was a serious racing enthusiast. In fact, his first new car was a 1962 Chevrolet Biscayne with the famous "factory lightweight" package. About six years later, Maher ordered a 1968 Corvette with the L88 V-8. The L88 was officially rated for 430 hp, though it is believed it produced more than that.

A few months later, he traded the L88-powered 'Vette for one with a ZL1 under its hood. Both engines were actually rated the same, but Maher knew that the ZL1's lighter weight should help in racing.

John Maher never sold the ZL1. If a hotter Corvette engine had come along, Maher might have traded up again, but, since no hotter Corvette ever came along, Maher just hung onto his car with the ZL1.

The Gulf Oil stickers on this 'Vette are there because Gulf sponsored John's car when it was new. Gulf Oil even wrote a letter to GM to help John get his "Corvette Masterpiece" ordered. John still has the original dealer invoice and gas tank sticker, both of which show that the car left the factory with the same ZL1 engine that's in it today.

◁ When John Maher rolled into the winner's circle at Corvettes @ Carlisle on August 28, 2000, perhaps some people in the huge crowd in the grandstands realized his Corvette was one of the handful of ZL1s ever made for 1969. Maher is the original owner of this 1969 ZL1 Corvette. That's the late and great Chip Miller announcing.

☐ Maher striped and lettered his ZL1 for racing.

Bunkie Knudsen's '63 Corvette Styling Twin

△ **Back "in the day" the GM guys who rose to the top were real car enthusiasts and drove customized rides like this racy roadster that belonged to "Bunkie" Knudsen.**

▷ **The car was put together in the GM Styling Studios.**

When Bill Mitchell mounted a shark he caught at Bimini on his wall, the blue body against a white belly, turning shimmery silver in the afternoon sun, gave him the inspiration for a new Corvette. That is the legend.

The styling reigns at General Motors would soon pass from Harley Earl to Mitchell and his "fish car" would become the Corvette Sting Ray. Mitchell created the first Sting Ray in 1959. He bought a Corvette dream car and may even have paid for its redesign out of his own pocket, though this hasn't been confirmed. This cut development time from three to four years to a few months.

The Sting Ray racer itself was put into service as a show car. Then, came more racing cars and show cars with Mitchell's "shark" look, like the fabulous 1961 Mako Shark. The revolutionary Sting Ray did debut for model-year 1963.

Following the Mako Shark came a roadster on a production car chassis that was seen at the Chicago Auto Show. It had a special set of side exhausts that really gave it a shark-like appearance. The pipes seemed to resemble the razor-sharp teeth of a shark.

This Corvette — called No. 352 — was put together by the styling department at Chevrolet. The general manager of Chevy at the time was a super car enthusiast named Semon

E. "Bunkie" Knudsen who liked the show car and asked Chevrolet Engineering to build him a copy for everyday use. This car carried No. 148, an even earlier number than the Chicago Auto Show car. This suggests that Knudsen's convertible was already in service when Chevrolet Engineering modified it.

By the early 1980s, the Knudsen convertible had passed through six Detroit-area owners who drove it regularly. It was in a sad state of repair. It had been stored in a garage and used as a step-stool. The rear deck was broken from people standing on it. The frame was corroded, the paint was in poor condition, the interior was worn out and the car had become undriveable.

△ Looking at the highly-detailed fuel-injected Corvette V-8 today, it's hard to imagine that this car was once barely driveable.

When you slide into the two-toned seat of this rare ragtop you're sure to feel like a character out of Arthur Hailey's book "Wheels."

BUNKIE KNUDSEN

△ **All of the styling gimmicks made the Knudsen 'Vette seem "piping hot."**

At this point, the car caught the attention of Corvette collector Wally Abella. He asked Werner Meier, a friend who worked at Cadillac, to look at the dilapidated car to see if it was unique. Meier knew the car was special and traded a 1971 Corvette for it.

After taking the car apart for a chassis rebuild, Meier realized the roadster needed more than a standard restoration because of its unique features. Standard reproduction parts did not fit it.

Werner found that the car started as a red, fuel-injected convertible. All the modifications were done after it left the assembly line and most likely after it was put into street use by Knudsen.

The most complicated part of the restoration was replacement of the side exhausts. They were reproduced in exact size and shape and made by the combined talents of eight craftsmen, starting with Werner's father, a toolmaker. He cut out and trimmed all the flanges. He then took the job to Chuck Watson of Watson Engineering in Detroit. There, some real artists fabricated pipes from straight tubing, using a mandrel to make bends. (A mandrel is a metal bar that serves as a core around which metal or other material can be bent and shaped.) After they were fabricated, the pipes had to be welded together. Then they were polished to erase all welding seams.

After completion of the pipes, craftsmen had to fabricate covers for the mufflers. They started with a flat, quarter-inch-thick sheet of aluminum, inserted it on a numerically-controlled boring mill and programmed it to cut grooves.

After the sheet of aluminum was machined, it was trimmed to size, placed over custom-built wooden mandrels and beat into shape with rawhide mallets.

△ **The sexy '60s were an age of flash and flamboyance and this car's interior treatment fits the mold.**

Once the pipes and covers were completed, the last job was fabricating the rocker moldings and "close-outs" that go behind the pipes. The original parts were done in brass. Werner wanted to make the reproductions last, so he used stainless steel, which is difficult to roll into shape. The inserts that go behind the pipes (where they exit behind the fenders) had to be made out of cold, rolled steel. It is more malleable and easier to work with.

Other metal parts had to be chrome plated or polished. It's amazing how difficult it is to get a shop to polish a seven-foot piece of stainless steel.

The rest of the restoration was no piece of cake either. Werner discovered the interior of the car was far from stock. The seats had been reshaped. The top of the seatbacks did not come to a point, but formed a square top as on 1964 models. This was replicated by adding foam pads at the top.

The interior featured floor grilles typically used in styling cars of that era. The door panels are Naugahyde panels with stainless trim. The steering wheel has unique dual spokes with two types of wood inlaid into the rim. The center console was a prototype part and kind of a forerunner to what came in

1964. The base is a large die-cast part, featuring a stainless steel insert around the shifter. The carpeting had a tight knit similar to what came along in late-'70s Corvettes.

Werner discovered the instrument cluster was updated when was the car driven by Knudsen, who told him it had been changed. The car has 1966-date-coded seat belts of a design that wasn't used in production cars until 1967.

The engine was stock, except for cosmetics like chrome and crinkle finishes. The engine bay had to be modified for the special pipes. The heater box was trimmed for clearance and the battery was relocated to the trunk instead of the passenger footwell.

Special metallic red paint with white Lemans-type stripes was used. Knudsen had Nova, Corvair and Impala convertibles built with the same red color. His wife drove the Corvette most of the time. It wore "M" series (manufacturer's) license plates. The car was turned back into GM about 1967.

Although not officially a styling car, this "Corvette Masterpiece" was built as a twin to one. It ties into the group of cars related to the Sting Ray sports-racing car and the Mako Shark. It's a piece of Corvette history that has been saved.

1964 World's Fair Show Corvette

If General Motors builds a show car today, it will probably never be sold to a private owner. In the '60s, when GM could do no wrong, company executives seemed to be able to do whatever they pleased. In some cases they had the GM styling studio make special cars for them. Werner Meier, an authority on mid-1960s styling studio Corvettes, has found that cars were also made for their family members and friend.

Some styling studio cars had only special paint and metal grilles in the floorboards. Others had unique show-car-type features. The 1964 New York World's Fair Corvette you see here was more of a show car than some of the other styling studio creations. It was not just a modified production-type Corvette like the cars built for the corporate brass.

Some cars built for family members of GM executives were Corvettes. Chevrolet general manager Bunkie Knudsen had a pink one built for his wife. So did styling chief Harley Earl. Some Corvettes were made for the executives' friends, too. "GM did one special (car) for General Curtis Lemay," said Werner.

△ Like many '60s factory show cars, this Corvette built for display at the 1964-1965 New York World's Fair represented a customized version of the current production model. It has some very attractive modifications that reflect design trends of that era.

△ **The custom side exhaust system was originally a show-only item made of plastic, but it was later replaced with functional pipes.**

△ **The rear license plates indicate the car is part of the Mid America Motorworks collection stored at the MY Garage Museum in Effingham, Illinois. There is one extra taillight per side.**

The coupe pictured here was originally created for exhibition at the 1964-1965 New York World's Fair. However, it later wound up in the possession of the son of a GM executive, who preserved it in very good condition for many years.

When the World's Fair ended in 1965, GM stored the car in a warehouse in New York. Werner Meier has heard a rumor that the car was vandalized, although he believes that story is "largely hearsay." For historical accuracy, we'll relate that the rumor said the car had a unique instrument cluster that was damaged by vandals. GM supposedly brought the car back to Detroit and installed the 1963 production-type cluster that's in the car now. Then Alex C. Mair saw it.

Alex C. Mair had access to the car. He was an executive vice president at GM. Mair thought the '64 World's Fair car would make a great birthday present for his 16-year-old son Steve.

For show purposes, the external exhaust pipes on the car were made of plastic and the car had no real exhaust system hooked up. Mair had the people in the engineering garage make the car drivable by putting a real exhaust system under it.

"It looked almost like a production exhaust system, other than the fact that tips did not exit through the valance underneath the rear bumper," said Werner Meier. "They had put some 'down spouts' on it so the exhaust passed straight down, rather than through the rear panel. So, the tips were very well concealed."

Many 16-year-old boys would have hot rodded and ruined a car like this, but Steve Mair treated it with respect. "For example, he would not wear his shoes in the car," said Werner Meier.

So, the one-of-a-kind car stayed nice and original. If you look at the car today, the leather seats still glisten and the paint sparkles. Steve Mair also held onto the car, resisting many offers to sell it until the late 1980s, when it's provenance grew and it became much more valuable.

Three car collectors bought the Corvette with the idea of selling it for a profit. Next, it wound up in Texas. Werner Meier flew down there to try to purchase it. "I had to line up buyers for five of my cars to try to buy that car," he told me. "Five nice Corvettes were going to bite the dust just to buy that car at the time." When a cat-and-mouse game started and the price went up, Werner walked away from the deal.

The car eventually went to California collector-car dealer Corvette Mike. From there, it landed in the Blackhawk Automobile Collection in Danville, California. In 2001, Mike Yager, the owner of Mid America Motorworks, bought the rare Corvette at the Monterey sports car auction.

Werner Meier followed the car's movements with interest. He knew that Mike Yager had a first-class Corvette museum at his corporate campus in Effingham, Illinois. Werner emailed Yager, offering his talents to restore the car completely to its 1964 World's Fair appearance.

Since the car had been "babied" its entire life, it remained in basically excellent original condition, but some small things needed attention. "Somebody had mismatched a set of knock-off wheels," Werner Meier explained. "The flashers weren't working in the doors and the radiator was oozing green liquid. The brakes weren't working and the rubber was falling out of the control arm bushings . . . small things like that. I told Mike Yager that if it was mine, I'd replace the show-car-style side exhausts, but make the exhaust system work."

Mike Yager agreed. He understood that Werner Meier was in a unique position in the hobby to restore such a car. He actually had the original plastic pipes, which were a big part of the show-car look. So, he fashioned a set of functional external exhaust pipes made of metal to use on the car.

While Steve Mair owned the car, his father could take it to the engineering garage at the GM Tech Center to get things fixed. As might be expected, a few parts were swapped. This probably explains why the car has a 1965-style clock and a 1967-type brake master cylinder.

Werner Meier walked us around the car and pointed out its many unique features. The showiest are the side pipes. He said the pipes on the car now are "dead ringers" for the plastic-fiberglass parts used at the World's Fair. Another unique feature is the fuel-injection unit rising through a hole in the hood.

"That was accomplished by just making a new lid for the injector," Werner pointed out. "The 'doghouse' has a very tall cover on it that sticks up and actually sits flush with the outer surface of the hood."

△ **Fuel-injection seemed like a technology of the future in the mid-'60s and made the car seem much more "experimental."**

△ **The interior broadcasted a sleek, modern look to fair goers.**

△ **The exhaust system was integrated into the overall styling.**

△ **The simulated brake cooling vents are non-functional, except for housing the radio antenna on the left.**

The drive train beneath car consists of a "basically stock" a 327-cid 375-hp fuel-injected small-block Chevy V-8. "The engine compartment was done in black crinkle finish, with a lot of chrome," Meier said. "They kind of went crazy with chrome on the car. We took some liberties under the hood. The engine was originally Chevy Orange, but it was painted silver and looked like crap. I asked Mike Yager what he'd like me to do and I said my preference was to paint it all black. We did it all in black because the silver doesn't contrast with the chrome. Other show car engines I'd seen were done in black." Werner had good photographs of other Corvette show cars of the period. "I think the silver may have been applied later," he said.

The car incorporates many distinctions. It has disc brakes, which were not available in 1964. It has six taillights, but they aren't stock '64 Corvette taillights. They are a much wider, with a larger-diameter lamp in the back. The Corvette emblem on the back is unique, as is the Corvette emblem on the glove box door.

There are simulated brake vents on the top surface of the rear deck on either side. They are similar to those used on Sting Ray racing cars. The grille is of an egg-crate design. It was fabricated out of aluminum plates.

The show car's interior is very special. The door panels feature three, sequential, flashing reflectors. It has high-back bucket seats featuring special leather trim. The carpeting is a cut-pile type, not the original loop style. The door weather-stripping is red. Werner Meier is really proud of the reproduction floor grilles he crated.

"My dad made a fixture to mount them in and we buffed the living daylight out of them," said the restorer. "They look like jewelry."

According to Werner, finding an unrestored show car in such great original condition is a rarity. "Especially with Candyapple Red paint," he pointed out. "There's so much lacquer, that the paint is starting to show some signs of distress, but we spent a lot of time finessing that paint." Werner also re-stuffed the seats and re-stretched the leather on the console, so this "Corvette Masterpiece" looks like a million bucks.

1963 Harley Earl Styling Corvette Convertible

The 20 years between 1930 and 1950 were immensely important in the evolution of automotive industrial design. It was during this period that the world's largest automaker, General Motors established a creative system to design cars in which talented artists worked almost anonymously.

By 1931, General Motors president Alfred P. Sloan established three important departments within GM that, together, had the responsibility to create new products. These were the Charles Kettering's Research Laboratories, the Engineering Staff and Harley J. Earl's Art and Colour Section.

GM's Art and Colour Section — sometimes called the Art and Colour Studio — was responsible for styling automobile bodies and interiors. Harley Earl was in charge of this function, although he was not a designer himself. In fact, it is heavily documented in C. Edson Armi's book *The Art of American Car Design*, that Harley Earl could not draw! "Although Harley Earl was known throughout the industry as a perceptive critic, his design contribution was limited to verbal themes," says Armi, a professor of art at the University of North Carolina. It is also said that Earl's authoritative way of dealing with his employees grew out of his frustration over not being able to express his ideas visually."

△ **Famed General Motors design chief Harley J. Earl was the first recipient of this factory-customized Corvette.**

△ **With an array of extra gauges, the dream car's dash really carries out the aircraft motif of the stock Corvette even better.**

What Earl did have was amazing ideas and a strong personality that gave him the will to make his ideas happen. Alfred Sloane's program of "coordinated decentralization" at GM allowed executives with strong personalities, like Earl, to play a guiding role at the corporation. When Earl saw something that he liked in a designer's sketches, he immediately knew he liked it and he had the will to turn it into a production reality.

The Corvette evolved from sketches that one of Harley Earl's stylists did during World War II. The concept was to design an all-American sports car. Earl code named his favorite design the "Opel," after the name of GM's German branch. This Opel sports car was the genesis of the 1953 Corvette. Not much has ever been written about this concept, because of Earl's secretive nature, which was mentioned earlier in this book.

After Word War II, Earl riveted a lot of his thinking on the modifying European styling trends to come up with distinctly American car designs. Sleek, tight curves were characteristics of European cars then and Earl pushed his designers towards more fully-rounded American monocoque shapes. He opened up the small-radius curves of European designers and came up with forms like the rounded front fenders and ample wheel wells seen on the first Corvette.

Once the sports car concept (not yet called the Corvette) was developed to Earl's liking, he knew that he had to find a way to sell the idea to the GM management. "That is why he built show cars, yes," said Earl's successor Bill Mitchell in Armi's book. "Those so-called dream cars had two meanings. He wanted to get the corporation off the duff. It was awfully hard to get the board to see ahead. So, by putting them in a show, someone would say, 'Why don't you build that!' That is how the Corvette was born."

After the Corvette concept became a production car, Harley Earl had an even greater appreciation of what a "dream

car" could accomplish. He created many such vehicles during his tenure at GM and even drove a couple of them himself. Earl retired from GM in 1958. Bill Mitchell replaced him as chief of design. During his fifth year of retirement, the Chevrolet styling staff created this convertible for Earl.

Widely known as "The Harley Earl Corvette Roadster," the car was hand-built at the GM styling studios in Warren, Michigan. It was completed in January 1963 and then sent to Harley Earl's home in Florida. The unique car is among the best-known of what are called "styling Corvettes." Such cars were generally not purpose-built for shows, like the corporate dream cars were. They were usually modified production cars provided to GM executives, their family members or a select group of friends.

Features of the heavily-modified Corvette convertible include leather-trimmed seats and door panels, knock-off style wheels, a 327-cid 340-hp fuel-injected V-8, a four-speed manual gearbox, special side-port exhaust manifolds and mufflers, a white racing "stinger" stripe running over the top, a specially-installed air conditioning system and a custom-crafted instrument panel that has over 15 monitoring gauges.

The car incorporates several advanced technical features that were not available on regular-production Corvettes until 1965. These include the special hood, disc brakes and a behind-the-passenger-seat battery mounting.

It is claimed that this Cobalt Blue Corvette was built by GM "without regard to cost." While that is probably debatable to a point, it certainly reflects — in a 1960s style — what could

be achieved when designers' minds were set at least somewhat free so that their imaginations could run to fanciful levels.

This one-of-a-kind Corvette is probably the most well known of the styling studio cars due to its popularity among Corvette enthusiasts. It was the first of the styling cars to be re-introduced to the public at the first "Special Collection" exhibition at the well-known Bloomington Gold Corvette show. This "Corvette Masterpiece" is currently part of the Bob McDorman Chevrolet Collection located in Canal Winchester, Ohio.

△ **This Corvette styling exercise got its own rendition of a custom side exhaust system.**

△ **The car's Cobalt Blue finish is set off with a White "stinger" hood scoop.**

Florence Knudsen's "Little Pink Corvette"

△ **Made for the wife of a Chevrolet general manager back in the "sizzlin' '60s," the pink color on the Corvette was patterned after the kitchen in her Florida home.**

Bunkie Knudsen was the general manager of Chevrolet in 1964. This customized Corvette was built for his wife Florence. She chose a Pearlescent Pink 1964 color for her car. The pink matched the décor of the Knudsen family home in West Palm Beach, Florida. The Corvette factory in St. Louis originally built this vehicle as an Ermine White car with a 327-cid V-8 and Powerglide automatic transmission.

Bunkie Knudsen, being a fan of big-block engines, probably had something to do with the engine under the car's hood.

The 396-cid V-8 wasn't available in production-line Corvettes until 1965, but Chevrolet Engineering swapped one into Florence's Corvette. To do this, they had to remove the 327-cid 300-hp base V-8 the car was originally built with.

Chevrolet didn't offer air conditioning as an option in big-block cars in 1964, but Florence Knudsen was going to drive in Florida and needed this option. It appears that Chevrolet Engineering had to machine custom pulleys from round billet to mount the accessory drives. These pulleys were not made by the usual stamping method.

△ The car left the factory with a 327, but a pre-production 396 was soon added.

◁ Chevrolet Engineering handled the job of customizing the car.

☐ Only one Corvette got this interior treatment and you're looking at it.

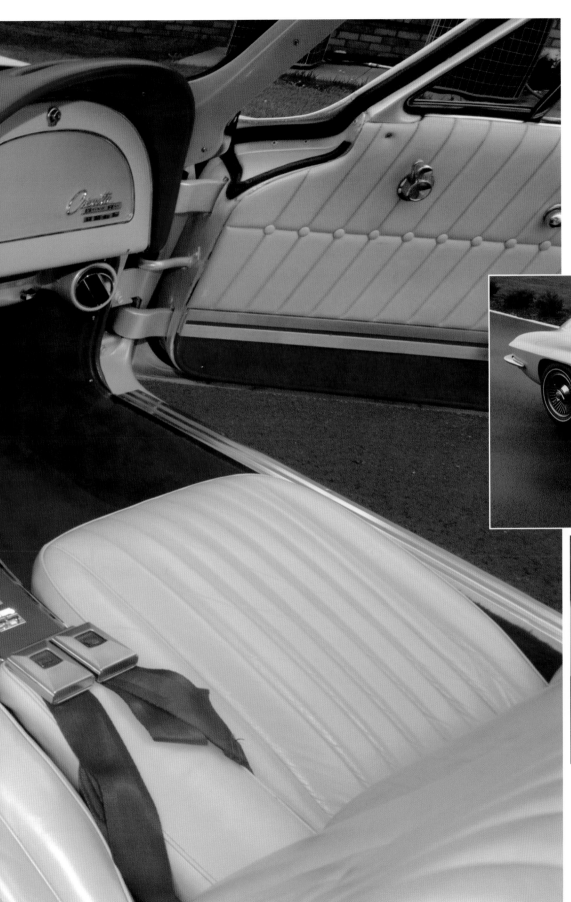

Just about everywhere you look, this '64 coupe has custom touches. It has six taillights instead of four. The grille is also a custom item. Its eggcrate design is the same one used on many of the "styling" Corvettes built by the Chevrolet design studio in the same era. Bunkie Knudsen had his own custom-styled Corvette.

Inside Florence's car, her initials "FMK" are inscribed on the seat belt buckles. The upholstery and dashboard have a two-tone pink-and-red treatment.

This low-mileage Knudsen 396 coupe resides in the Bob McDorman's collection in Canal Winchester, Ohio. This "Corvette Masterpiece" has its original paint and just 18,273 original miles as of July 11, 2006.

△ The custom front end treatment and grille was shared with some other styling cars.

△ Seat belt and console show the amount of design detailing on this car.

1970 LT1:
"My High Performance Zora Rocket"

△ **This LT1 still has its California emissions equipment intact.**

Car collectors are enthusiastic about Corvettes with the LT1 V-8, especially 1970 models. "This is my high-performance Zora rocket," LT1 owner Terry Ricer said.

Of all small-block Corvette engines, the '70 LT1 was the hottest. In fact, Chevrolet didn't surpass its 370 gross horsepower (290-310 net horsepower) for another 20 years. Then, to pay homage to history, Chevy resurrected the LT1 option code in 1992.

The '90s LT1 is a great Corvette, but it's the 1970 LT1 that originated the legend. It captured the hearts of Corvette enthusiasts in the early '70s, when performance was starting on a downslide.

'Vette fans didn't know what they had until it was gone. The 350-cid LT1 V-8 of 1970 was awesome. It had an 11.0:1 compression ratio, GM's last mechanical cam, a huge 850-cfm Holley four-barrel carburetor and a set of two-and-a-half-inch exhaust pipes (shared with big-block V-8s). The LT1 is not a

smooth engine, but you just know it's hot from the way it idles. It literally "thumps" through the dual exhausts.

Although the original LT1 V-8 stuck around through the 1972 model year and continued to be a hot offering with 330 hp, it was de-tuned to operate comfortably on 91-octane fuel. This change was needed to satisfy new government emissions standards. The compression ratio was dropped to 9.0:1. This was a sign that the classic muscle car era was on its way out.

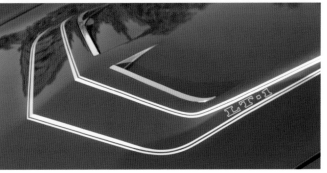

△ The egg crate grille was new for 1970. Corvette production dropped to its lowest level since 1962 in 1970. They built 10,668 coupes and 6,648 convertibles for a total run of 17,316.

◁ The LT1 is easy to spot. Pinstripes incorporate LT1 and outline the sides and front of the reverse facing scoop.

△ The tachometer reads up to 6,500 rpm for the high-winding small block.

Still, the LT1 designation has, over the years, become synonymous with the image of a high-output small-block V-8. The early '70s LT1 also contributed to a Corvette with great handling, since the lighter engine gave it 50/50 weight distribution. To a degree, the first LT1 won bragging rights over the last of the Corvette big-block V-8s, the 454-cid engine of 1970-1974.

When Terry Ricer was diagnosed with cancer a few years ago, he threw the idea of "saving for a rainy day" to the wind. Then, he started looking around for the Corvette of his dreams. What he found was this Bridgehampton Blue '70 convertible with the LT1 engine.

Behind the car's 370-hp V-8 is a four-speed manual transmission spinning a set of 3.70:1 gears in a positraction rear axle. As Terry knows, that's the hot set-up for an LT1.

Terry also knows that production was fairly limited on the 1970 model LT1. Chevrolet built only 1,287 "Corvette Masterpieces" with this engine. Of the total, Terry says less than 500 were convertibles.

☐ Terry Ricer trailers his '70 LT1 to shows that are long distance from home. Otherwise, he pleasure drives and cruises with his 'Vette.

Elfie Duntov's Favorite:
1971 Corvette LS5 Convertible

△ **This '71 'Vette ragtop won the prestigious Duntov Award in 1997.**

On August 30, 1997, Bobby Chestnut — the owner of this 1971 Corvette LS5 convertible — received an award he will cherish forever. That was the day Elfie Duntov presented him with a wooden carving of the Chevy Bow-Tie emblem. Elfie, Dave McLellan and other famous Corvette celebrities had signed the award.

"That was the year Zora passed away," Chestnut remembered. Chestnut had his LS5 at the Labor Day weekend gathering at the National Corvette Museum. "I don't know how many thousands of 'Vettes were there," he said.

In 1997, the museum had unveiled a new monument dedicated to Zora Arkus-Duntov, the Corvette's famous first chief engineer. Elfie — Duntov's wife of many years — was there to help with the ceremony.

"They took her around the whole show and wanted her to pick out a Corvette that best exemplified her husband Zora's philosophy of Corvette ownership," Bobby Chestnut recalls. "That's what they said on the stand when they gave this award to me."

Zora liked to drive and race Corvettes, so Elfie wanted to

☐ Under the chrome air cleaner under the hood is a big-block 454-cid Turbo-Jet V-8 with 365 hp.

△ Although this car is in mint condition, its owner prefers to drive it to events.

▷ Bobby Chestnut, owner, proudly displays his Duntov award.

What convinced Elfie to give the award to Bobby Chestnut and his 1971 Corvette with its 454-cid 390-hp LS5 engine was that he wanted to drive the car four or five miles to nearby Beech Bend drag strip, where he planned to race. Bobby fired his engine and started driving when National Corvette Museum employees on golf carts stopped him to ask where he thought he was going.

Chestnut told them he was driving to the drag strip to race his car. "You're going to race this car?" said an NCM employee. "Yeah, I'm going to race it," Bobby answered. "I didn't trailer it here; it's my favorite car and I use it."

When Elfie Duntov heard about this, Bobby got the award. "He actually enjoys his car, races it and drives it; he doesn't trailer it," Elfie pointed out. "That's just like Zora's philosophy of Corvette ownership. That's why I want to give this award to the owner of this car."

Bobby still had time to drive out to the quarter mile drag strip, so that's what he did. And since his car is all-stock, his numbers at the track that day reflect what an LS5 would actually do when it was new, back in 1971. For the record, Bobby's best run was 13.9 seconds at 107 mph.

That wasn't bad, considering that the gorgeous Sunflower Yellow convertible is on the luxury side with air conditioning, power steering, leather seats, an AM/FM radio and automatic transmission.

For Elfie Duntov, Bobby Chestnut's '71 big block convertible is a real "Corvette Masterpiece."

give the award to a Corvette that saw plenty of use. "She didn't want to give it to a car that had been trailered to the event" Bobby explained.

"Corvette Summer" Movie Corvette

△ The unusual customized body on this Corvette was created for the motion picture "Corvette Summer."

This car appeared in the motion picture called "Corvette Summer." That explains the car's special attraction. Millions of people have seen "Corvette Summer." When people see the movie car, memories of the film come flooding back. Many of us wanted a "Corvette Summer" and didn't get it. Some of us are still hoping and looking for one.

The car itself is unusual. The hood is gargantuan and none of the nine air scoops are functional. The strange boat-tail front end has no bumper. Like the rest of the car, the engine is like a "rhinestone cowboy" with a huge 10-gallon hat, but no ranch. The car has multiple carburetors, but they don't have a high-performance engine to feed the fuel to.

Nevertheless, this car packs 'em in at the MY Garage Corvette Museum on the Mid-America Motorworks campus in Effingham, Illinois. "A great percentage of the people who view the car recall the film after they see the Corvette," admitted Dennis Gunning, the MY Garage Corvette Museum curator. "They either hate the car or love it, but, either way, they are in awe of it."

Mid-America Motorworks displays this "Hollywood" Corvette with a movie theater for a backdrop. Hardly a week goes by that Dennis Gunning doesn't get a letter or an e-mail from a fan wanting to purchase a body kit or a mold of the car so they can make a replica.

As far as we know, nobody has yet made a replica, but if

△ The engine now in the car is a 350-cid V-8 with twin four-barrel carbs on a tunnel-ram intake.

△ The movie car Corvette looks as unusual from the rearview as it does when seen from the front.

△ The steering wheel inside the car is on the passenger side, but under the hood the steering box remains on the left-hand side of the vehicle.

they did, we doubt very seriously that they'd convert the steering to the right-hand side of the car, which is a curious feature of the real vehicle. You have to see "Corvette Summer" — or read this chapter — to understand why it has what the British call "right-hand drive."

It seems the star of the movie — a character named Dantley — wants to be next to girls as he cruises the streets around Los Angeles, especially on Van Nuys Boulevard.

When Dennis Gunning got the car, he was surprised to see the steering wheel on the right, but he was really flabbergasted at the conversion. The stock Corvette steering box remains on the left-hand side of the car. The steering action is transmitted to the right side of the vehicle via a Harley-Davidson motorcycle chain and two sprockets bolted under the dash. Obviously, this film car wasn't meant to be driven very hard.

A clamshell hood is the car's most impressive custom feature. This alteration was done before the C4 Corvette, with its clamshell hood, debuted in 1983.

In the movie, the car is powered by a 350-cid V-8 with an Edelbrock manifold and a single four-barrel carburetor. Somewhere along the line, the car's engine got souped up. The Chevy small-block now sports a tunnel-ram intake and dual four-barrel Holley carbs.

The paint appears to be a Candyapple color and was applied with 6-8 coats, like hot rodders did in the good old (school) days. Gunning says the base coat color is gold metallic. It is topped with candy-colored clear coats. When a painter removed the tape to redo the striping, the gold in the base coat showed through. The old painting system is simplistic, but it provides dazzling results, as you can see.

The car's original moon roof, a popular feature in the 1978-1982 era, has been replaced. The modified tops used in the movie had a border of about three inches painted to match the body. The interior upholstery was originally saddle color, but it has been dyed black.

Overall, the heavily-customized car remains pretty much as it appeared in the movie. It retains its original paint, mirrors, wheels, tires, exhaust system and just about everything, at least as far as Dennis Gunning can tell.

There were actually two "Corvette Summer" movie cars. This one was the "hero car" or "camera car." There was also a "stunt car." It was sold to somebody in Australia about 15-20 years ago.

You can see this "Corvette Masterpiece" at the MY Garage Museum in Effingham, Illinois. Admission there is always free.

△ **A flip-up nose allows a good look at the wildly-customized car's innards.**

Red '73 LS1 Modified
with Original Paint

△ **It isn't common to see a Resto-Modded Corvette, like this '73 convertible, with its original factory paint.**

It's hard to beat a red Corvette, no matter the model year. Just ask Charley Mornout of Bismark, Illinois, owner of this red '73 convertible spotted at the National Corvette Museum's "C3 Extravaganza."

Though the '73 'Vette might be low on factory performance, it is still a Stingray and it still screams "great style." Plus, it makes a great starting point for modifications.

The sun was peaking in and out from behind a cloud, creating a sunset line on the side of the body. The light really showed off the lines of the '73 Corvette.

Although modified, Charley's '73 convertible looks pretty much stock. He painted the side-pipes a factory color and added a set of American Racing Torque Thrust II wheels.

With 190 hp, the stock L48 350-cid V-8 proved uninspiring. The period from the early-'70s to the early-'80s was the era of "smogged" motors. Detroit automakers were struggling to meet tough new emission standards. To satisfy the U.S. government, they had to choke down engine performance.

Charley Mornout pointed out that his TPI (tune-port-injected) engine "sucked gas" at an alarming rate. His car got

□ The 5.7-liter LS1 V-8 in the car is a definite upgrade.

△ The car is a nice blend of mods like the side exhaust system and factory items like the chrome trunk rack.

△ The interior retains the original theme overall, but sports a couple of nice custom touches.

Charley quickly realized that he needed an LS1 engine that attached directly to the transmission — a Camaro engine, in other words. On eBay, he found an online auction that was offering an LS1 engine and 460LE transmission for the price of just an engine. He bought it, of course.

"I couldn't see spending $5,000-$6,000 for a crate engine without a transmission," said Charley. He also claims that the 4-speed automatic overdrive transmission he got is great for highway cruising and contributes to good gas mileage.

Most builders would probably stop with a deal like Charley got and be happy. Not him. He also bought a "Competition Plus" suspension from a company called Vette Brakes. This setup replaces the stock '73 Corvette coil springs with fiberglass front and rear springs. It also includes tubular A-arms.

With the hot LS1 engine and upgraded suspension, Charley claims he can burn rubber with his car in second gear. The car is faster and more fun to drive. As a plus, it gets better fuel economy.

Charley said the official name of the factory color on his car is Mile Miglia Red, which sounds more glamorous than the factory listing, which calls it red. Charley stressed that the paint on his car is the original coating it left the factory with. This proves that modified cars can retain a measure of originality.

The mention of paint revealed an interesting story. Charley's Corvette originally belonged to a GM plant manager in Dayton, Ohio. When the car showed up at the dealership, the manager refused delivery due to paint quality. The dealership re-squirted the paint. Charley met the original owner at a car show in Valparaiso, Indiana, in 1990. That was two years after he bought his car. The plant manager was glad to see the car being babied like a "Corvette Masterpiece."

only 15 miles of travel per gallon of fuel — on the highway that is. Around town, he calculated 12 mpg efficiency!

Eventually, Charley got on eBay to look for an LS1 Corvette engine. GM installed this version of the 350-cid small-block V-8 in newer C5 Corvettes, as well as in 1997-2002 Camaros.

To modify a Corvette, the car "builder" has to play the roles of auto engineer, auto designer and bean counter. Charley, for instance, discovered that the transmission was mounted right behind the engine in 1997-2002 Camaros. That was the same layout used in his '73 Corvette. The C5 Corvette, on the other hand, mounted the transmission at the rear of the car.

Modified 1977 T-Top Runs a ZZ4 Crate Engine

Nineteen-seventy-seven Corvettes don't have to be "lap dogs" — at least not as long as the owner has the guts to provide the glory.

Dick Countryman knows the score. He's owned this black '77 T-Top Corvette for 20 years. He admits that the stock 180-hp L48 was not a hot V-8. With 350-cid it pumped out 180 hp, which is anemic. Power-robbing amenities like air conditioning, power steering and power windows didn't help, either.

△ The car is driven to Corvette shows and events across the country.

◁ The Keisler five-speed overdrive transmission aids the performance of this '77 'Vette.

☐ After 1976, it appeared that true convertibles were going to be "outlawed" so Detroit invented the removable roof panel to replace the ragtop.

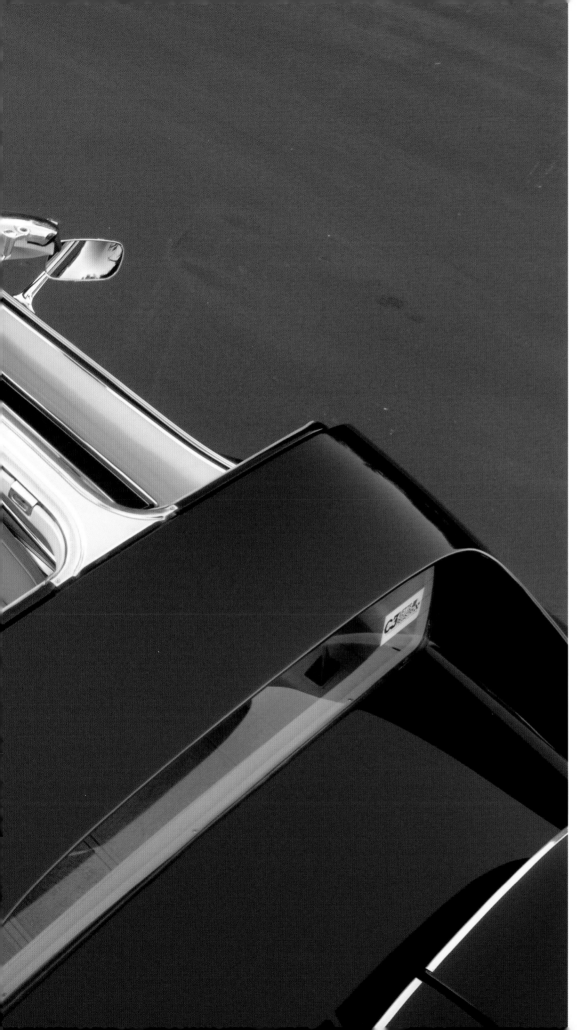

When General Motors first offered the ZZ4 crate motor five or six years ago, Dick was one of the first to order one. He jumped on board the ZZ4 wagon early.

"A lot of the guys in our C3 'Vette Registry have gone to the GM crate motors," said Countryman. "The ZZ4 is probably one of the most popular motors available."

Numbers don't lie. The ZZ4 delivers 335 hp and 405 pounds-feet of torque. Those kinds of performance numbers gave Dick something to work with. Now each year when the car goes into hibernation, he "upgrades" the drive train. He hunts for even more improvements, such as his Keisler five-speed overdrive manual transmission. Dick's now planning to install a hydraulic clutch and rack-and-pinion steering.

Upgrades like these are put to good use, too. Dick and his wife Jill drive the '77 Corvette thousands of miles each year, traveling to various Corvette events across the country.

"I do run it, too" Dick added, referring to occasional blasts down a quarter-mile raceway. One year, at Beech Bend drag strip, his ZZ4-powered '77 'Vette beat a '94 LT1 'Vette in a race. Both ran in the high 13-seconds bracket. To outrun a C4 Corvette powered by the hot LT1 engine is impressive. It means that this '77 "Corvette Masterpiece" is a lap dog no more.

▽ **When Dick Countryman slides behind the wheel, his wife Jill climbs into the passenger seat.**

Radical Wide-Body Greenwood 'Vette

△ **There's no mistaking the wide-body Greenwood creation with a stock-bodied Corvette.**

ohn Zandy's '78 coupe is one of those Corvettes you either love or hate. It's long, low and wide and looks like it's going 200 mph standing still.

The car is a modified Greenwood wide-body Corvette. It features American Custom Industries body components. ACI, a company located in Sylvania, Ohio, is right down the road from where Greenwood's shop used to be.

The Greenwood name comes from John Greenwood, a man who was catapulted to fame in 1971 when his red, white and blue Corvette won the 12 Hours of Sebring with comedian Dick Smothers co-driving. Greenwood's racing Corvettes stood out because of their low, wide bodies,

Zandy, a Chicagoan, said, "When I first saw this car, it just hit me right between the eyes like a sledgehammer." It was love at first sight. Zandy got a chance to buy the wild coupe and acted on it.

The car was a modified or street variation of a Greenwood racing car. Overall, the car was in pretty sad shape and the body needed extensive work. Zandy didn't care.

Zandy knew he was buying a project. Asked to reveal the amount of work he invested in the car, Zandy said, "The only things that haven't been touched since I bought it are the seats, hood and steering wheel. I've replaced *all* the running gear: the engine, transmission and driveline. The brake system, ex-

◁ The car has a real "Darth Vader" look and was sinister enough to scare competitors off.

◁ Everything under the hood has been replaced with something that looks brighter or runs hotter.

△ The steering wheel is one of the few untouched items on the car.

haust system, cooling system and electrical system have *all* been changed. I modified the front end with an aluminum nose. The headlight covers are a custom item."

A government agency had seized the '78 Corvette from a drug dealer and then auctioned the car in a public sale. "What I heard is that they also seized two or three other custom Cor-vettes and three or four more cars from him," Zandy recalled. When the sale took place, Zandy was high bidder.

Zandy's work on the rebuilt Corvette is a sight to behold. The extra-wide Greenwood body was designed to create down-force during high-speed racetrack use.

△ **Wide rear tires require wider rear body panels.**

△ **Turning a racer into a modified street car doesn't always work out this well. It looks awesome!**

It is hard to imagine improving the looks of a Greenwood wide-body Corvette, but that's exactly what was done with the hood. Zandy told us the four scoops on the passenger side are fender vents from either a 1968 or 1969 'Vette. They evacuate air to help cool the engine bay. At one time in the car's racing history, they also provided clearance for a Gale Banks turbocharger.

Zandy switched to a 350-cid small-block V-8 that he bored .060-inch over. "I used Corvette heads on the car," he said. "I had those ported and got 2.02/160 valves. It's basically a full-race engine with a forged crank, forged pistons and forged rods. Power is probably in the neighborhood of 425-430 hp."

In keeping with the car's distinctive exterior looks, Zandy built a novel air cleaner intake from scrap chimney flashing. It has snowmobile louvers on its side. For wing nuts he used Harley-Davidson point covers that happened to fit the hold-down bolt for the Holley carburetor on his "Corvette Masterpiece."

Pop Art 'Vette:
A Real "Psychotic Reaction"

Troy Noren's '85 C4 Corvette might best be described as pure American pop art. The "artistic side" of Troy's car goes much deeper than the wild paint scheme on the customized fiberglass body. This '85 'Vette embodies a *total* departure from stock.

"I went extreme," Troy said. "I *completely* re-did the whole car. I went over the edge."

Noren's build has a retro theme. He is in charge of the maintenance of 170 fleet vehicles at the University of Chicago. And he is slightly "anti-computer" in his thinking.

"I just feel that with more computer stuff, there are more problems," says Noren. "With these newer cars, one little sensor doesn't work and the whole car doesn't run. On my 'Vette, when something is bad, at least you can start the car."

Troy's engine reflects good, old-time-hot-rod technology. No computer is needed, thank you. Brodex heads and a single-plane intake are not what you expect to see on a 383 "stroker" engine under a C4 Corvette's clamshell hood.

The ignition system Troy used comes from MSD. It's a complete system from the billet distributor to the 6AL spark box and

△ **Is this a Corvette book or an art book?**

△   **The design blends several different custom body parts.**

◁   **Hot rod engine is fully exposed by the clamshell hood.**

coil. As the old hot rod magazines that Troy likes to read would put it, "The Hooker headers expel the hot exhaust gases."

Troy's car proves that an early C4 Corvette makes a great starting point for an old-fashioned hot rod build. Just look at all that elbow room under the hood. Drag racers love to have engine bay access like that.

Noren kept the retro theme going inside the car. Sounding like a man on a mission from God, Troy boasted, "I ripped out everything; all the air conditioning ducts, every piece." The car has no air conditioning and no heat either. When Troy was finished, there wasn't even a door-ajar buzzer left. Of course, the digital dashboard was gone.

"I made a piece of aluminum to fit this hole where the digital dash used to go and bolted it right in," said Noren. "I installed AutoMeter gauges with a tach, shift light and mph indicator."

Stock body panels wouldn't do on Troy's 'Vette. More out-of-the-box thinking was called for. Few people pick up on the fact that Troy used a mixture of different C4 body panels from American Custom Industries. "It's got a '98 rear clip and a '96 front nose with a 3.5-inch cowl-induction hood," he pointed out. "It's got a Greenwood ground-effects kit, too. The kit included the rear wing."

The roof of the car used to be solid fiberglass painted to match the color of the car. Now, it has a transparent glass top. Eighteen-inch Weld Racing blade wheels are mounted front and rear. Troy also lowered the body a full three inches. Wheel simulators block the rotors and calipers, giving a cleaner look.

The result of all Troy's modifications is a great-looking car that Troy drives occasionally and takes to car shows. The wild paint scheme is what really turns heads. Treating the fiberglass like some kind of swoopy artist's canvas was a creative addition to building the car.

"It was something the painter and I were just playing around with on paper," says Troy of the crowning touch for his "Corvette Masterpiece." The two men sketched the design out. "It came off a lot better than I thought it would," Noren admitted.

△   **The graphics on the car are pretty wild and the owner helped pick them.**

△ The car has a low-slung appearance and a transparent-glass top.

◁ The interior has its share of changes, too.

1989 Corvette Challenge Racing Car

△ **By making all the cars identical, the Corvette Challenge racing series turned racing into a true test of driving skills, but the cars involved were still beautiful.**

What if every racing driver had an identical car? Then, the winner would be the driver with the most talent. Nobody would have an unfair advantage. This was the rationale behind the Corvette Challenge, a racing series that ran for two seasons: 1988 and 1989.

Canadian racing driver John Powell, who retired in 1987, after four straight years without a loss in Sports Car Club of America Showroom Stock series racing, came up with the idea. He got together with Chevrolet and the SCCA to make the dream a reality.

Each 1988 or 1989 Corvette Challenge race car came from the factory with a 350-cid 245-hp Tune-Port-Injected L-98 V-8, a Doug Nash 4 + 3 manual transmission, the Z51 Performance Handling Suspension, an AC3 6-way Power Driver Seat, a UUB Delco-Bose Stereo, the Z6A Side Window and Side Mirror Defog System and the 245 Blue Tint Glass Removable Roof Panel package.

A company named Protofab, located in Wixom, Michigan, equipped each Challenge Corvette with a full roll cage, an onboard fire extinguisher, racing seats, Bilstein shocks and special wheels.

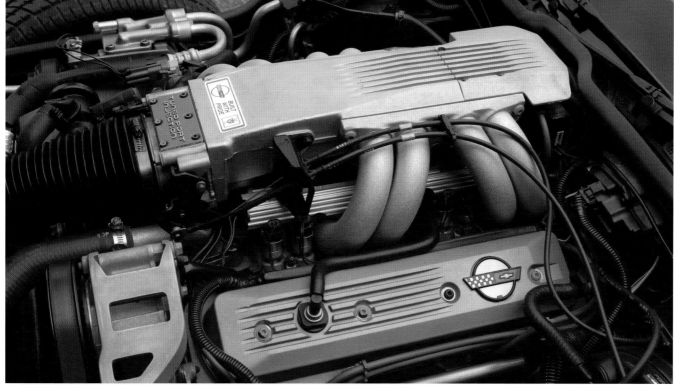

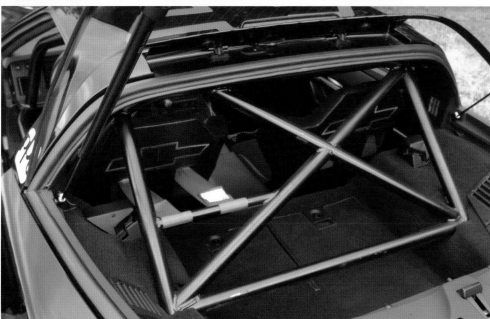

◁ All of the 350s sourced from the Flint, Michigan engine plant were equalized at very close to 245 hp.

◁ Protofab fabricated the full roll cage and other competition components.

Chevrolet sourced the engines for all of the racing cars from the Flint Engine plant and equalized them to within 2.5 percent of the stock 245 hp. They were then sealed with tamper-proof paint that was visible only under a special light source. This green paint on the bolts would rub off on a wrench, tipping off tech inspectors to possible internal engine modifications.

That's where our featured car — the No. 30 "back-up" Corvette Challenge car of 1989 — comes in handy today. It is one of two Challenge Corvettes that stayed out of the action for the entire season. It is exactly as Protofab prepared it to race.

Racing can age a car beyond its years, but this vehicle is a literal "time capsule." It appears exactly as it was when new. Nothing on the car has ever been changed, altered or revised.

△ As far as seating went, comfort and safety came first, but the interiors looked pretty nice for a racing car.

◁ This Corvette was one of the back-up cars in 1989.

The stakes were high in Corvette Challenge Series racing. The teams were competing for a $1 million dollar purse. From the start, car No. 30 was only intended to be used if someone crashed and needed to buy a new car to stay in the competition.

Lance Miller remembers when his late father Chip bought the black Corvette from John Powell. The sale took place the year after the series ended. Chip was a successful promoter of car events in Carlisle, Pennsylvania. He was also one of the country's top Corvette enthusiasts and collectors.

Lance Miller now maintains a Website for Corvette Challenge history at www.showyourcorvette.com. On the Website, he recalls when the transporter delivered the black No. 30 Corvette Challenge car to Carlisle and he and his dad took a ride in the car.

"I'll never forget when this car was delivered," he wrote. "We both ripped around the fairgrounds with huge smiles on our faces. This car was the car that truly launched me into loving cars . . . and especially Corvettes. It was the sound of the exhaust, the way it handled and the sheer beauty. This is the car that started it all for me; it's a car that will always remain in our family collection because of the sentimental value. We've taken this car on various tours and cruises; one of us would drive half of the time and the other would finish the trip."

Each Corvette Challenge car is identified by a unique option code, so there can be no question of a vehicle's authenticity. In 1988, the unique option code for a Challenge Corvette was "B9P." Chevrolet produced 56 total cars with this option. Protofab converted 48 of these Corvettes for racing. Exactly 46 were raced. That left two back-up cars that were never raced.

In 1989, the unique option code for a Corvette Challenge racing car was "R7F." Chevrolet produced 60 cars with this option. Protofab converted 29 of these Corvettes for racing. Exactly 27 were raced, leaving two back-up cars that never raced.

The original colors for 1988 Corvette Challenge cars were Red, Black, White, Yellow, Gray, Dark Blue and Dark Red. In 1989, the colors offered were Red, Black, White, Charcoal and Medium Blue. Entrants applied racing numbers and sponsorship decals.

The 1988 and 1989 Corvette Challenge cars are a very interesting chapter in Corvette racing history. They will make excellent vintage racing cars.

My prediction is we'll see some of the races re-enacted, in the future, with the original cars. If that's the case, it's likely that 1989 Challenge car No. 30 will not stay on the sidelines. Lance Miller will be behind the wheel, racing, with fond memories of the first day he and his father took their "Corvette Masterpiece" out for a spin around the Carlisle Fairgrounds.

◁ Painted 5-spoke wheels were fitted.

The car is part of the Chip Miller Collection and Lance Miller remembers when his father bought it.

Fastest Little Street 'Vette in Texas –
All Dressed to the Nines

△ **Fat tires on David Stone's '92 'Vette provide "bite" during hot runs down the drag strip.**

Car magazines can get you in trouble. "In '95, I was reading *Hot Rod* and they were talking about Vortec superchargers and how good they'd make a car run," said David Stone, of Arkansas, "So, I got a hold of some guys, had a Vortec put on my '92 'Vette and liked the way it ran."

The Vortec supercharger knocked more than a full second off David's 1,000-foot elapsed times. They went 12.20 seconds to 10.90 seconds. That was fast, but not fast enough for Stone.

In 1999, David won the "Fastest Street Vette in Texas"

title. In the process, he went through five engine builds. The last four were done by Absolute Performance, a small tuner from Jacksonville, Arkansas.

How fast did Stone have to go to win his title? It took a 10.81-second *quarter mile*, at 133 mph, to beat everybody out. That was after David slipped past the safety people at Texas Motorplex in Ennis. (He'd have won the following fall, too, except he failed the safety check when a hawk-eyed inspector noticed he didn't have "door bars" on his roll cage.)

David's consolation that fall was that he did record the fastest ET of the day, a 10.42. He was preparing to hit the high 9-second bracket once he got racing slicks installed and kicked in a full shot of nitrous oxide.

We caught up with David Stone at the Viper/Vette Shootout at River City Raceway in Marion, Texas. There he ran a best ET of 10.22 seconds at 140.6 mph. He wasn't running slicks, either. Instead, he went with a set of Mickey Thompson ET Street tires on 10 x 15-inch Weld wheels.

With 580 hp flowing to the rear wheels, plus a 175-hp shot of nitrous (Nitrous Works), Stone was spinning all the way through first gear. His 60-foot times were far short of their potential.

▷ **With nearly 600 hp flowing to the rear skins, a little smoke is inevitable.**

▽ **The Vortec supercharger gave the Corvette a lot of snort.**

▷ Looks pretty sleek inside for a racing car, doesn't it?

△ The 'Vette is 100 percent legal to drive on the streets.

△ This is the view that driver's of most supposedly-hot street cars get.

David's car is a very *serious* C4 Corvette, but amazingly it is completely street legal. "I drive it to church and to get something to eat," he said. "I take my girlfriend on dates in it. My parents live about an hour and a half away from me. I drive it to their house. I drive it to Jacksonville where the tuners work on it. That's 130 miles."

David is quick to credit Aaron Salisbury and John Simms at Absolute Performance for building his sturdy '92 LT1/automatic. He met them at the drag strip about a year after he'd installed the blower. His car had "slowed down a good bit," he told Aaron. "Man, I'm having trouble with my car." Aaron said, "We can help you with it."

The duo did a compression check and found out the pistons were shot. Superchargers are hard on stock pistons. The ring lands were broken off and the cylinders were leaking down 25 percent. They rebuilt the LT1 and installed "blower" pistons.

David didn't start off with the killer build he now has. As his enthusiasm grew, he came up with new ideas. Each time, the guys at Absolute Performance listened and got the job done. David remembers the first engine build. "They said I'd probably run high 11s at best, but the first time I ran an 11.06. When I saw I could do 11.06, I set my sights on 10s."

David's current setup is on the exotic side with 580 hp at the rear wheels. Of course, the original LT1 block has been replaced. Absolute Performance started with a two-bolt block out of a "police cruiser." With splayed billet caps, it's stronger than the four-bolt 'Vette LT1.

Absolute Performance installed a 3.825-inch Cola crank, Lunati Pro Mod rods and Lunati blower pistons. Comp Cams even ground a special cam for the new engine. All David will admit is, "It's a pretty big roller."

The heads on the engine come from Air Flow Research. They are re-worked and fitted with big 2.02/1.625-inch valves. The intake tubes are a big deal. They were custom built for Absolute Performance by race car builder Bobby Shahan of "Quick Time Race Cars."

David made another big change by switching speed-density technology, which was stock on the 1992 Corvette, to a 1994 Corvette MAF (mass air flow) fuel-injection unit.

The extra power necessitated a stronger automatic transmission. Absolute Performance installed a race-ready THM 400 built up by TPI. David swapped the Dana 36 rear end (stock for automatic 'Vettes) for a Dana 44 (stock for six-speed 'Vettes). He also installed 3.73:1 "digger" gears (3.42:1 gears were stock) and a Gear Vendor unit mounted on the end of the transmission tailshaft. This device splits the gears, allowing a driver to go from first to first overdrive, second to second overdrive and third to third overdrive. At 60 mph, David taps 2300 rpm and gets 21 mpg.

David has a Line Loc, which he uses to heat the tires on burn outs. He also has a 3,500-rpm-stall converter, but stalls to only 1,000 rpm, before launching. "It is amazing how the car runs, being as heavy as it is," Stone said. "With a quarter tank of fuel it weighs 3,513 pounds, so with me inside, it weighs over 3,700 pounds."

This September, David Stone promises a big surprise for the folks at Ennis, Texas. This time, he will have a set of those door bars on his "Corvette Masterpiece," plus a set of wider Hoosier racing slicks. These tires have more tread and a softer rubber compound, so his 'Vette will be "dressed to the nines."

(In case you didn't get his drift, the gold old boy from Arkansas is suggesting he'll be doing the quarter in the 9-second bracket! Won't that be a hoot?)

Tuner King of the Hill

aul Dehnert's '95 Corvette twin-turbo ZR-1 is fast. "When the boost comes on, all hell breaks loose," he says. "It feels like you've been shot out of a damn cannon."

When you have a car that produces 850 hp at the flywheel and 742 pounds-feet of torque at the rear wheels, it's not surprising that you feel like Quaker Puffed Wheat shot out of a field weapon.

Apparently, the ZR-1 "King of the Hill" Corvette is also the car on the top of the heap when it comes to tuner Corvettes of the street variety.

Paul Dehnert could not think of a more powerful 'Vette that acts so docile in everyday traffic. "I'm sure there are more powerful racing cars," Paul admitted. "But, this ZR1 is de-signed to run on the street, with the air conditioning on and all the creature comforts of a stock ZR-1. I mean, the car will idle around town. I could send my wife down to the grocery store for a quart of milk and would run so much like a stock ZR1 she'd never know the difference. That's how docile it is when it is not on the boost."

Dehnert, who lived in Austin, Texas, took his low mileage ZR-1 to the well-known tuner Lingenfelter Engineering, located in Decatur, Indiana. He had a twin-turbo system installed.

"The thing I like about the ZR-1 is its engineering unique-ness," said Paul, who has always favored the double-over-head-cam LT5 engine. "The fact it is a Lotus-designed dohc engine built by Mercury Marine means the engineering is phenomenal."

△ **The ZR-1 had a hot-car reputation, but this masterpiece ups the ante a bit.**

△ Are you ready to rock-and-roll?

▷ The stock six-speed gearbox was upgraded for the Twin Turbo V-8.

▷ If you think Paul Dehnert donned a pair of Viking horns, look closer. Those are the fat exhaust pipes on his car.

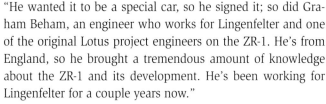

△ John Lingenfelter and engineer Graham Beham both signaturized the hot 'Vette.

Dehnert knew that GM built an experimental twin-turbo version of the LT5. Such an engine is on display at the National Corvette Museum in Bowling Green, Kentucky. GM's twin-turbo engine produced 650 hp.

Paul wondered what John Lingenfelter could do and Lingenfelter said he was interested in taking on the project. Dehnert got together with another ZR-1 owner in Austin to order a pair of Lingenfelter twin-turbo ZR-1s. Dehnert's contract with Lingenfelter specified that no more than four of the twin-turbo cars could be built. The third one was made and went to a Houston, Texas, enthusiast. At the time this was written, the fourth car was waiting to be built on custom order.

Lingenfelter even made up special passenger-side dashboard plaques to denote that each Twin-Turbo ZR-1 will be one of a maximum of four built. "That little badge is one of the things Lingenfelter put together for us," Dehnert explained.

"He wanted it to be a special car, so he signed it; so did Graham Beham, an engineer who works for Lingenfelter and one of the original Lotus project engineers on the ZR-1. He's from England, so he brought a tremendous amount of knowledge about the ZR-1 and its development. He's been working for Lingenfelter for a couple years now."

Fitting two full-ball-bearing turbos into the engine bay was not an easy task. Packaging was probably the most difficult engineering task. Lingenfelter had to route air to the turbos via stainless steel pipes inside the frame. The turbos are hidden from the top. The engine bay looks pretty stock, except for a big air box in the front. You've got to put the car on a lift to see the turbos.

Lingenfelter fabricated new exhaust manifolds which fit right up underneath the exhaust ports. The object was to get the turbos as close to the exhaust system as possible, to minimize turbo lag.

The double-overhead-cam LT5 retains its stock engineering features. Lingenfelter upped the cubic inch displacement to 368, cut the compression ratio back to 8.0:1, ported and polished the heads, changed to a turbo cam, installed special liners and blueprinted the rotating masses.

The stock 6-speed manual transmission is equipped with a McCloud twin-disc clutch to handle the increased power. The suspension is also slightly modified for the added horsepower and torque. A special computer chip for the suspension controller flips the shocks to their "soft" setting, with no compression damping, so the rear end will squat for good weight transfer.

Dehnert commented, "If I don't have slicks on it, you can be driving along in fourth gear, at 50 mph, and spin the rear tires when the turbos spool up."

His best ET in the quarter mile has been 11 seconds flat at 138 mph running Mickey Thompson ET Street tires. Paul believes these tires are almost as good as racing slicks.

Will Lingenfelter build more than four of these "Corvette Masterpieces?" John said he is limited by contract to build only four cars, unless Paul says differently. So, until a hotter model comes along, the Lingenfelter ZR-1 Twin Turbo Corvette is apparently "King of the Hill" in *Tunerville*.

△ **We can guarantee that you won't see too many Lingenfelter 4-Cam 32-Valve Corvette V-8s.**

Ertl Model Box Photo Shoot:
The Rest of the Story

△ **When your "job" is photographing Corvettes you can run into all sorts of challenges.**

The Ertl company makes model cars. One of my assignments was to photograph a '95 Corvette ZR-1 for the cover of one of their model boxes. Chevrolet said they would leave the ZR-1 coupe in the parking lot at Detroit Metro Airport.

It was early on a summer afternoon and there was still time to get some pictures. This seemed like a good idea because rain was in the weather forecast for the next day.

Ertl wanted a front three-quarter photo for the box cover, plus five specific shots of the side, engine, rear three-quarter view, interior, profile and a detail, such as an emblem.

To get the right pictures, the car had to be moved around to get the light just right. It was late. The sun was low in the horizon and the Torch Red paint glowed wonderfully.

Along came a young man wearing a colorful jacket. He was curious about what was going on. He was intrigued by how the job of photographing a new Corvette for the cover of a toy box was done. He agreed to hold a 42-inch diameter silver photographic reflector over the engine compartment and got a big kick out of helping with the photography.

We struck up a conversation. The young man's name was Willie. He had trouble explaining what he did for a living and where he worked. The best he could offer was that he "worked with kids."

After a while, we both got thirsty and decided to drive to a store to get something to drink. Willie was invited to ride along if he wanted to. He did and we talked more. Willie told me he would like to be a photographer. He wondered if he could take good photos. He was encouraged by a positive answer and said that maybe he could get into the business of taking pictures for a living.

We got Cokes and headed back to the same photo location, but we didn't get the chance to take more pictures. As soon as we parked, two cops jumped out of their squad car and rushed us.

At first it was hard to understand why a cop was pushing

me against the Corvette. Then, I heard the word "drugs."

Being from a small Texas town, I was a stranger to illegal drugs. But the cop was sure I was buying drugs. He wanted to know where they were.

The cop searched and searched and couldn't find any drugs in the car. He said the other cop was questioning Willie and that our stories better match or we would both be going to jail.

The cop kept saying over and over, "We'll take your pretty little car from you and you won't see it again." Of course, I wasn't worried about losing the Corvette, since I didn't own it anyway.

The cop had a hard time believing I was a photographer and that Willie had just showed up and offered to help me by holding the reflector.

"Okay, let me see your photo equipment," the cop said. So, I opened the hatch on the ZR-1 to show him the aluminum

Haliburton case holding a hasselblad500cm, lenses, a tripod and reflectors.

The cop finally started to get it. He didn't want to see more photo gear. "Do you know who that is you're dealing with?" he asked. "That's Little Willie."

I told the cop that Willie had introduced himself and told me he worked with kids. "Yeah, he works with kids," the cop answered. "We suspect that he sells them drugs. And certain drug dealers have been known to put a 'cap' in your head quicker than you can say Hasselblad."

One policeman saw on my driver's license that I was from Texas. "Don't come around here with an $80,000 Corvette trying to shoot photos in Inkster," he warned.

The other cop had Little Willie in handcuffs. I don't know what happened to him.

Before I could leave, another black-and-white pulled up and a third cop got out. He opened the ZR-1's door and started

△ **In the author's line of work, you get to photograph interesting cars and meet unique people, like Little Willie, who posed with the ZR-1.**

△ Going on assignment for Ertl can be educational. You get to see the insides of new cars and what's going on in the outside world.

the same inquisition. He even said, "I'll take your pretty little car away from you and you'll never see it again."

The other cops came over to straighten the new cop out. He was in my face and I was getting fed up. I figured what the heck and said, "I don't care if you do take my pretty little car, because it isn't mine anyway." At that, the cop stared at me like I was insane. He didn't know what to say. He must have thought I was admitting to stealing the car.

"Chevrolet loaned the car to me to take pictures of it," I told him. "I'm a photographer." Then, the first cops arrived and began explaining the situation. That's when the last cop said he would fix it so I never got another car from Chevrolet or any other manufacturer.

After the dust cleared, I completed my pictures in Dearborn, which is another 10-15 minutes down Michigan Avenue. The toy box cover pictures of the ZR-1 — another "Corvette Masterpiece" — came out just great.

I've always wondered what happened to Little Willie and if he got into photography. You may think I'm naive, but I felt he was really interested in learning how to take pictures for a living and was not going to put a "cap" in my head. Maybe I'm not Crocodile Dundee, but I'm from Texas, I'm six-foot three-inches tall, I weigh 200 pounds and I wasn't scared of anybody I met in Detroit. In fact I met some nice people in that neighborhood.

4 CAM 32 VALVE

CORVETTE

☐ If you shoot it, they will come.

Corvette's Second Chief Engineer Drives a '95 ZR-1

△ Though McLellan's one concession to vanity may be his "Z-Rex" license plate, the former Corvette Chief Engineer is about as unpretentious a fellow as you'll meet anywhere. And he always has a smile for 'Vette enthusiasts.

Corvette chief engineers are celebrities at Corvette shows. Zora Arkus-Duntov, the first man to hold that job, passed away in 1996. His successor, Dave McLellan was chief engineer from Zora's retirement thru 1992.

When he was alive, Zora enjoyed meeting and talking to Corvette enthusiasts at car shows. He was always a great speaker when it came to relating tales about his favorite car. McLellan is also an articulate speaker and though retired, he keeps busy going to shows and working on various projects.

With a full head of white hair, McLellan is easy to spot at Corvette events. He drives to shows in his green 1995 ZR-1. Glenda, his wife of over 40 years, is always by his side.

"I drive it," Dave said of his Corvette. "I don't show it."

McLellan is not out to compete with car hobbyists and he doesn't restore or collect cars. "I love cars," he said. "I like cars from the 'teens, '20s, '30s and other eras, but I chose not to collect a whole bunch of them." McLellan might tinker with cars if he had the time, but he keeps very busy, so he has just one Corvette in the four-car garage at his Holly, Michigan estate.

McLellan authored the book *Corvette From the Inside*. Now, much of his time at car shows is spent autographing copies of it. He has another Corvette book in the planning stages.

McLellan is still involved with performance-car engineering, specifically the Mosler program and its MT900 supercar. He's also working with a military truck manufacturer, a computational fluid dynamics company, Georgia Tech Research Institute and the Society of Automotive Engineers. Dave says he has, "a whole bunch of balls in the air."

△ **Although Dave's personal car is an off-lease purchase, he keeps it clean as a whistle and treats it like a rare, one-of-a-kind show car.**

The McLellans have interests other than cars. Dave and Glenda built a Frank Lloyd Wright "student house" 32 years ago. The student is John Howe, who trained under the famous architect in 1935 and stayed in his employ until 1959, when Wright died. "We're in the process of bringing the house up to modern sub-systems and technologies," Dave said.

Built in a "triangular module," the house is novel, featuring about 1,000 square feet of window wall glass wrapping around the living space. It can be snowing outside, but when you turn on the outdoor lights, you lose the window wall as a barrier. The effect is to feel like it is snowing or raining *inside* the house. Apparently, the house is an evolving mechanism, not unlike the Corvette.

McLellan was born in 1936. He grew up in Michigan and attended Redford High School in Detroit. He graduated in 1954.

While in high school, McLellan participated in the Fisher Body Craftsman's Guild competition. Entrants in the nationwide competition had to design a model car, build it and paint it.

"I think I went through three cycles of that and made enough prize money to buy a trombone," McLellan recalled. Dave was not into sports cars then, but he constructed his vision of a dream car.

McLellan graduated from Wayne State University in 1959. He earned a BS in mechanical engineering, then started working for General Motors his first summer out of college. He was assigned to the "Noise and Vibration" lab at the GM Proving Ground.

After moving to Chevrolet, one of the first cars McLellan helped engineer was the 1970-1/2 Camaro. He became Corvette chief engineer in 1975, succeeding the legendary Duntov.

△ **After the fabulous job he did creating the ZR-1, Dave just had to have one in his own garage.**

"I started in Corvette just months before he retired, so my involvement with him prior to that was little," McLellan revealed. "Over the next 15 or however many years, until he passed away, we were reasonably close to one another."

Perhaps the technical highlight of Dave's tenure with Corvette was the ZR-1, which he calls "an important step in the history of the Corvette."

Dave's personalized Michigan license plate reads "Z-Rex." It has a special meaning. When the ZR-1 was introduced, Chevrolet treated journalists to a trip to France so they could drive the dual overhead cam super car code named the "King of the Hill."

McLellan was there. "Totally by serendipity, we had a number of the cars on Michigan license plates that were three letters and three numbers," McLellan remembered. "The three letters were 'REX,' which is Latin for king. So, I picked up on that."

As we looked over Dave's C4, he popped the hood and grabbed a rag to wipe road dust from the LT5 engine's intake and valve covers. "Don't take a picture yet," said Dave. "This thing is filthy." We assumed McLellan had bought his car brand new, but he corrected us, "The first owner was actually a lease holder," he revealed. "I bought the car from GMAC."

From stem to stern, the ZR-1 that Dave calls "Z-REX" is as stock as can be. Nothing has been changed from the way GM built the car. This makes sense if you consider that the ZR-1

was built on McLellan's watch. He told us he's not planning to sell it.

Dave was very much identified with the ZR-1, but modestly pointed out, "It was the program of a lot of people. I was certainly in the middle of it, but Lloyd Royce defined the engine program."

Life is good for McLellan. He's in demand at shows as a speaker and autograph signer. He's written a great book. However, he is not resting on his laurels. He has both an appreciation of history and an investment in the future of cars.

"There was a chapter in my book that was ultimately broomed out of there by my editor Jonathan Stein," Dave said. "It was really a fast walk through the history of the sports car and it contained a discussion of a lot of the early cars that had some seminal reason for being. They are important for the future. You can't understand where you are if you don't understand the past."

Looking to the future, McLellan speaks of a 'Vette based on the Mosler structure with a 0-60 mph time of 3.0 seconds, quarter mile ETs of 11.0 seconds and a top speed above 200 mph.

History has shown that Corvette chief engineers never really retire. Nor do they fade, fade away. In Dave's case, they drive their personal "Corvette Masterpiece" to shows all over the country and share their love of America's sports car with other enthusiasts.

Supernatural 450 Grand Sport

☐ Street time in this driver's seat is a real kick-in-the-pants driving experience.

hevrolet dropped the ZR-1 high-performance model in '96 and added the Grand Sport in its place. The automaker pumped up standard power with a new 330-hp LT4 V-8. The way to get even more horsepower than the ZR-1 had was to send your Corvette to Callaway Cars for their "Supernatural" upgrade.

This was the same idea that Randy Flock had. He and his wife Judy first saw the Grand Sport at the Black Hills Corvette Classic, in the summer of 1995, when some Corvette engineers, including Jim Minneker, were tooling around South Dakota in the soon-to-be-introduced Grand Sport.

△ There's no mistaking what you're looking at when you pull up behind this powerful white-striped 'Vette.

☐   This is either a signed set of golf clubs or a 450-hp customized LT4. What's your guess? Callaway name promises a powerful golf swing or "powerfully engineered automobiles."

The Flocks liked the Grand Sport's looks and found that its Admiral Blue paint and white stripes grew on them as time passed. By the following summer, the East Greenwich, Rhode Island couple decided they had to have a GS, but finding one was difficult. All of the cars seemed to be gobbled up. Then, an area Corvette show brought out a dealer who had a new '96 Grand Sport for sale. It even had the red interior Randy wanted.

The couple purchased the car and, in February of 1997, they sent it to Callaway Cars in Old Lyme, Connecticut, to have the engine upgraded. At first, Randy didn't order Callaway's aero body package, because he felt he loved the stock look of the Grand Sport. Randy also fretted over altering the stock LT4 V-8 that pumped out 330 hp, 30 more than the base LT1.

After their first ride in their completely-customized Callaway-tuned 450-hp Grand Sport, the Flocks knew they'd done the right thing. "We came home and I said 'oh my god, it's a rocket,'" Randy recalled. "We were in dreamland there for about a week. Getting on it was definitely like wow!"

One good thing led to another. By the summer of 1999, Randy and Judy were back at Callaway for the complete aero body treatment. Randy wondered how the special features of the Grand Sport would integrate with the Callaway aero body. For example, where would the Grand Sport's factory stripe intersect the four openings in the front of the Callaway hood?

Randy had confidence in Reeves Callaway. "I knew from Reeves' reputation that we wouldn't have any problems," Flock said. "Reeves backs everything he says. Even if it's just verbal, he will back it up. We were mostly concerned about taking a unique car and making it more unique. We didn't want to go too far and make it choppy looking. The way it came out was very nice."

Installing the Callaway aero body components is no small task. The Corvette's entire rear end, all the way up to the gas cap, has to be removed and replaced. The whole front nose is also replaced. The scoops added to the lower front fenders are functional; they exhaust hot air from the engine compartment. Installing them takes work.

Randy's car is the only Callaway-modified Grand Sport that includes the aero body package and the Supernatural LT4 engine. Randy has seen one other Grand Sport with a Callaway body, but on that car the owner did the body install.

Callaway also built at least three LT4-powered Supernaturals, but they are no more powerful than LT1s with the same modifications. Callaway Cars offered 400- and 435-hp Supernaturals at the start of the 1996 model year. Later, the 435-hp engine became a 450-hp job. Both LT1s and LT4s were offered in 450-hp tune.

On Randy's car, Callaway kept the original look of the Grand Sport engine intact. It has unique red highlights. Callaway added his signature on the fuel rail covers. Another appearance upgrade is the chromed valve covers that replace the stock black valve covers. They carry the inscription "Callaway Powerfully Engineered Automobiles."

Randy felt no need for suspension upgrades. He thought the extra braking performance of the Grand Sport was sufficient and nice to have with the hotter Supernatural LT4 propelling the car. He could have modified the interior with leather and Callaway signature items, but instead decided the car was just right as is. The Flocks are very content with their "Corvette Masterpiece" — the one-and-only Callaway Supernatural 450 Grand Sport.

△ **Randy's car is a one-of-one 'Vette.**

◁ **This looks like "over the river and through the woods" Grand Sport style.**

1997 Corsa Tiger Shark

△ **Wheel-to-Wheel made this once-stock C5 a Tiger Shark.**

After 75,000 miles and six years of normal driving use, Jim Browning turned his very early 1997 C5 Corvette with chassis No. 2324 into a test and show vehicle. For maximum attention, he made it look like GM's Tiger Shark show car. This was logical, since Browning's company, Corsa Performance Exhaust, built the exhaust system for the real Tiger Shark factory show car.

A company named Wheel-to-Wheel turned Browning's C5 into a Tiger Shark look-alike. Kelley Longwish is a manager for this Warren, Michigan firm. He explained that Wheel-to-Wheel's front fascia, which sits lower than a stock fascia, tends to give the car a Ferrari 355 look. Longwish said the rear-end treatment adds a more European flavor by integrating the reverse lights and turn signals into the taillights. "This gives a cleaner look," Longwish said. "There are no other lights anywhere, except in the taillights."

Wheel-to-Wheel has links to General Motors. That's how it got the assignment to build the real Tiger Shark. The show car's exhaust was farmed out to Corsa, another firm with GM connections. Wheel-to-Wheel got the rights

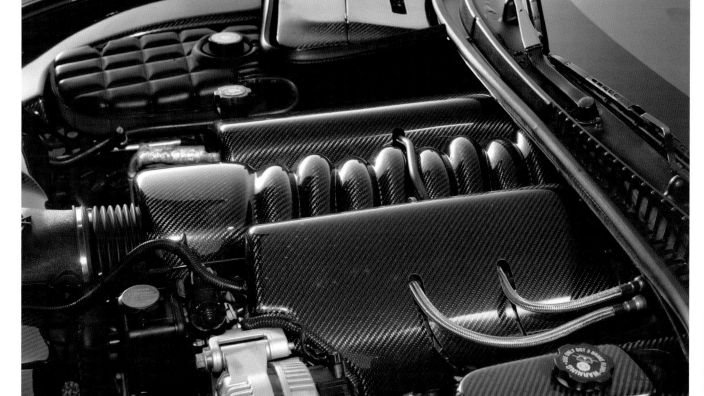

◁ The engine has been styled in a sophisticated appearance package.

▽ Browning's 'Vette is a show car.

to market a Tiger Shark body kit and Corsa has an exhaust system to go with it.

Browning knows the strong points of the LS1 engine used in the "Tiger Shark" C5 Corvette. He rattled them off as, "New camshaft, Z06 intake manifold, CNC cylinder heads, forged pistons, blueprinted and balanced reciprocating assembly and long-tube headers with high-flow catalytic converters."

The Corsa exhaust system in the Tiger Shark eliminates low-frequency noise. It promotes extreme airflow and delivers higher performance without bringing unwanted sounds into the car. The system consists of mufflers and over-the-axle pipes. The Tiger Shark body kit squeezes the four exhaust tips together.

Jim Browning drives the Tiger Shark on the street and his "Corvette Masterpiece" also serves as a test vehicle and show car. "It's a good way to test the performance of our exhaust systems, as well as showcasing our products," he said. "Those are the reasons why we decided to build it."

△ The interior has a rich, fluid look to it.

◁ There's a Euro image to the car's rear end treatment.

The American Heartland Creates a Monster
The "Green Thing"

△ **In this case "Green vehicle" equates to "hi-po."**

Quiet and reserved, Chuck Mallett is above all else a top-notch Corvette tuning guru. His company, Mallett Cars, based in Ohio, serves as a source of research and development for many C5 Corvette endurance racers.

Chuck Mallett's "Green Thing" is a tuner car that would be easy not to take seriously. To be quite frank, we've never seen a Corvette tuner that looks so *Hollywood*. Yet, the Green Thing is a serious Mallett test mule.

If the car's performance lives up to its looks, the Green Thing is one of those *ultimate* rides. Though it sounds noticeably docile, you can't help noticing that the carbon-fiber fuel-rail covers on the GM Motorsports race block that read "435." Stripes, fashioned of hand-carved urethane, give the Green Thing a "Hulk" cartoon-like image.

"That's just some crazy thing I came up with," says Chuck Mallett.."The car is green cause I've always been a fan of green. I think green makes it stand out."

△ When you put the hammer down on this Mallett those fat tires bite the pavement.

◁ The corporate logo pounds home a message.

The fact that Mallett doesn't race himself, though he's in the business of developing racing parts, gives his company a "Skunk Works" image, as if he's doing "back-door" development for Detroit-based automakers. His windshield decal boldly states his slogan — "Mallett, More Than Just Power."

"We do chassis development so the cars turn right and left," Mallett said. "We do brake development so they stop and go. We do everything, not *just* power. Mallett sells a totally handmade suspension. "We change the pick-up points," Chuck explained. "We use production-type A-arms, but we move them around."

Mallett talks about "roll centers" and "anti-squat" hardware like a race car builder. He understands that the tough part of selling *extreme* power is not so much building a car as it is building in reliability and getting the horsepower to the ground. Mallett's supercharged 435 will light up the tires of a Corvette in any gear, but that alone won't win checkered flags.

In addition to suspension tuning, the Green Thing is designed to slip through the wind, thanks to its use of unique, Mallett-developed body parts. Even the caps on the outer bottom edges of the rear fascia have a function. Chuck says, "They keep the air attached to the car and make it more slippery."

Mallett mentions a friend, Randy Witine, who is in charge of GM's wind tunnel testing. Witine will call and say, "I've got a Corvette in the tunnel and will be here until midnight, in case you want to bring some of your body parts up and test them."

△ **The 435-hp power plant hooks to a bullet-proof gearbox.**

▷ **Chuck Mallett is the "real deal" when it comes to building and tuning Corvettes.**

Mallett markets 396 and 435 tuner 'Vettes. The Green Thing is his test mule for future high-performance models. Customers have ordered engines like the one in the Green Thing. What they want is a power plant that delivers 608-hp and 620 pounds-feet of torque to the rear wheels.

The 3,200-pound Green Thing has a full-carbon-fiber body fitted with wind-tunnel-tested aero body parts. Its top speed is 225 mph. For the drag strip, Mallet estimates quarter-mile elapsed times in the mid-10-second range at close to 150 mph.

The car has had five or six engines starting with a Z06 V-8. Others included the famous 372-cid "Hammer" — a muscle motor written about in many magazines. Later, he installed a blown 372-cid engine. His latest and greatest creation is a supercharged 435-cid monster.

The Green Thing is not for sale, though Chuck admitted he did list it once in an eBay auction. "I was going to peddle it and put it on eBay for a week," he said. Someone bid $101,000. Another guy e-mailed a $125,000 offer. "I had a $150,000 reserve on it and I told him that was it," Mallett advised. "I wasn't going to sell it for $125,000."

More than just a tuner shop, Mallett Cars provides good, old-fashioned American ingenuity from the Ohio Heartland. And Chuck Mallett's Green Thing is certainly an unusual "Corvette Masterpiece."

Callaway C12

The 1999 Callaway C12 bears little resemblance to a production Corvette. The basic layout is still engine up front with rear-wheel drive. Inside and out, the car is a high-performance exotic. From the start, Reeves Callaway chose to build a "Corvette Masterpiece" from the bare bones of a fifth-generation Corvette.

The construction of a C12 begins in Callaway's Weingarten, Germany shop. Craftsmen bolt replacement upper and lower A-arms to the Corvette's strong perimeter frame. These A-arms are hand-fabricated by IVM Engineering of Munich. Then, the workers add coil springs and adjustable shocks to the Corvette's stock transverse plastic springs.

△ **This Callaway Corvette Speedster listed on the window sticker for $178,700. It does 60 mph from a standing start in 4.7 seconds and hits 100 mph in 9.7 seconds.**

◁ **Stylized logo carries the model name.**

△ **Based on the Corvette "dual" theme the cockpit sports upgrades.**

▷ **The 5.7- liter LS1, as modified by Callaway, delivers 465 hp at 5700 rpm and 473 foot pounds of torque at 4500 rpm. The engine is silky smooth and unstressed in this "Supernatural" configuration.**

▷ **There is not one "stock" Corvette panel surviving in the C12 Speedster, which is Callaway's most exotic Corvette.**

Callaway upgrades the brakes with 12-inch diameter rotors. Massive 295/30ZR/19 series Pirelli p-zero tires are standard equipment on the C12.

To create the swoopy shape of the C12 body, Callaway called on designer Paul Deutschman. If it wasn't for his exotic design, some of the chassis, suspension and running gear upgrades might pass unnoticed.

The use of fiberglass, carbon fiber and space age Kevlar in construction of the Callaway C12 provide strength and save weight. The car comes with unique fenders, door and hood panels and doorsill plates. Even the B-pillar panels are completely new.

Our featured C12 is a Speedster with a distinctive rear deck lid incorporating headrests. Callaway also offered the C12 in a Fixed Roof Coupe and a hardtop with a removable center roof panel.

The C12 interior has the Corvette "dual-cockpit" layout and lots of upgrades. Callaway swaps the standard seats for custom Koenig buckets. Custom gauges and carbon fiber around the console further upgrade the original Corvette interior. A Callaway badge on top of the console is stamped with the consecutive unit number of the build — "012" in this case.

Power for the C12 comes from a Callaway "Supernatural" V-8 that is installed in the car at Callaway Engineering's

facility in Old Lime, Connecticut. The "Supernatural" name indicates normally-aspirated. The car has no turbocharger or supercharger.

The engine starts as Corvette LS1 power plant. The block is fitted with a Callaway crank and forged 4340 steel connecting rods. A specific cam times a set of lightweight, forged-aluminum pistons. CNC machines a set of new Callaway-designed aluminum heads with improved flow characteristics. The result is 465 hp at 6500 rpm.

As hot as the car is, luxury abounds. It has a climate-control system, heated exterior mirrors and deluxe contour seats.

Our featured C12 has the optional leather interior including adjustable electric sport seats and two-tone leather on the steering wheel, door panels, console cover, and lower part of the dashboard.

This C12 was the first Speedster built in the series. Callaway displayed this "Corvette Masterpiece" at the Detroit and New York auto shows in 1999. Later, Sony Music CEO Tommy Mottola bought it. Christopher Pliaconis of Oldfield, New York is the current owner of the like-new car, which remains in its original auto show configuration.

△ **Customers could order their C12 interior in virtually any color or color combination.**

Excess and "Wretched Excess"

△ **This LT1 still has its California emissions equipment intact.**

Rich Rembold's '98 C5 is currently the one and only twin-turbo 427-powered wide-body Corvette in the world. With 725 hp, Rich's car is in a league with the likes of the $1 million McLaren F1. In that perspective, the $150,000 Rembold spent for his Lingenfelter Corvette is a bargain.

At first, Rich merely wanted a Lingenfelter-modified Corvette, so he sent his '98 coupe to Lingenfelter Performance Engineering. He initially had a Stage 1 twin-turbo setup installed on his stock LS1 motor.

A year later, Rich went back to Lingenfelter for an upgrade to a twin-turbo 383-cid " stroker" engine. He also had LPE install the wide-body kit they had developed in 200-plus-mph testing.

"After John Lingenfelter turned 225-226 (mph) in his Stage II twin-turbo (Corvette), the body got a little light," said Rich. "The new wide-body kit may have been a response to the need for high-speed stability."

At those speeds, a Corvette body needs more down force for stability and good road-holding. Another benefit of the

△ **"Rare Vet" plate is accurate.**

wide-body modification is that it can accommodate wider wheels and tires.

After making a hit with his stock-bodied C5 twin-turbo, Rembold became the darling of the Corvette concours circuit with his wide-body C5. He placed second in the entire Eastern Region. However, stone chips eventually took their toll on judging points.

Rich shipped his Maryland-based 'Vette back to Indiana-based LPE for paint. Then, Lingenfelter told him that a 427-cid C5-R racing-type engine block had become available. Not one to pass up a rare opportunity, Rich gave the OK to put the hot-ter power plant in his car.

To justify his actions, Rembold — an Associate Provost at Coppin State College and law professor at the Johns Hopkins University in Baltimore, said, "There is *kind of* excess and *wretched* excess."

Rich stressed that he is a responsible driver and does not have the skills to take his re-worked car to its limits in either the quarter mile or top speed. The car's 0-60 mph time is 2.97 seconds. As he described it, all you got to do is put the beefed-up automatic transmission in gear, aim the car, floor the pedal and hang on.

As for the quarter mile, Rich has done projections based on the performance of another car with the 427 twin-turbo LPE drive train and automatic transmission (but without the wide-body modifications) that did a 9.36 second quarter mile at 151.7 mph. Top speed, according to Rich, is estimated at "over 240 mph."

For now, Rich and his wife are content just to exhibit their "Corvette Masterpiece" at car shows and to occasionally fracture the speed limit (since cars this fast don't just break the limit.)

▽   This is the one-and-only car of its type to carry the 427-cid Lingenfelter Twin Turbo V-8.

▽   The car is in a league of its own both out and in.

☐   Steve Coffey of Crossville, Tennessee bought this car at the January '07 Barrett-Jackson auction. He purchased it at midnight on Saturday. He has since done some research and found that Lingenfelter built seven wide-body cars.

Kaizen C5

△ **As Tracey's tags suggest, this Corvette is "one to show."**

Corvette enthusiast Tracey Richardson is tall and attractive and in her early 30s. She laughed good naturedly when she said, "Most women strive to get diamonds or gold or jewelry for Valentine's Day, but all I ask for is parts for my Corvette."

Tracey owns a modified '98 coupe. "Sometimes people don't understand my involvement with Toyota, when I have such a love for the Corvettes," Tracey pointed out.

Richardson started working at the Toyota assembly plant in Georgetown, Kentucky, when she was 19. She quit college for the job there. "The guiding principles Toyota manages by are different than what you are used to," Tracey explained. "They talked about the 'problem-conscious mindset' and I had to go to class for four weeks before I was even allowed on the factory floor."

Tracey said she received 360 hours of classroom training — equivalent to masters degree study — to learn Toyota's problem-solving attitude. Ten years later, armed with this knowledge, she started her own consulting firm.

"I do consulting work in the educational and business

communities that teaches quality methods of problem solving and teamwork," she explained.

Tracey put Toyota's continuous-improvement principle — represented by the Japanese word "Kaizen" — to work in the process of modifying her C5 Corvette.

In January 2000, she and her husband Ernie bought this silver '98 Corvette. Their original intention was to have a show car to exhibit in little hometown events. They also expected to enjoy driving the sports car. As they did better and better at winning awards in the little shows, they improved the Corvette more and more.

First, they added chrome wheels and a Corsa Performance Exhaust system to make the coupe stand out from stock vehicles. Soon, Tracey was winning "Best Chevy" awards and then "Best of Show." The *Kaizen* Corvette had begun to emerge.

"Really it just started to *evolve* into a show car," Tracey recalled. "What they call this on CorvetteForum.com is the 'Mod Disease.' And it kind of bit me. When I started showing Corvettes back in the early '90s, it was like I was never going to do anything except win regular awards. At that time, I couldn't afford to do anything to the car. It was enough just to own a 'Vette."

△ **Design Specialties show-styled the 5.7-liter V-8.**

As her financial status improved, Tracey found she had more resources to invest in her show car. The question then was how far she wanted to go with her *Kaizen* Corvette.

"It was the Christmas of 2001 when we decided to put the paint graphics on," Tracey recalled. " We went to Bob Taylor's House of Color in Louisville. He was recommended by several of our friends. Ernie and I had come up with a design. It was a C5 emblem with the flag trailing all the way down from the gills and all the way to the back end of the rear quarter panel."

The next decision made was to stop driving the car and show it indoors. This involved participating in International Show Car Association events.

"The ISCA really looks for certain criteria," Tracey explained. "They are real nit picky. You almost have to have the car to where you can eat off of it. It has to be *that* clean."

Today, Tracey has racked up an enviable record in ISCA Eastern Division Championship shows with her "Corvette Masterpiece." She has been a consistent class winner in the "Conservative Sports" category, which covers 1983 to 2000 two-seat sports cars.

☐ Bob Taylor's body side graphics have a unique racing theme to them.

Cavallo GT
Blends 'Vette Sophistication with Viper Boldness

△ **While most Corvette fans want to vaporize Vipers, the designer of this car set out to Viperize the 'Vette.**

Although unmistakably a Corvette, designer Ken Grant says that the Cavallo GT is "an exercise in restraint because we wanted to take the sophistication of the C5 and bring out the raw, bold proportions of the Viper."

"The C5 design never *grabbed* me when it came out," said Grant. "It was not until we started talking about this project that I saw stuff in the car I really didn't know was there."

"It doesn't scream at you," Grant felt of the C5. "It's very subtle and refined; our idea was to take its design elements and exaggerate them." The designers had to consider the C5's existing lighting and hardware mounting points, however.

Ken Grant came to the Cavallo GT project after 10 years as a Ford designer. His Ford efforts included the 1999 redesign of the Mustang and the 2002 two-seat Thunderbird.

After that, Ken started a company doing cosmetic accessories. He designed the front fascia of a Harley-Davidson package for the Ford F-150 pickup. After he sold that business, he and Paul Burke started Blue Dot Design, of Livonia, Michigan. Paul owned a new C5 and said, "It's the ideal car to re-body. Noth-

△ It's the "Dodge Boys meet the GM Styling Staff" and somehow it all worked out fine.

◁ Burk and Grant stitched up the leather-trimmed interior and hit a home run with a baseball-sized gearshift knob.

◁ The wheels are a full three inches larger than stock to carry the big, fat tires.

ing on the C5 was sonic welded."

Doing the 'Vette on an impulse, Ken and Paul had nobody to please, but themselves, and came up with a clean design. "We wanted to enhance the car, proportionally. With the C5, width and fullness of shape were a little on the thin side. The Cavallo has a little bit more volume. You can see it when they're side by side."

The Cavallo GT is wider than a C5 front and rear. "Take the ZR-1 where it exaggerates C4 proportions," said Ken. "Then, go a little bit further. That was the idea and we did more than

design new quarters and a rear fascia. Look at the side scoop — the 'Vette has one that kind of hints 'I got a little scoop here.' Damn it, if you're going to put a scoop on a car, make it a scoop."

The hood is also more pronounced. The C5 has a traditional GM dual-cowl-induction look. The Cavallo GT's hood is a little higher, a little bigger, a little flatter, a little harder-edged. It has a bit of a more-pronounced shape.

For the pilot car, Paul and Ken wanted a bright color to make a splash in car magazines. They thought yellow was a

hot color, so they started spraying panels to look for just the right shade.

"I thought maybe we would do a metallic," said Ken. "But, it was coming to the 11th hour and I couldn't find just the right shade. We were two days away from paint. I was driving and a yellow Viper went by and I thought it looked re-ally good. If it ain't broke, don't fix it, so we went and bought stock Viper paint."

Blue Dot Design sells Cavallo GT body kits. Performance enhancement of a Corvette is up to the car owner. The three-inch-larger-than-stock wheel wells *can* accommodate some *very* large, performance-enhancing wheels and tires.

Since it was built for show, the Viper Yellow Cavallo GT is hotter than a stock C5 Corvette. The factory LS1 engine has been replaced by a 383-cid "stroker" motor with 500 hp built by GTP Technical Performance in Houston, Texas. The suspension features T1 sway bars and Penske racing shocks. The body sits an inch lower than the stock C5 body. The car has 18 x 10-inch front wheels and 19 x 12-inch rear wheels.

Inside the car, Burke and Grant added a white leather seat insert, a leather-covered steering wheel cover and baseball-style cover for the stock gearshift knob.

The Cavallo GT debuted at SEMA '99. Back then, the company sold it as an unpainted body kit, so you might see various builds at Corvette shows. Blue Dot Design also offered installs by its own professional staff. If you went looking for a used Cavallo GT to buy today and keep as your "Corvette Masterpiece," a Blue Dot installation history might be something worth spending extra for.

1999 Specter Werkes'
Fixed-Roof Corvette Coupe Demonstrator

The C5 Corvette is a car that aftermarket tuners loved to modify. Specter Werkes/Sports, Inc. was a company that produced its own variation of this world-class Corvette.

John Thawley was part owner of Specter Werkes and the full driver of the head-turning '99 Corvette C5 "demonstrator" vehicle seen here. When Thawley drove this Torch Red Fixed-Roof Coupe, it always generated lots of questions from people who saw the car. It was like a car salesman's demonstrator car.

"When I went out at night, I really needed to leave early, just to be nice to people and answer their questions," Thawley said. "Everywhere I went, this C5 drew a big crowd."

The most stunning feature of the tuner demonstrator was a set of unique "projector" headlights. These featured C5-R internals and they were a plug-and-play install. You simply removed the old ones and dropped these in.

Thawley's demonstrator doubled as his part-time personal driver. John revealed that he sometimes put as much as 1,000 miles on the 'Vette in just three months. It did *that* good of

△   **Every car salesman would love a demonstrator like this one.**

△   **Group 5 'Vette logo.**

◁ In keeping with its solid design philosophies, Specter Werkes went back to the drawing board to develop the Group 5 collection.

△ Group 5 has proven to be one of the most popular aftermarket body packages available for the C5.

a job demonstrating Specter Werkes products and services to potential customers.

Though Specter Werkes offered Matrix 1 (top end) and Matrix 2 (stroker) engine packages, Thawley was most concerned with the *looks* of his demonstrator. It had a wild, fiberglass "extractor" hood that pulled hot air out of the engine compartment via a pair of reverse-facing functional scoops that were partially concealed inside the black center stripe.

Ground effects were another big product line at Specter Werkes that this car helped demonstrate. The GE kits gave Group 5 Corvettes a lowered look through the use of side panels, a rear deflector and a lower front chin spoiler. The rear fascia integrated a molded-in spoiler that installed separately.

Specter Werkes contracted Corsa Performance Exhaust to make hot-looking, semi-oval exhaust tips. They were of an exclusive design and could also be used with stock C5 exhausts or a full Specter Werkes' GTR stainless-steel exhaust system. The demonstrator let people see the system up close.

Specter Werkes' most radical Group 5 option may have been the 19-inch front blades and 20-inch rear blades the demonstrator wore. The 3-piece HRE wheels fit the stock wells with no problem and were mounted with 30 series B.F. Goodrich tires. This gave the demonstrator a tire-and-wheel combination that had the same overall diameter as stock ones.

☐ Group 5 components allow C5 owners to capture Specter Werkes GTR's styling queues without the expense or build-out involved in the handcrafted version.

◁ Specter Werkes allows you to give your interior a custom look and feel with this "Touch" package. The system includes recovering your steering wheel, shift knob, emergency brake handle, door pulls and console lid.

▽ Specter Werkes' Euro-Lights system takes its queque from exotic imports. It features quality construction complete with waterproof connectors and a straight forward installation.

△ This is the Group 5 Carbon Fiber C5 Cover Set, Each component is crafted from hi-temp, hand-laid carbon fiber for strength, durability and outstanding fit and finish.

Under the hood, Thawley kept the modifications on his demonstrator very simple with a set of carbon-fiber fuel rail covers, a cold-air box and TPIS headers.

The interior of Thawley's car featured a two-tone steering wheel, red leather trim and leather accents on the door pulls, emergency brake and the console lid. This was called the "Touch Package" and it came in Millennium Yellow, Gray or Oak, as well as in Torch Red.

The titanium gearshift knob and pewter paint on the demonstrator car's console, gauge surround and radio stack were Thawley's personal additions. The pewter accents in the car took considerable work. They required a heavy primer and lots of sanding. John traded bucket seats for stock Corvette sport seats that the factory didn't put in Fixed Roof Coupes in '99.

A set of Euro taillights added a continental touch to Thawley's demonstrator. The Group 5 emblems on the body of this "Corvette Masterpiece" gave the demonstrator a special identity and prompted many questions from curious onlookers.

Wide-Body GT-R:
Another Future Corvette Collectible

Rick Moroso knows a good car when he sees one and he has the ability to drive precisely what he thinks is good. One car Moroso drove with passion was this Specter Werkes Wide-Body GT-R. It is sure to someday become a collectible Corvette.

The GT part of Moroso's car's designation indicated "Gran Tourismo" and hinted at exotic looks and style. The R suffix stood for racing. Was it any coincidence, then, that well-known Corvette race car driver Jeff Nowicki was president of Specter Werkes/Sports, the company that built the car?

Moroso's GT-R was three inches wider than a stock C5 Corvette at the front and six inches wider at the rear. In fact, its dimensions were very similar to those of the C5-R racing car campaigned by Corvette Racing. That's the team behind the first-ever, factory-backed, Corvette competition program. Was there a connection between the GT-R and the C5-R? Of course.

"When we were doing the original clay model of our car, Chevrolet got involved," Jeff Nowicki said. "They basically asked us how wide we were going to make the car. We told

△   The competition-inspired wide-body GTR left C5 owners breathless.

△   Specter Werkes' GTR was first developed in 1998.

▷ Building on the C5's existing good looks, Specter Werkes designers massaged the C5 silhouette into a hefty 77-inch wide car.

▷ By merging race inspired performance and knowledge, Specter Werkes put the C5 on steroids.

them and they said if we would do this and that, they would buy parts from Specter Werkes for their original test car."

While companies like Callaway create body kits that lead to drastic changes in the stock look of a C5 Corvette, Chevrolet wanted the Corvette Racing fleet to retain some brand identity on the racetrack. The Specter Werkes GT-R design, as seen on Moroso's car, has more of a relationship to the assembly line Corvette.

While Specter Werkes built GT-R racing car bodies for the factory team and others, the company also sold tuner versions of the GT-R (plus the much more affordable Group 5 model pictured in the previous chapter) for customers like Rick Moroso. His GT-R represented an exotic tuner and one of relatively few constructed. Specter Werkes built the panels, door skins and

other parts from either fiberglass or carbon fiber, depending on customer needs. In Moroso's case, the end result was a gorgeous GT Corvette with racing-oriented wide-body mods.

The wide-body mods were necessary to accommodate the widest tires ever mounted on a street vehicle. The 19 x 12-inch HRE 57 rear wheels rolled on 345/30 tires. "When you start to grow the body work, proportionally you really need a bigger tire/wheel combo," Nowicki explained. "There was quite a bit of wheel and tire on that car." Moroso's 'Vette also had charcoal body stripes that were color-matched to the HRE wheels.

Specter Werkes modified the car's suspension with Hotch-kiss front and rear anti-roll bars featuring spherical rod ends. Coil-over Bilstein shocks provided racing-type adjustability.

Under the car's hood, the big deal was a Vortec blower with 7 psi boost. Other upgrades included an LS6 intake, ported-and-polished heads with 2.05-inch valves, a GT-R specific cam grind and TPIS ceramic-coated long tube headers. With all this, the supercharged 350-cid V-8 delivered 530 hp to the rear wheels.

In keeping with its road-racing capabilities, the braking system on Moroso's car had Alcon four-piston calipers all the way around with 14-inch rotors.

Moroso opted for a sophistication inside, too. The seats, door panels and steering wheel were re-trimmed in a gray reptile print to contrast with the blue, spiny-back, smooth leather. The whole center console was done in the reptile print. It was quite a feat to get that material to wrap over all the compound surfaces. White-face gauges by RK Sport went with the light interior colors.

Each GT-R carried a unique serial number. Rick Moroso's "Corvette Masterpiece" was numbered 99-004-12. For future collector reference, that breaks down like this: 99 = 1999, 004 = fourth 1999 build and 12 = 12th GT-R built overall.

△ Adding a full six inches to the rear width and three to the front allowed for an aggressive "coke bottle" shape through the middle.

△ All GTRs are painted and trimmed using state-of-the-art finishes and fabrics.

◁ The interior package includes GTR seat embroidery and appointments, as well as a registry dash plaque.

Friyantha Weerasuria's Z07 Corvette

△ **The super-sano black-on-black C5 sports an elevated hood, a lowered body and 18-inch Fiske 5-spoke rims.**

There are tuners and tweakers. Friyantha Weerasuria of Elite Motorsports, in Austin, Texas considers himself a tweaker. His goal was to build the fastest C5 Corvette with a six-speed transmission. "You can make an automatic run faster," Weerasuria reasoned. "A fast six-speed takes more skill."

Weerasuria had MTI, in Houston, Texas, build the motor and modify the drive train on the hardtop you see here. He did the rest.

Take a close look at Weerasuria's black-on-black car. It's a clean-as-a-whistle, GT-type Corvette with an RK Sport elevated hood, a slightly-lowered body and a set of 18-inch Fiske wheels.

Inside, the Corvette has "Wet Oakley" seat covers to keep Weerasuria from sliding on the stock leather. The air blows cold. The car seems ready to drive to the country club.

On the front fender, the car has a set of eye-catching Z07 front fender badges. "Everybody knows what a Z06 is," Weerasuria smiles. "But they can't figure out what a Z07 is."

The '99 C5 was built two years prior to the release of the Z06. And the starting point for MTI's engine build was the stock LS1 motor, which is the shop's specialty. MTI bored and stroked the motor to 422-cid — about 7 liters — and used many Z06 parts on it including an LS6 intake and LS6 cylinder heads. That's why the Z07 fender badges made a lot of sense.

Motorsport Technologies of Houston can convert a 1997–2004 C5 or Z06 Corvette into the supercar of your wildest dreams. With over 100 conversions to date, MTI has the expertise and product combinations to perform this conversion to exceed your expectations.

This build — done two years prior to release of the factory Z06 — started with a '99 C5 'Vette and turned it into a "Z07."

△ **The car looks "street" inside and has no roll cage.**

The modified C5 runs a 9.98-second quarter mile. With its TNT nitrous system engaged, it gets an extra 135 hp shot all the way down the dragstrip. Friyantha can stab the clutch and grab gears with his shortened throw shifter and end up in fourth gear traveling through the traps at a phenomenal 145.2 mph!

The need for speed pushed Weerasuria's "Z07" modifications past boundaries. "Every time we modified something, we created a new problem," he admitted. "We were experimenting a lot."

One example is the solid-roller cam. It has a custom grind that's being kept a secret for now. "With the solid roller, we had problems with the lifters making noise," Weerasuria said. "We'd adjust them, run the car for about an hour and they started backing off. We had to buy the racing setup the C5-R uses. The lifters alone cost $2,000. You adjust them and you are done. They're almost like hydraulics. We've only adjusted them once."

Weerasuria and MTI didn't bolt all the parts together, go to the dragstrip and run a 9.99-second quarter. Making the Z07 perform took a "learning curve." With 620 hp at the flywheel and close to 800 hp with the nitrous shot, a lot of testing was required.

The learning curve continued at the strip. "You've got to be able to launch correctly," noted Weerasuria. "I've broken an inner stub axle. I've broken a clutch and I've twisted the long input shaft from the back of the motor to the transmission."

Weerasuria's first runs at the strip were 10.3, 10.2 and 10.3, at 143-144 mph. "It took me quite a while to get into the high 9s," he admitted. "I went from a 10.2 to a 10.15 and then to a 10.09. The secret is proper launching. When I ran my first ET in the 9s, I had a 1.48-second 60-foot time and that's pretty good with IRS."

The Z07 has no roll cage. Weerasuria's original goal wasn't to build a drag car, so it is a very streetable Corvette. It doesn't overheat and the air blows cold. It can be driven anywhere.

Weerasuria's tweaking continues. The Z07 should get faster. He has decided to install a 6-point roll cage so he can compete in more events. He'll up the nitrous boost to a 200-hp shot, which is going to require a larger fuel system. On the test dyno, the air/fuel ratios already reads on the lean side. "I'm running the same fuel pump and fuel lines rated for the 345 hp LS1," said Weerasuria.

One has to wonder if this "Corvette Masterpiece" is the fastest street C5 around. Weerasuria says, "As far that I know, it is the world's fastest C5 with a six-speed. It's surely the fastest Z07!"

Wheel-to-Wheel Built C5 Tiger Shark Precursor

f you're a "car guy" and own a company that builds prototypes and show cars for auto manufacturers, you're likely to own really special cars. Jeff Bietzel's firm Wheel-to-Wheel makes such cars and he has owned everything from a '23 T-bucket to a tubbed, big-block '70 'Cuda."

GM cars are Jeff's favorites and make up the bulk of his stable. This Millennium Yellow Corvette, that looks very similar to GM's own "Tiger Shark" show car, belongs to Bietzel. "Wheel-to-Wheel makes all those Tiger Shark parts," Jeff said.

Wheel-to-Wheel actually constructed GM's 740-hp "Tiger Shark" show car. Its highly-stylized features were reminiscent of Corvette-based "Shark" show cars of the past. However, the Tiger Shark used a modern Corvette platform and body.

Wheel-to-Wheel has staff engineers and designers, but Bietzel is a driving force when it comes to design concepts. Fortunately, he has long-time connections to the Corvette. Jeff's company built CERV-4, the Chevrolet Engineering Research Vehicle that many enthusiasts feel saved the Corvette in 1993.

△ The build on this Millennium Yellow Corvette gave it looks to rival the "Tiger Shark" show car that took all the resources of GM to create.

△ Not liking the Tiger Shark's squared-off rear-end treatment, Jeff Bietzel took a different design direction with his yellow C5.

△ The yellow car became the "demonstrator" for Wheel-to-Wheel's product offerings.

△ Like most tuner 'Vettes, this one has interior upgrades to personalize it.

△ This 371-cube LS6 got the stroker treatment to boost output to 485 ponies.

The Tiger Shark featured in this chapter of *Corvette Masterpieces* evolved when Wheel-to-Wheel was building the real Tiger Shark. It was actually put together a month before the show car.

"It's kind of like the Tiger Shark, only it is a little different," Jeff revealed. "The Tiger Shark (show car) has a slightly different front and a slightly different rear end. The two are close, but mine isn't exactly the same as the one we made for GM." Jeff admitted his car has some hints of the Ferrari 355.

Bietzel disliked some aspects of the original CERV-4. "I wasn't real happy with the way the front end ended up looking," he admitted. "And I was particularly unhappy with the way the back end came out." Apparently, the squared off back was dictated by wind tunnel testing. Jeff got to dictate the design of his own Tiger Shark-like car.

"First, I fixed the back end, because I never liked where the quarter panel met the rear fascia," he pointed out. "The front end looked too Pontiac-like to me, so I took a stab at changing it." When the body tweaking was done, Jeff's coupe was fitted with a 373-cid "stoker" LS1 engine that rated 485 hp.

Once Jeff's car was finished, Wheel-to-Wheel made the same body parts available to anyone. Kelley Longwish of Wheel-to-Wheel explained, "We made that 'Corvette Masterpiece' a demonstrator to showcase the things we do at Wheel-to-Wheel."

Fastest Street Legal Corvette: Lingenfelter 427 Twin-Turbo

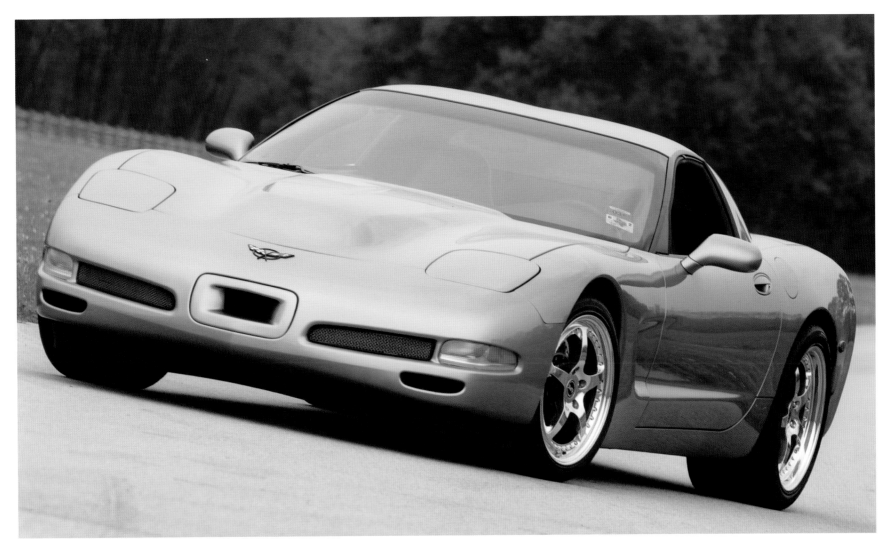

S peed can be measured in a number of ways: top speed, quarter mile speed, 0-60 mph speed. Steve Dumler was not concerned with top speed, only acceleration.

"I've always liked acceleration," Steve mused. "I'm not much into road course racing. I just love the feel of power and acceleration. Ever since I've been a kid, I've always had quick cars and tried to make them work a little bit better than other cars like them."

Dumler got the motivation to the build you see here after reading about two different tuner 'Vettes built by John Lingenfelter in the same magazine article. One car featured a new 427-cid engine. On the very next page, Steve read about Lingenfelter's 550-hp twin-turbo package.

"The thing I liked about the 427 was that its 0-60 speed was awesome, because of the way it put the power down, it would really hook up. And the thing I liked about the twin-turbo was, that once it was rolling, the acceleration was awesome.

△ **This Corvette is fast enough to outrun a jet aircraft — at least for the first 10 seconds or so.**

▷ It looks stock, but isn't.

▽ Twin-Turbo owner Steve Dumler.

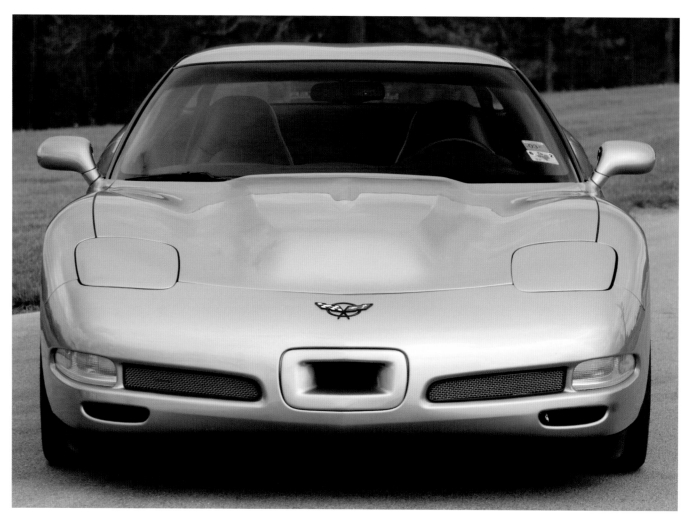

△ Twin Turbo builder, the late John Lingenfelter.

So I thought well is there a way to marry these two together? So that's how I came up with the twin-turbo 427."

Steve wasn't the only one with the idea, but he was one of the first customers to order such an engine. Lingenfelter Performance Engineering (LPE) agreed to do the install in Dumler's Corvette hardtop, which had an automatic transmission. "This was a first," Steve claims. "They took it to the next level."

The surprise when you see and hear the car is how docile the C5 seems at idle and normal speeds around town. Even the catalytic converters are still in place and the engine passes the "sniff test."

"John told me he could make this thing sound however I wanted it to," Steve recalled. "He said he preferred to keep it *stealthy* and I agreed. So, we put on Borla titanium exhausts; they're a little more expensive, but John said they wouldn't hurt the flow and would perform very, very well."

After installation of the twin-turbo 427 and the 4L60 automatic (hardtops came with a six-speed manual transmission), Steve took the car back to LPE a second time to increase the size of the turbos and boost the air flow. This particular twin-turbo package is not the standard one. Steve said it's "all custom."

In the June, 2002 issue of *Motor Trend*, Lingenfelter and Dumler raced an FA-18 Hornet jet, on the ground of course. Dumler's Corvette reached 60 mph in 1.97 seconds. The jet took 3.57 seconds. The Hornet was still far behind at the 100 mph. It took 6.32 seconds to get there, compared to 4.33 seconds for the Lingenfelter Twin-Turbo.

Admittedly, the jet was starting to catch up by the end of the quarter mile, although the car was still ahead. The aircraft registered an ET of 10.45 seconds at 158.14 mph, which was over a second slower than Dumler's Corvette.

Soon thereafter, the jet's 12,000-hp took over, right before the craft became airborne.

Keeping his car street legal was extremely important to Steve Dumler. "That makes it even more of a prize in my mind," he explained. "As long as you can truly drive your car on the street, you're accomplishing something when you go for the 'fastest' title. It's hard to beat the clock and keep it legal." Dumler even cancelled installation of a roll cage. "This car is going to see the drag strip just a little bit," he said. "I don't want to put this in here and leave it like that."

◁ The car has "killer" looks and the legs to go along with them.

◁ You're viewing 427 cubes and 550 ponies.

Dumler uses a 6-point unit with sidebars that move out with the door. "We're not that fast so often," says Steve. "But Texas Motorplex won't let us run if we go under 10 seconds."

Another go-fast consideration is fuel. "When we run a high, high boost, like 19 or higher and we are on the strip, we have to run 118 octane leaded fuel," Dumler explained. On the street, however, he drops down to pump gas and the engine — with a 9.2:1 compression ratio — stays happy."

Dumler also removes the catalytic converters for track runs in his "Corvette Masterpiece." He notes they really have no effect on speed. "I only take them off so I don't restrict the flow at all," says Steve.

△ The roll bar is a necessity in this monster.

◁ Most people are very familiar with this view of the Twin Turbo.

Stage 4 MTI World Challenge For The Street

△ **MTI Racing is a leading automotive shop in the Southeastern U.S. It specializes In GM performance vehicles. No where in the "tuner" market will you find the level of experience, on and off track, that you'll find at MTI Racing.**

Reese Cox's Stage 4 Corvette was all about function. Nothing existed in the car that wasn't there to produce higher lap speeds on a racecourse. Of course, the Stage 4 was a *street* Corvette. Basically, what was being delivered, in Stage 4 terms, was a wide gamut of features developed on the World Challenge racing circuit.

Once in a while, I like to get to *drive* a feature car like the Stage 4. Maybe I don't get to go full tilt, as I'd like to do out on a racecourse, but at least I get to drive it, within the speed limit, on public streets.

Reese Cox, the owner of MTI — a Marietta, Georgia company that builds racing cars — needed a few minutes to get

◁ The steering wheel looks like something out of a Salvatore Dali painting.

△ Inside the car there's a definite competition look.

◁ If you see this sight in front of you, the drafting should be excellent.

△ For the performance-minded customer, MTI Racing offers a full spectrum of products and services from dyno-proven engine packages to track-tested upgrades.

used to the concept of letting me drive the car, but he finally got it. Then, I got my chance behind the wheel.

My first concern was whether Reese's "bad boy" Corvette was going to provide a compliant ride on the street. Or was it going to be a case of the car is King Kong and I'm Faye Raye?

After a dozen or so turns (some gentle, some sharp), plus some liberal doses of throttle on Kentucky back roads, I could honestly say that Reese's machine was amazingly graceful. It was truly easy to drive. The suspension was firm, yet smooth; it was no King Kong . . . no Faye Raye beat-you-up car.

The first challenge with the Stage 4 was getting over and down into the high-bolstered, body-gripping bucket seat. Anybody with a wide girth would need the optional wider seat. Being 6-foot 3-inches tall, I particularly liked the flattened bottom of the steering wheel and knew at once its purpose. It gave my

▷ **Sounding like something from the mid-'60s, the new 427 is a high-tech underhood masterpiece.**

△ **The car is essentially a racer made for the road.**

legs room to do what they're supposed to do . . . heel-and-toe the clutch and throttle pedals.

Cox looked young enough to get carded at a nightclub. He seemed way too young to know so much or to have accomplished all he has. "We worked with GM on development of the Z06," Reese told me. "Then, we worked with GM on development of the C5-R kit car for professional racing." (The kit car was not done for the factory, but for the privateer racing teams).

"A lot of the development we did with GM in 1999-2000 led to parts that went on the Z06," Reese explained. He then ran down some of the parts: steering rack, wheel bearings, transmission, heavy-duty differential, camshafts, cylinder heads.

Reese told me he had built his own Corvette racing cars and competed with privateers in the Motorola Cup, Grand Am Cup and World Challenge Series. He explained that parts developed on the racetracks made their way into the Stage 4.

As I drove on, I was intrigued that my Stage 4 driving experience was similar to racing a World Challenge Corvette. In reality, the street car is not bound by the same rulebook and limited to maximum cubic inches, so I was controlling more power with my foot than the racing car had.

Reese Cox definitely talks in "engineerspeak." Most people don't use the term "i.e." in everyday conversation. Most of us don't build racing cars, either.

"We can actually run larger cubic inches, i.e. the 427, and we can actually make more power in our street car than we did in World Challenge," Reese said, confirming my earlier thinking. He pointed out that the racing displacement limit was 346 cubic inches.

As the Stage 4 wound around the Shania Twain-style country curves north of Nashville, I could feel the acceleration in the seat of my pants. The MTI street racer ran through the bends like a big slot car. It was tempting to push it, but I do not promote breaking speed limits. So, I stayed the course, save for some high G -blips powering out of corners. We were satisfied this car qualified as "streetable."

What was this car? Who would want it? I guessed that the top speed had to be supersonic. Reese gave us the profile of his target customer: "A guy who's contemplating buying a Ferrari 360 Modena or a Porsche 911 turbo and wants to purchase something faster, for less money. It's our attempt at building a budget supercar."

The Stage 4 definitely had a supercar feel. Reese said it sold for about $90,000. I thought, "Now, there's maximum bang for your supercar buck!"

Reese rattled off the quarter-mile numbers: 10.90 seconds at 130 mph with drag-type radial tires. 11.4 seconds at 128 mph with Michelin Pilot Sport 2 "street" tires. The 0-60-mph times

△ **Reese Cox behind the wheel of his "bad boy" 'Vette.**

◁ **The car serves as a development vehicle for MTI's "tuner" aspirations.**

△ **Visit mtiracing@yahoo.com.**

were 3.9 seconds with "sticky drag radial DOT tires" and 4.2 seconds with the Michelins.

"At Road Atlanta, where we do a lot of testing, there's a little kink in the back straightaway called turn 9," Reese related. "At 150 mph you could barely go full throttle through that kink. After we put an aero package on the car, you could drive through turn 9 with one hand on the steering wheel. It held that much."

Reese had another story about an elevated, carbon fiber, air-extractor hood he had engineered. "GM did validation testing on that hood at a drag strip," he said. "They found they picked up two miles per hour." According to Reese, the reason behind this was related to the evacuation of high-pressure air trapped in the engine compartment, plus the creation of more down force with no drag penalty.

MTI's Stage 4 super car may have been the highest-performance, series-produced Corvette ever made out there. To date, 10 have been built. This model remains a bit obscure though, since it originates from a shop that exists mainly for the purpose of winning races. A side benefit for Corvette fans was the street version of the racing car that I drove. I would describe this "Corvette Masterpiece" as a competition-prepped 'Vette that is street legal.

A Tuner's Rendition Of A C5-R
For The Street

△ "Oh, you handsome devil . . ."

Rarity, high performance and great looks build a strong case for collecting cars like this "tuner" Corvette. It is John Caravaggio's 2001 LM — a car that's sure to be highly sought after in the years ahead.

If you look at what's happened with the Corvettes built by early tuners like Motion Performance, Carroll Shelby, Don Yenko, Dickie Harrell and Nickey Chevrolet you will see a trend. Prices on these cars have entered the stratosphere. I believe the same will happen with Caravaggio Corvettes, which are works of art.

Caravaggio, located in Woodbridge, Ontario, Canada, has been in business for more than 20 years. He operates one of the premier shops in the world that turns out series-produced, custom Corvettes.

This yellow LM, which is short for "Le Mans," is a hotter-than-stock 2001 Corvette Z06 with a host of unique features intended to thrill the enthusiast.

Though far from a racing car, the Caravaggio LM plays up many racing queues from its blacked-out taillight panel to its pumped-up LS6 V-8. It has upgraded seats, powder-coated

△ **The interior is even more radical than the outside.**

◁ **The wheels carry forth the car's functional beauty.**

◁ **Power is boosted eleven percent from stock level up to 420 hp.**

black wheels and "side splitter" rocker panels. The LM is lowered to boot and features a lift-off targa roof of Caravaggio's own manufacture.

A Ferrari influence is definitely present in this car. In profile, with the targa roof panel lifted off and out of the way, the LM looks decidedly exotic. In fact, Caravaggio feels that the stock Z06 should look like this.

"A lot of people want a Z06," Caravaggio said. "But they all complain about the same thing . . . that you can't take the roof off the car. So, what we did is give them that option."

Caravaggio's reference was to the fact that factory-made Z06 Corvettes were based on the Fixed Roof Coupe body style, which didn't offer roof options. Caravaggio Corvettes figured out how to convert any Fixed Roof Coupe to a targa body style. The company used the factory rear backlight and manufactured the exterior fiberglass rear section and one interior trim piece to make it all work.

The LM model was based on the Z06 Fixed Roof Coupe,

but John Caravaggio said his inspiration was really the C5-R Corvette racing car. "If Chevrolet was to bring out a special model styled after the C5-R, this would be it," he insisted.

Although every Z06 offers high performance, Caravaggio figured that a car visualized as a street version of the C5-R needs even more oomph. That's why he tuned the stock LS6 to make it race-worthy. The modifications include ported-and-polished cylinder heads, bigger valves and a larger cam. They boosted power from the stock 385 hp to 420. That's 15 more ponies than a Z06.

By merely adjusting spring bolts, Caravaggio was able to lower the body an inch and a half. "Aesthetically, the lower car looks a lot better," John said. Side splitters multiply this lowered effect for an even hotter appearance. "We call it a side splitter, but it is actually a rocker panel that we added to the bottom," Caravaggio stressed. "The top surface of the rocker or splitter is painted the same color as the car. The edge of it going underneath is black and gives a racing car appearance."

As racy as the LM's exterior is, the interior is even more radical. The big change inside the car is new seats with two holes in the top and one opening in the bottom to fit racing belts. The second big change is a roll bar, which is of Caravaggio's own manufacture and wrapped in leather. Caravaggio copied Ferrari by stitching the seats in yellow.

A leather-wrapped console and steering wheel are featured. "What we do is take the existing Corvette steering wheel, strip the leather and re-cast it so it's got a different shape," said Caravaggio. "It's still round, but with thumb grips like a Momo wheel. Then, we re-wrap it in leather or suede and stitch it to match the seats."

Just the targa roof on the Fixed Roof Coupe makes for an exotic appearance. Caravaggio set out to take the Z06 and tune it for special looks and performance. What he wound up with is a "Corvette Masterpiece" that reminds you of a C5-R for the street.

△ The tuner's telltale tag.

☐ Like the famed Italian painter of the same name, Caravaggio is a creator of masterpieces and this car is one.

Hennessey Z500:
Vetter's Venomous 'Vette

▷ The cabin contains copious custom conveniences.

▽ Why couldn't the tuner famous for his venomous Vipers do a Corvette with a poisonous bite?

▷ The basis for this super Hennessey Corvette is the Z06.

As we all know, "dog bites man" isn't new, but "man bites dog" will make big headlines. The same reverse dynamics came into play when a Texas shop famous for turning Dodge Vipers into venomous snakes decided to give a Z06 Corvette bigger fangs.

Jon Paul Vetter, owner of this "'Vette with a bigger bite," just happened to be in the right place, at the right time, to make tuner-car history. As far as timing, he had just bought a 2001 Corvette Z06. As far as place, he lived five minutes from Hennessey Performance Engineering, the Houston, Texas tuner shop famous for its Viper Venom package.

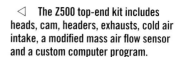

▽ The wheels have a high-tech, functional look.

△ With slicks and skinnies the car's best time was 11.59/123.76 mph.

◁ This car was the prototype for the Z500 line.

"Lingenfelter did a Viper," Jon Paul pointed up, attempting to show that there was kind of a "mirror-image" precedent to the Hennessey Z06 Corvette project that he got involved in. Corvette tuner John Lingenfelter's dalliance with a Dodge had already been widely reported. Vetter's view was that if Lingenfelter was going to do Vipers, why couldn't his friend Hennessey hop-up a 'Vette for him?

A "Better 'Vette for Vetter" so to speak (Yes, that is Jon's real last name). "All's fair in love and super car wars," Vetter re-emphasized, as he explained that he and Hennessey had been friends for years. So, why couldn't Hennessey, the tuner famous for his poisonous Vipers, make Vetter a 'Vette with an even more poisonous bite?

Jon Paul met Hennessey way back in 1994. "When he opened his shop, I just stopped in and met him and I've known him ever since," he said. "Years later, we were shooting the breeze one day and John (Hennessey) mentioned his plan to offer tuner Corvettes."

Vetter says he had actually been considering the purchase of a Viper. When Chevrolet brought out the high-performance Z06 Corvette, he changed his mind quickly. "With my last name, it was a natural," Vetter noted.

Hennessey told Vetter he was going to offer two different Corvette tuner packages, both of which were in prototype stage at the time. Vetter's Vette became the first of the Z500 models. This was denoted as "No. 001" right on the car's valve cover.

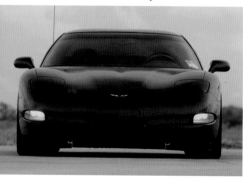

△ **For now, you are seeing the very first car, identified by the Hennessey signature and No. 001 on the top of the fuel rail. This valve cover was also signed by Will Corskey, the manager of the Corvette factory.**

△ **With computer re-programming. Owner Jon Paul Vetter feels he'll be able to dip into the 11.20s in the quarter mile.**

The Z500 content added to Vetter's Z06 consisted of a heads-and-cam package. The second offering was the Z600, a "stroker" motor in a Stage 2 configuration.

In both cases, the "Z" part of the model designation indicated that the package was for the Z06 Corvette. The 500 part of the 500 designation related to the dyno readings the car registered. Tests showed that Vetter's high-tuned Z06 was generating 520 hp at the flywheel.

Even in bone-stock condition, Vetter found his Z06 capable of running the quarter mile in 12.42 seconds at 114.24 mph. This was comparable to a Viper. He was told that the Z500 package would put the Z06 ahead of the V-10-powered Viper Venom 500. Now, Jon Paul feels he's in the same league as Hennessey's even more powerful Venom 550 and Venom 600 Viper models.

The Z500 top-end kit included cylinder heads, a hotter cam, headers, a performance exhaust system, a cold-air intake, a modified mass-airflow sensor and customized computer pro-

gramming. The head work featured larger valves and extensive high-flow port work. Vetter said Hennessey modified the heads to flow what he called "serious air" (318 cfm). A ceramic-coated Belanger exhaust system with 1-3/4-inch primaries emptying into B & B PRTs was installed on the car.

Vetter's car was considered to be a "test mule" with a prototype buildup. "There's more work to be done," Jon Paul told us when our photos were taken. "We're going to have the computer redone to make some final fuel and spark curve changes and we should get another 10 to 15 horsepower."

Vetter's prototype did not have Hennessey badges at first, because the car was the first Z500 and the badges (along with some Z600 badges) were still being made up.

"The car is a monster now," Vetter said of his "Corvette Masterpiece." With slicks and skinnies, he registered a best time of 11.59 seconds at 123.76 mph with stock computer programming. In the end, he expected to be running 11.20s and to have a car capable of winning any 'Vette/Viper Shootout event.

Z06 and a Half:
How Do You Describe An LS6 With Twin Turbos?

What happens when Lingenfelter Performance Engineering bolts a couple of their high-tech ball bearing turbos onto an LS6? The answer is that all hell breaks loose.

Graham Behan, a Brit who is project engineer at Lingenfelter and former developmental engineer on the LT5, likes to compare the kick of the company's twin-turbo Z06 to that of a normally-aspirated, big-cubic-inch V-8. "You don't feel some huge delay then a big kick when the turbos come in," he said. "There is virtually no turbo lag; it just feels like you're driving a big block."

This is precisely what LPE worked towards with their new twin-turbo Z06, a car we discovered in the pits at Beech Bend drag strip during a classic C5 Bash hosted by the National Corvette Museum. A white-haired man in a black shirt with an LPE monogram was leaning on top of the roof and writing notes on his time slip. The man was John Lingenfelter, fresh from a 10.84-second 134-mph pass.

Our feature car was the very first twin-turbo Z06 that Lingenfelter built. The decals on the sides of the car read "550 hp." Inside, the badge on the center console read "500 hp." Behan, who was helping Lingenfelter prepare and race the car,

△ **This car was the result of upgrading an LS6 Corvette engine with a pair of turbochargers to produce 500 hp.**

▷ The builder put his name on the valve covers during the Millennium year of 2000.

▽ A much-missed smile.

△ A masterpiece is never done.

explained the variation. "The horsepower is 550, but we don't have a 550 center decal yet," he said

Originally, the owner of this car — New Yorker Greg Kordix — was going to pick up his new twin-turbo LS6-powered 'Vette at the National Corvette Museum in Bowling Green, Kentucky. When Kordix wasn't able to make the trip, Lingenfelter showed up. Then, he raced the 'Vette at Beech Bend.

In his stiff British manner, Behan, who oversees this project, gave us technical details. "We do quite a bit more to the engine than people actually realize," he said. "We take the LS6 (engine) out of the car, lower the compression ratio slightly and modify the oil pan to receive the return feed from the scavenge pump. We do a little bit of intake work . . . just a little porting around the valve-seat areas to reduce compression ratio. We change the camshaft to the turbo cam. We have our own cam design that we put in there. Basically, it's pretty similar to a stock cam, with slightly less overlap. With the pressure charging, it doesn't like overlap. We fit heavyweight valve springs to cover the fact the valves receive boost on the back of them. We port match the intake."

The modifications were done to accommodate the twin turbos, which were very special. Graham stressed how much turbo technology had improved.

◁ **The car was built with all of the goodies and they sure looked good.**

◁ **Wheel designs varied front and rear on this car.**

▽ **The car could be driven around town with no muss or fuss.**

"Buick Grand National," Behan laughed. "That technology is over 20 years old. With the advent of ceramic ball-bearing turbos, the new designs are significantly better. Technology has increased so much, with the right turbo match you don't see big problems with lag and taking a long time to spool."

Behan said LPE had the match "pretty close" with a hybrid Garrett T27/T30 turbo. This is a Garrett T27 exhaust stage with a Garrett GT30 compressor stage and boost is set at 5.5 psi, which is actually quite moderate.

"There are many naturally-aspirated engines with higher specific output," Behan told us. " We started with 5.7 liters and we didn't really need to hit it that hard to make 550 hp. We were not even making 100 hp per liter, so the stress on components was not that great."

With the stress factor low, Lingenfelter could supply a two-year/24,000-mile warranty with cars like this one. "The beauty of the package is that it drives like a stock Corvette, until you put your foot to the floor," Behan explained. "You're not paying for performance with a noisy, rough-idling, difficult-to-drive-about-town car. It's none of that."

With 550 hp and 500 pounds-feet of torque, the twin-turbo Z06 Corvette's 350-cid engine makes this "Corvette Masterpiece" a Z06 and a half.

Killer Z06 Corvette
Doug Rippie Motorsports

▷ Final tuning of the signaturized engine revealed 406 hp at the rear wheels, which equates to about 477 hp on a dyno.

▽ DRM graphics decorate doors.

△ The car sits low to the ground.

Minnesotan Ron Marks said, "These Z06s are amazing cars. In bone-stock configuration, they are damn near racing cars." Marks has great respect for the latest-generation Corvette. Still, like the rest of us, Ron appreciates a car that's even a wee bit hotter than a stock C5 Z06.

When tuner Doug Rippie offered to build our feature car for Marks, he was all ears. That was back in 2001. "I had my car three days and Rippie called asking if my Corvette could be the prototype test mule for their head-and-cam package," Marks remembered. "They told me to drop the car off in the fall. They would play with it all winter and have it ready in the spring. Here in Minnesota, my car sits all winter anyway, so it worked out fine."

Ron's very early Z06 was built the third day of production. It was the first Z06 sold in Minnesota, the home state of Doug Rippie Motorsports. Ron already had plans for his 'Vette. Note the "Corvette Racing" name on the rear pillar.

Marks and his wife are both Corvette enthusiasts. "Susan and I both autocross quite a bit and do high-speed road racing," Ron said. "Not wheel to wheel (racing), but timed stuff." However, their Z06 was not strictly a racing car.

Mark and Susan drive their car all over. It traveled over 20,000 miles. At Route 66 Raceway, in Joliet, Illinois, Ron clicked off the best time of 50 'Vettes running on street tires. Both he and Susan had wins in class 3H. They racked up even more impressive results in the high-speed events, where a Doug Rippie head-and-cam package really helps.

☐ Ron appreciated the chance for his car to be Doug Rippie's Z06 test mule and has the DRM name on the side.

Rippie didn't want to change the valves in the car, partly out of cost consideration, but he wanted to port the heads and change cams and do little tuner tricks with the computer to see if he could get rear wheel horsepower over 400.

The final tuning showed 406 rear wheel horsepower on Rippie's dyno, right where he wanted to be. That's about 477 horsepower at the crank. A stock '01 Z06 delivered 385 crank horsepower and about 330 hp at the rear wheels.

Ron doesn't feel he's a skilled drag racer and 12.8 seconds at 121 mph with street tires was the best he did at a drag strip. Ron's forte is autocrossing. He says it "lasts longer." Using the Z06 for high-speed autocrossing necessitated adding a roll bar and harnesses to the car.

Brainerd is a three-mile, 10-turn course about an hour and a half northwest of Minneapolis and one of the fastest road courses in the whole country. Ron said he hit 165 mph on the straightaway there running on street tires.

Ron tapped his brakes to drop the speed down to the "mid-130s" for the "sweeper," a banked turn. "I kept them on until I reached the apex of the corner," he said. "Then I came back on full gas to exit the corner under full power. I probably came out of that sweeper at about 145 mph." After that, there was another short straightaway. "I got back to 150 mph again," said Ron. "Then, there's a second sweeper, not banked, but long and flat, where you drop to the 120s again."

With this kind of track performance, Ron Marks' comments about his Doug Rippie-built "Corvette Masterpiece" being close to a racing car are understandable.

△ Interior styling reflects a competition image.

"After Hours" Effort Created "Skunk Werkes" Z06 Convertible

 If someone had to go build a Z06 ragtop, why not the Skunk Werkes?

Chevrolet did not build a "factory" Z06 convertible, so the unofficial team known as "Skunk Werkes" did.

"Skunk Werkes" is a term that appears throughout Corvette history. It refers to engineers and designers who work together on special Corvettes on an "after hours" basis in their spare time. The classic racing Sting Ray was Bill Mitchell's "Skunk Werkes" project. The original Grand Sport was also done "skunked out" by Zora Arkus-Duntov.

A similar "Skunk Werkes" project was the Mako Shark, a Corvette concept car that "jarred" automotive designer John Cafaro in the '60s, when he was in grade school.

Cafaro and a man named Henry Iovino ultimately became GM employees. Both were key members of the team that designed the C5 Corvette. Both are still very much "'Vette guys" at heart. They continue to work on the car they love in their spare time after work and on weekends.

The current Skunk Werkes that Cafaro and Iovino belong to is a little different than such groups in the past, because it offers the public a chance to own a distinctive "tuner" type Corvette. This Skunk Werkes operates in a small shop in the basement of Iovino's house.

◁   John Caravaggio (see page 294) also got involved in the creation of this drop-top masterpiece.

◁   The awesome interior includes carbon-fibre door panels.

"We consider ourselves a tuner, but on a very small scale," said Cafaro. "Luckily we don't depend on Skunk Werkes to feed ourselves."

Cafaro explained that "Skunk Werkes" was a term that evolved out of aircraft maker Lockheed, but it became a real part of Corvette history. In a Skunk Werkes you shut the doors, go underground, do things that nobody would even attempt to try at "work" and kind of go against the grain a little bit. "The whole operation can be cloaked in secrecy," Cafaro added.

Since there was a certain mystique involved in initially combining the hot Z06 performance Corvette with an open body, the Z06 convertible seen here was the perfect Skunk Werkes project.

This black-on-black Skunk Werkes Z06 convertible was the first one built. With help from Cafaro, Iovino at Skunk Werkes and the well-known tuner Caravaggio, this car came together just the way the factory would have done the job.

After this car was finished, Caravaggio assembled three or four more of these "Corvette Masterpieces" and offered to build more of them to fill customer orders. The Skunk Werkes Z06 convertible filled a hole in the Corvette by giving high-performance seekers the chance to get the hottest 'Vette in "topless" format.

▽ Skunk Werkes' Z06 ragtop.

Skunk Werkes' Z06 Convertible Content

Skunk Werkes Body Kit

Rear Spoiler

Rockers

Body Side Strakes

Canards

Red-and-Black Suede Skunk Werkes Interior

Steering Wheel

Seats

Shifter Boot

Parking Brake

Door Pulls

Red Leather Wrapped Cosmetic Bars

Red Door Sill Trim

Billet Shifter Knob

Billet Inside Rearview Mirror

Brushed Metalized Interior Trim

Carbon Fiber Door Panels

Simpson race belts

Performance Upgrades

High-rise Hood

Donaldson Airbox

100-hp Engine Upgrade

Exhaust Headers

Corsa/Skunk Werkes Titanium Exhaust

Short-throw Shifter

Enhanced Baer Brake Rotors

Lowered Suspension

Chrome Wheels

△ The stock Corvette mill gains 100 ponies.

△ High-rise hood hints at muscle below it.

◁ Corsa/Sknunk Werkes titanium exhaust system exits near center of rear.

A Red Z06 Convertible From The Skunk Werkes

Chuck Conkle, a Pontiac dealer in Kokomo, Indiana, custom ordered this red Z06 convertible, one of the early cars built by the Skunk Werkes operation of GM designer John Cafaro and Henry Iovino.

"We take an AMG approach," said Iovino, referring to the famous Mercedes-Benz tuning house AMG in Stuttgart, Germany. "We use more high-tech, exotic materials than found in a regular production car. That's why we use metalized trim and carbon fiber and re-style our seats."

One of Skunk Werkes' goals was to move cars like this red Corvette ragtop upscale into the same niche as a high-end Mercedes, Porsche or Ferrari.

Cafaro agreed. "We're trying to interject premium materials into the Corvette," he said. "We're trying to move the Corvette up to the next level."

Iovino described the task at hand as the refinement of an already superior design. "We were very proud of the C5," he said. "But, we also realized that GM was not able to do certain things with it as a production car." One of Skunk Werkes' goals was to do the things GM couldn't.

△ **Pontiac dealer Chuck Conkle's red ragtop was one of Skunk Werke's early efforts.**

▽ This C5 ragtop has a very special character.

Skunk Werkes' Z06 Convertible Content

Skunk Werkes Body Kit

Rear Spoiler

Rockers

Body Side Strakes

Canards

Red/Black Suede Skunk Werkes Interior

Steering Wheel

Seats

Shifter Boot

Park Brake

Door Pulls

Red Leather Wrapped Cosmetic Bars

Red Door Sill Trim

Billet Shifter Knob

Billet Inside Rear View Mirror

Brushed Metalized Interior Trim

Carbon Fiber Door Panels

Simpson race belts

Performance Upgrades

High-rise Hood

100-hp Engine Upgrade

Corsa/Skunk Werkes Titanium Exhaust

Exhaust Headers

Short-throw Shifter

Donaldson Airbox

Enhanced Baer Brake Rotors

Lowered Suspension

Chrome Wheels

As you can see, the end result of the Skunk Werkes effort was a C5 with a very special character. The vehicles they did — like this red ragtop — were definitely "tuner" cars, but they had a factory-type edge to their modifications. Buyers like Chuck Conkle loved the finished product.

"Henry Iovino is a stickler for quality and the way the car came out, I just can't be happier with it," Conkle said about his "Corvette Masterpiece." The car was not supposed to be a daily driver. "Now, I like it so much I drive it to work every day," Conkle admitted.

△ Black and red suede interior "werkes" for the car's owners.

△ A lowered suspension helps the car hug the earth better.

Tuner-Modified C5 Corvette Z06 Grand Sport Convertible

W ell-known tuner John Caravaggio's wife loved the '96 Grand Sport Corvette. "She kept bugging me to buy one," he said. "To this day she wants one."

What Caravaggio decided to do, instead of buying an "old" Grand Sport, was to take a 2001 Corvette Z06 and turn it into a Grand Sport. "The Z06 already had the red accents on the motor," Caravaggio noted.

John — the owner of Caravaggio Corvettes of Woodbridge, Ontario, Canada — had been modifying Corvettes for close to

20 years. Before the 1986 Corvette convertible came out, he was custom building drop-top Corvettes.

Caravaggio also works with John Cafaro, the chief Corvette designer, on various *aftermarket* Corvette projects. Cafaro liked the idea of a custom-made C5 Grand Sport. Their original plan was to build a custom C5 Grand Sport from a Z06 Fixed Roof Coupe. The project went as far as making drawings what such a car would look like.

Then, Caravaggio came up with an even better idea: cut

△ **It seemed like a good idea to craft a ragtop, so…**

▷ The front end treatment is wider than what the factory did.

△ Adding 35 ponies made good sense.

▷ Black powder-coated Z06 wheels turn the car — and turn heads.

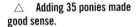

the roof off. "Why don't we do a convertible Grand Sport?" Caravaggio asked Cafaro. "They didn't make many of those." According to Caravaggio, that's basically how this feature car came about."

Cafaro wanted to get much wilder than the stock Grand Sport theme by adding spoilers and front canards. "We were going to do all that and I decided not to," Caravaggio explained. "I wanted to build, as John would say, a *boring* car."

The project included Admiral Blue paint and a white center stripe. "The red hash marks on the left fender are the original hash marks they used on the '96 car," Caravaggio explained. "We basically ordered everything from a '96 Grand Sport — the fender emblems, the hash marks, the stripes, the decals up top for the stripes. All of it is original Grand Sport material."

They used Z06 wheels, which Cafaro powder coated in black, in the style of the '96 Grand Sport. He left the brake calipers Z06 red. They stand out nicely against the Admiral Blue paint and match the hash mark on the driver's side front fender.

The Grand Sport heritage is racing and goes back to the original Duntov creations of 1963. In '96, the LS4 Grand Sport carried a V-8 rated at 330 hp or 30 more than the base LT1 V-8. Caravaggio, likewise, tuned the stock Z06 engine to produce an additional 35 hp. "We kept everything stock, but we ported the heads and put in a different cam. The cam was not too outrageous. It was mild. But, at the same time, we went from 385 to 420 hp."

Cosmetically, the Z06 engine was also a perfect Grand Sport choice. The Grand Sport engine had a red intake and the

☐ **Custom-made suede trim pieces enhance the factory interior.**

Z06 engine has red valve covers. "You could almost cross the two," said Caravaggio. "If the factory were going to do something, that's pretty much the way they would have done it."

Inside, every '96 Grand Sport had either black or black-and-red trim. Caravaggio upgraded the Z06's stock black interior using his own custom-made suede covers for the steering wheel, console, shifter knob, boot, brake handle and seats, but he stitched them with red piping. Individual custom roll bar hoops, chrome-finished, added to the racy appearance and function of the restyled interior.

The build is so close to the look of the original 1996 Grand Sport it could fool some onlookers into believing this car is a C4. Just 190 of the 1,000 Grand Sports built in 1996 were convertibles and the ragtops are very rare and collectable today.

This 2001 Grand Sport convertible was a one-off prototype in a C5 wrapper. Maybe this is why Caravaggio insisted on keeping this "Corvette Masterpiece" very close to what GM designers would have created if they had actually done a C5/Z06 Grand Sport convertible.

△ **Light, pipes and stripes add to the racy image.**

Andy Pilgrim Special Edition C5

△ **This special 'Vette is a racer's dream machine.**

▷ **Special badging tells the horsepower story.**

An Andy Pilgrim Corvette? What's that and who's Andy Pilgrim?

Pilgrim is one of the original Corvette Racing C5-R drivers. The Andy Pilgrim Special Edition C5 is the racing driver's interpretation of what a high-performance street Corvette should be. His business is racing, so he should know and this car proves he does.

Although he did not have a shop to build tuner 'Vettes, Pilgrim did have a connection with Grabiak Chevrolet, a large dealer in New Alexandria, Pennsylvania. Joe Policastro owns Grabiak Chevrolet. He is Andy's friend, in addition to the fact that he raced with him in the American Le Mans series.

◁ **The stylish looking V-8 develops 440 hp.**

◁ **Fixed racing-style headlights hint at the frog-eye look.**

Andy Pilgrim was born in Nottingham, England, but is a U.S. citizen. "I'm from Del Rey Beach, Florida," he said. "Ron Fellows and I have been on the C5-R race team since the beginning." Andy first raced Corvettes in 1985 when, "Somebody let me use a Corvette in a club race. This guy said come and drive my car. You can do it. So I did and that was my first experience in a Corvette and it was great." Andy needed points for a national championship and got hooked on the 'Vette.

Andy says Policastro came up with the idea for the Andy Pilgrim Special Edition C5. "I'll be honest with you, I had not really thought about it; I like production cars," Andy said. "The Z06, for instance, I had a 2001 and a 2002. During 2002,

Joe Policastro called me up and said he wanted to build Andy Pilgrim Special Edition cars."

Policastro thought he could sell such cars. "After I picked myself up off the floor, I told him he was out of his mind," said Pilgrim. "I told him nobody would want to buy an Andy Pilgrim car and he was crazy."

Later, Andy agreed to think about what an Andy Pilgrim Special Edition C5 should be. He really got into the job of coming up with a workable concept. Eventually he was calling Joe Policastro in the middle of the night with ideas. "We're just working on another brake package," Andy would say. "We're changing the calipers."

△ **Race driver Pilgrim is a 'Vette fan.**

▷ **Three-piece racing wheels are chromed up and have a black annodized finish.**

▷ **Pilgrim's Special Edition Z06 is a low-build item.**

Brakes were actually a big deal in the building of the car. People who race are usually quite fond of *stopping* in a timely manner on a consistent basis. Yet, Pilgrim was defensive when we asked if his special edition 'Vette was built mainly for handling. Apparently, to earn your status in the tuner field, additional horsepower is a must.

"We've done an 11.9-second quarter mile at 121 mph," said Andy. "It's quick. It's very quick. It's quicker than a standard Z06 by quite a bit. It's got a lot more mid-grunt and top end grunt. It's got more torque and horsepower."

Actually, the horsepower figures are built right into the name. Officially, the badges read, "Andy Pilgrim Special Edition 440 HP."

Road racers were impressed by the opportunity to buy a tuner car set up by a C5-R racing car driver. Essentially, what Andy Pilgrim wanted to end up with was a "track day" car. Of course, such a 'Vette had to also be totally street legal and suitable for daily driving.

"I'm lucky enough to have a Corvette that I drive it everyday, in all weather conditions," said Andy. "When I called Joe back, I told him that if we did this deal, I wanted a car that handled and could be an everyday driver, because (I knew that) the Z06 was already a great car." He also told Policastro, "I don't like cars that are lowered for the street, because they crash into everything."

Policastro, the entrepreneur, was ready to rock and roll. The project got off the ground and the first car debuted in February of 2002.

The goal of the build wasn't all out horsepower; this "Corvette Masterpiece" was a total performance package refined in all aspects of the car.

"ANDY PILGRIM" SPECIAL EDITION Z06 CONTENT

Andy Pilgrim Design Long-tube Headers

Enhanced Rear Spoiler

Increased Air Flow with Advanced Andy Pilgrim Power Duct

3-Piece Racing Front Wheels, 17x9.5, Chrome, Black Annodized

Enhanced Titanium C5 Exhaust System

3-Piece Racing Rear Wheels, 18x10.5, Chrome, Black Annodized

Andy Pilgrim enhanced heat resistant front rotors

Andy Pilgrim enhanced Front Sway Bar

Front HP Plus Performance Brake Pads

Andy Pilgrim Enhanced Rear Sway Bar

Rear HP Plus Performance Brake Pads

Interior Enhancements

Stainless Steel Braided Hoses with Zinc-plated Fitting Brake Line

"Special Edition" Graphics

Reinforced Front Spoiler

"Andy Pilgrim Special Edition" Serial Number Plaque

Fixed Race Style Headlights

Autographed Certificate from Andy Pilgrim

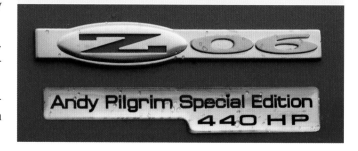

FA-427 Predator: World's Ultimate, Street-Legal, Naturally-Aspirated 427

P eer under the hood of Gary Greenwood's 2002 Corvette Z06 and you'll find a far more potent engine than it left the factory with. The car's original LS6 V-8 has been replaced by a 427-cid V-8 based on the illustrious 7.0-liter, C5-R racing block.

Painted Electron Blue with the Mod Red interior, Gary's Z06 looks pretty much stock from a distance. If you got up close, you might notice the Kinesis three-piece wheels, the Wilwood race brakes and, finally, the massive P345-30-19 rear tires that give away the secret that the back end of the car is *tubbed*.

"I grew up in the era of the late 1960s muscle cars," Greenwood explained. "My dad was a GM dealer. I grew up around 454 Corvettes, SS 396 Chevelles, SS Camaros and all those old muscle cars. I guess that's really what I ended up making this car."

Greenwood works in the chemical business from 8 to 5. He lets his passion for hot Corvettes run wild in his spare time. He bought a new Z06 Corvette in 2002.

"I had trouble finding this color combination at the time," he said. "It seemed like the dealers were scared of Electron Blue with the Mod Red interior." Gary had to go to Florida

△ **The Electron Blue Predator looks absolutely "nasty" from this angle.**

▷ The front looks like a piece of sculpture.

▽ Big wheels front and rear.

△ Racing engine develops 545 hp at the rear wheels.

▷ Like the front, the rear end has been lowered.

to find one like that. He trailered it home and had his dream Corvette. Even in stock tune, the Z06 is an awesome car, but Gary got ideas.

"I started off doing cosmetic things," he said. "Then, I decided I wanted to do engine things. I did mainly bolt-on's at first, like a cat-back exhaust. Then, I decided that I was going to do a head-and-cam package. After considering that, I got to thinking a stroker package sounded better. Then, that sounded so good that dropping in the 427-cid C5-R block sounded even better."

To dress up the inside of the car, he eventually bought everything that Vette Essentials makes: the steering wheel, door pulls, a shifter handle, the shifter boot, the brake handle, the brake boot and the console lid, all done in Mod Red.

Gary chose red mats and red carpets front and rear. The red-and-black partition in the back is a one-off done by "Twisted Interiors."

Gary worked with a talented builder named Sean Freese, who put the car together and tuned it in house, using LS1 edit with the stock PCM (power control module in the car's computer system).

This car offered what Gary called "Ultimate Street Performance," meaning that it's legal to run on the street. With 544.5 rear-wheel horsepower, Gary's Z06 is one of the highest-horsepower street-legal, naturally-aspirated, 427-powered "Corvette Masterpieces" in the country. He calls it his "F/A-427 Predator."

"F/A-427 PREDATOR" CONTENT

BASE CAR

- Electron Blue Exterior
- Modified Red Interior
- All factory options

EXTERIOR

- Rear tub kit with shock travel limiters
- A&A Corvette Specialties rocker rails
- A&A Corvette Specialties frame savers
- Cleartastic bra
- Shorty antenna
- Lowered front and rear
- Red Corvette lettering front and rear

INTERIOR

- Modified red parts by Vette Essentials (steering wheel, door pulls, console lid, shifter knob and boot, brake handle and boot)
- Custom partitions by Twisted Interiors (modified red front panel with raised panel, Plexiglas inserts and C5 logo, black rear panel with raised panel and red neon Twisted Interior logo, and custom formed wheel well covers)
- Vinyl lettering on steering wheel, dash, and door sills

ENGINE RELATED

- GM C5R 7.0 liter race block (installed at 1,249 miles)
- Lunati rotating assembly
- All internal friction surfaces coated
- All heat exchange surfaces coated
- Cam – custom grind
- Ferrea one piece steel valves – 2.100 intake / 1.670 exhaust
- Isky 295D Gold Series Tool Room springs
- Ferrea titanium retainers
- T&D 1.70 shaft mounted roller rockers
- New LS6 head castings – custom hand finished porting
- ATI Super Damper
- FAST 90mm intake manifold
- TPIS 90mm throttle body
- Holley 36lb injectors
- Vararam
- Breathless Performance air bridge
- Meziere electric water pump
- Katech belt tensioner
- Katech tall valve covers with coil relocation kit

HEADERS & EXHAUST

- Bassani 1-7/8-inch Tri-Y headers
- Bassani high-flow catalytic converters
- Bassani 3-inch exhaust from catalytic converters back

CLUTCH RELATED

- Fidanza aluminum flywheel
- Ram 910 disc
- Ram 402 pressure plate
- McCleod billet adjustable clutch master cylinder
- B&M Ripper shifter

WHEELS / TIRES

- Kinesis K18R – Front – 18" x 9.5"
- Kinesis K19R – Rear – 19" x 12"
- Michelin Pilot Sport – Front – 275/40ZR18
- Michelin Pilot Sport – Rear – 345/30ZR19

BRAKES

- Wilwood Superlite 6-piston front
- Wilwood Superlite 4-piston rear
- 13.8-inch replaceable, slotted front rotors, red-anodized hats
- 13.8-inch replaceable, slotted rear rotors, red-anodized hats
- Goodridge stainless steel, Teflon coated lines
- Speed bleeders
- Motul brake fluid

△ **Vette Essentials interior looks great.**

▽ **The car hugs the earth.**

△ **The car started as a cosmetic exercise.**

Mallett Z06 Hammer:
Clearly A Case Of One-Upmanship

△ **This "Hammer" hits the nail on the head.**

▷ **Car sits low to the ground.**

You say you want a little Z06, but you don't want to be like the rest of the LS6 owners on your block? You say that 0 to 60 in a stitch under four seconds is fine for the masses; that quarter mile ETs in the low 12s at close to 110 mph are great for Joe Schmoe, but you want to dip into the magic 11s?

If you want superior handling and a Z06 that's special, you should check out Mallett Cars (www.mallettcars.com) for their latest tuner 'Vette. Built on the Z06, Mallett's "Hammer" is awesome.

◁ **Mallet builds a total package including interior upgrades.**

△ **Pounding home a point.**

◁ **It kind of looks like a "police-car" 'Vette — and goes like one, too.**

Mallett Cars bills itself as "The C5 Experts." They have a Mallett 396 and a Mallett 435, too. With a heritage involved with building and racing cars clear back into the 1950s, this family is very experienced in the racing car arts. They know also how to put together a hot street-tuner version of the Corvette. Mallett is located in the small town of Berea, Ohio.

Our Screaming Yellow Mallett feature car has that unique tuner look that says "hotter than stock." It is that, but it's also been engineered as a "total package."

Mallett agrees that precision tuning is necessary to create a car that really works, but they also believe that power advances must be mated with suspension upgrades.

The Z06 engine in the Mallett Hammer had a custom-ported cylinder head, but retained the factory lightweight valves. Mallett put in its single valve springs with dampers. This particular car also has a 1.8 roller rocker arm on it. This modification alone is good for about 10 hp at rpm peak.

Mallett uses custom-made stainless-steel long-tube headers with a D-port to match the exhaust ports on the custom Z06

▷ The "Hammer" is a hotter-than-hot Z06.

▽ The car has many serious engine upgrades.

▽ The scoops cool the brakes.

cylinder head. Lightweight pushrods and new valve spring retainers complete the internal engine mods. The stainless steel mufflers that Mallett uses feature dual outlets instead of the factory quads.

The suspension gets a set of Mallett/Penske non-adjustable shock absorbers. The car sits about an inch to an inch and a half lower thanks to the short-shafted shocks and custom mounting hardware on the rear springs. The feature car seen here has optional stiff sway bars front and rear.

Mallett's custom billet gearshifter is part of the package. On the outside, the optional 18-inch rims are Mallett's optional one-piece, cast-alloy design. They are 9.5 inches wide in the front and 11 inches wide in the back.

The end result of the Mallett upgrades is a "Corvette Masterpiece" that provides something special. The Z06 is the factory's top-of-the-line performance offering and the Mallett version takes things one step up from there.

△ Mallet promotes itself as a C5 expert.

2006 Commemorative Edition LS2 Twin Turbo 427

The Lingenfelter 2006 Commemorative Edition LS2 Twin Turbo 427 may be the hottest tuner 'Vette sold brand new that year. And for 2007, the performance is going to go up again. The question is when it will stop.

The horsepower race of the '50s, '60s and '70s fizzled out after 1972. Then, things were calm for about two decades. In the early '90s, Chevrolet and other Detroit automakers picked up where they left off.

Corvette added the exotic and extremely powerful ZR1 model in 1990. The modern Corvette LT1 V-8, introduced in

△ **Perhaps the steamiest of all tuner 'Vettes.**

◁ **Corsa's stainless 304 exhaust juts out back.**

John may be gone but his name carries on.

▽ The big 427 generates 725 ponies.

△ Fast fiberglass!

1992, matched or slightly exceeded the horsepower output of the '70 LT1 engine, which is considered a legendary high-performance engine. Since that time, the Corvette's performance has continued to improve. Where the horsepower race will end this go-around is anybody's guess.

The end of the horsepower race will be the model year that the brand new Corvette has *less* performance than the hottest factory stock Corvette of the preceding model year. We're not there yet and may never be. The performance levels are astounding.

Rumors of a 700-hp Corvette SS are circulating. In May 2006, we attended the Lone Star Corvette club's annual show at the Texas Motorspeedway, just north of Fort Worth. The C6 Corvette you see on these pages — a red Lingenfelter 2006 Commemorative Edition LS2 Twin Turbo 427 — rolled out from among hundreds of Corvettes attending the show.

The 505-hp Z06 is a high water mark for a "factory" Corvette. Cars like the Z06 make it harder and harder for the tuners to top the factory. Nevertheless, Lingenfelter Performance Engineering continues to modify factory cars and make them hotter still. LPE added twin turbochargers to the LS2 to achieve 725 hp in this C6, which is called the "Commemorative Edition."

Lingenfelter's website claims a 0-60 mph time of 3.9 seconds, a 0-100 mph time of 7.3 seconds and a quarter-mile time of 11.6 seconds at 136 mph for this car.

▽ 19-inch wheels carry "Commemorative Edition" centers

△ Caravaggio supplies custom leather seats.

Vehicle Specifications

Year: 2007

Make: C6

Model: Corvette

Body: Coupe or Convertible

Colors: Black, Victory Red or Yellow

Interior: Ebony or Cashmere

Gearbox: 6 Speed manual

Springs: Z51 springs

Suspension: Sway bars & custom-built shocks

Other: Navigation system with XM Radio

Export specification vehicles are also eligible to be included in this series

Lingenfelter Package

Engine: 725-hp 427-cid V-8

Turbo: Lingenfelter GEN-2 twin intercooled twin-turbo

Exhaust: Corsa 304 stainless steel exhaust system two 4-inch pro series tips

Clutch: Heavy-duty dual disk clutch assembly

Brakes: Brembo 4-piston calipers, two-piece rotors, stainless lines front and rear with Lingenfelter logo

Interior: Custom Caravaggio Connolly leather seats, console cover, shifter knob/boot, e-brake knob/boot, steering wheel and duffle bag

Body: Unique body enhancements including: Lingenfelter C6 hood, Lingenfelter front spoiler, Lingenfelter side skirts and unique one-piece rear fascia with Lingenfelter logo embossed. The large embossed center logo is only available on this special edition car

Tires: Michelin Pilot Sport tires with Lingenfelter mini tub kit and 345/30/ZR19 series in the rear

Wheels: Lingenfelter 756 Series 19-inch C6 forged 3-piece aluminum wheels by HRE

Special: Special seat embossing, serial numbered plaque, wheel centers, Lingenfelter brushed finished fender badges, Special commemorative C6 coil covers complete with the classic John Lingenfelter signature, Commemorative Edition Hypertech HyperPac Onboard Diagnostic Computer, Excellent drivability, highway mileage not adversely affected, Lingenfelter 3 year/36,000 mile warranty

Price: $86,995.00*

* Price does not include base Z51 vehicle. To be included in the commemorative edition series, all cars must be ordered specifically for this Lingenfelter package as specified above. Vehicles with other options cannot be substituted and this package will be installed only on new vehicles. Corvettes will be drop shipped to Decatur, Indiana from Bowling Green, Kentucky. Once all 25 are sold no further orders will be accepted for this very special limited edition Corvette. Specifications subject to change without notice depending on availability of parts or design changes. Last update January 2, 2007. This package is for off road use only and is not represented to be emissions legal for public highways.

Corvetteforum.com's Cruise-In

△ **Daytime finds Corvette Forum members showing their cars at the National Corvette Museum.**

Corvette Forum's national show is planned to have fun. The shows are refreshing since they have nothing to do with judging, restoration or classic car values. The things people enjoy at these shows today are the same things Corvette enthusiasts enjoyed in the '50s and '60s.

It seems like the hobby went through the low-performance era of the '70s and early '80s, the escalation of prices and the "let's not drive it phase," only to re-emerge as it was in the good old days.

The people involved with the Corvette Forum are young and energetic and concentrate on doing the things their sports cars were meant to do: autocrossing, drag racing, road racing, cruising and other "active" things.

This car is about more than restoring. It involves a whole

▷ $8 for Roscoe's cookout food buys an assortment of smoked meats along with potatoes and veggies.

▽ Friday night at the Baymont Inn is one big party.

lot more than getting a big shiny trophy, although there's certainly nothing wrong with that if it's all good and all fun.

Although Corvette Forum shows at the National Corvette Museum have weekend dates, the beer keg goes operational about Wednesday. Soon, hundreds of Corvette people will be gathering to applaud and cheer for more and more smoky burnouts. Friday night, it's paper plates and treats like Roscoe's smoked turkey and pork. Roscoe cooks up his culinary delights right there on the grounds. The Forum event isn't a catered affair.

△ A red, white and blue 'Vette burns rubber at Beech Bend Drag Strip, near the National Corvette Museum in Bowling Green, Kentucky.

△ Donna Littlejohn drove her multi-colored C5 to the Corvette Forum show and conversed with another Forum member.

▷ Mark Gearhart goes by the Internet handle "Mean Green." Badges reveal such names at the Corvette Forum show.

Corvette people like Donna Littlejohn are colorful and exciting. She goes by the Internet handle "earnedit" (matching the license plates on her C5 Corvette). She told me she was surprised when she met "Mean Green." With a handle like that, she expected Mark Gearhart to look like Hulk Hogan, but he was of medium build with a ponytail. "He's really a sweetheart," said Donna. "And a really big part of the forum. Everybody knows him."

◁ The owner of a '79 'Vette with "Ole Yello" plates was encouraged to do burnouts to the crowd's cheering approval.

△ A 'Vette "advertises" the owner's club.

◁ Forum members smoked big cigars and posed for a group shot.

Gearhart, of Tampa, Florida, was smiling ear to ear under a blue cap and a white Corvetteforum.com T-shirt. "Everybody talks to everybody on line and you build online relationships," Mean Green explained. "You talk to people on a daily basis or every other day and then when you get a chance to get everybody together and talk cars, it's just great."

Gearhart pointed out Troy Roberts, the owner of Corvetteforum.com. In a later interview, Roberts stressed that "show" is not the Forum's preferred description for the national Cruise-In. His view was that the keynote to forum activities is fun. "Show" is hardly a good term to get across the idea that a Corvetteforum.com event is like a college frat party featuring much older folks who drive $50,000 Corvettes.

△ **This could only happen in a parallel universe or at a Corvette Forum drag race at Beech Bend Drag Strip.**

▷ **This license plate inscription is typical of Corvette Forum bravado.**

National Cruise-In activities include a People's Choice Car Show, drag racing and autocrossing at Beech Bend raceway, a burnout contest, a Poker Fun Run & Scenic Tour and tours of the Corvette Assembly Plant. Almost everybody *drives* Corvettes to the event.

"We drove 980 miles in one shot yesterday," Doug Bruggeman of Sioux Falls, South Dakota said. "I can drive my C5 all day long at 85 mph, keep the air conditioning on, get 27 mpg and not worry about breaking down."

Roberts characterizes his constituency's passion as, "A love of Corvettes — America's sports car." As Troy pointed out about the Internet, "Online, you can have somebody from Alaska, somebody from Europe, a low-wage worker who spends every penny on his Corvette and a wealthy corporation head; it doesn't matter. They like to get together . . . have a

Corvette Forum members take over the lawn of the Baymont Inn in Bowling Green.

Dave Hill, Corvette chief engineer, joined the Corvette Forum party.

Adam Boca gets sheared for a good cause. He believes he raised $18,000 for the National Corvette Museum by doing this.

"Joecooool" and "Ohyealiz."

good time . . . get out and drive their cars . . . show them off. That's the Corvette lifestyle."

Indianapolis resident David Edmonds — who goes by the handle "Leadfoot" — may have explained this common interest best when he said, "The people who own 'Corvette Masterpieces' have the same DNA."

Lingenfelter Shop Tour

△ **Rows of customer cars in the fenced back lot wait their turn with Lingenfelter.**

ohn Lingenfelter was a quiet man who thoroughly enjoyed building high-performance cars and racing them. On October 27, 2002, John was critically injured in a crash at a National Hot Rod Association Summit Sports Compact drag racing event at Pomona, California. He died Thursday December 25, 2003 at Adams County Memorial Hospital in Decatur, Indiana at age 58.

His name lives on through the special Corvettes he built. His company, Lingenfelter Performance Engineering continues to stress high-performance. This chapter is based on a visit to Lingenfelter Performance Engineering in 2001, but the shop continues to build engines and cars in the same tradition.

Overall, Lingenfelter Performance Engineering is pretty much what you'd expect from one of the premier Corvette tuners in the country. It began as a machine shop and engine-building facility. Then, it grew to encompass a business that tore down cars and built them up a different way. LPE builds about 100 cars a year and turns out an engine almost every working day.

◁ The largest part of LPE's shop is devoted to building mostly (but not only) Corvettes. The yellow C5 in the center was slated to get one of the new Lingenfelter wide-body conversion.

◁ This C5 was getting a "top end kit." With a set of CNC ported heads, modified intake, cat-back exhausts and a fresh cam, the 350 pumps would put out 430 hp. The car is a daily driver with a good idle and good gas mileage.

Though sometimes LPE sounds like an overnight success story, things didn't happen that way. John Lingenfelter raced and built competition engines for over 25 years. But Lingenfelter was lucky enough to become more than an engine builder. He became the consummate "tuner" of late-model Corvettes (and other cars) and gained an enviable national reputation.

LPE's home was a small town called Decatur, Indiana, about 30 miles south of Ft. Wayne. The business had no sign on front. "When we added onto the shop five years ago, we took it down and never put it back up," said Tim Dyer, one of the company's 30-odd employees. It was obvious that Lingenfelter's customers were scattered far beyond the Decatur area. There was no need to advertise locally.

The place was easy to find. There were big transporters with Corvettes and Camaros spilling out of them. An old brick two-story house with a cellar door stood at the front of Lingenfelter's shops. John used to live there. Then he rented it out. Later, the building was torn down.

◁ The machine shop where LPE does its in-house engine builds.

▽ John Lingenfelter posed beside this timing light found inside the shop.

△ This is the engine teardown room. Notice the cars outside.

▷ Lingenfelter builds ASA engines in big quantities. They were stacked everywhere around the shop and the lot.

America's premier Corvette tuner was housed in a mishmash of steel buildings. But the cars around the buildings were impressive. There were rows of Corvettes, Z28s, Trans Ams — even an early '90s rear-wheel-drive Impala SS and a GMC Cyclone pickup.

"We do crank balancing, block boring, block honing, cylinder head work and valve jobs," Tim Dyer said. This was really the nuts-and-bolts of the Lingenfelter operation. In fact, everything seemed to revolve around nuts and bolts. There were engines on stands everywhere. And there was even a "secret engine" room — no cameras allowed in it.

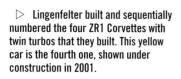
△ Steve Lambert does the final assembly for all engines.

▷ Lingenfelter built and sequentially numbered the four ZR1 Corvettes with twin turbos that they built. This yellow car is the fourth one, shown under construction in 2001.

Another room is a "clean room" where Steve Lambert worked doing final assembly of all Lingenfelter engines, as he's done since 1981. Any enthusiast who has a car with a Lingenfelter-built engine has Lambert's fingerprints. He has done over 5,000 builds.

"I've probably built more ZR1 motors than any other type", Lambert explained. But he has also done some pretty interesting other motors like Viper V-10s.

One room behind a set of hanging plastic curtains, split into long streamers, was full of just engines. A worker explained that it was the Engine Teardown Room. "It's my job to take the engines apart after they come out of the cars," he said. This room was open to the outside and there were Corvettes lined up in rows. Apparently, the engines had come from these 'Vettes.

The biggest room in the shop held 12 cars (11 Corvettes and one street rod) in various states of disassembly or assembly. The most interesting was a C5 Corvette that was high in the air on a lift. The car was in the middle of a complete Lingenfelter body kit installation. Workers were putting in one of Lingenfelter's 650-hp twin-turbo engines in that particular "Corvette Masterpiece."

△ **Lingenfelter has quite a racing history. Trophies and framed pictures on a wall tell part of the story. In the foreground are completed engines.**

◁ **Lambert has had his fingers in many projects.**

Burnout Basics

△ **Smoke 'em.**

▷ **Step 2, stand on it.**

A ll Corvette masterpieces can do tire-spinning "burnouts" by accelerating rapidly from a standing start. We tend to associate burnouts with juvenile delinquency, vandalism and "smoking in the boys' room." Yet, a burnout is an essential part of drag racing. It's as important to a good drag strip "launch" as a set of traction bars and leaves an all-American image like "Mom, Apple Pie and Chevrolet."

☐ Step 3, give it some more gas.

◁ Step 4, start with the "right" car
— a 'Vette, of course.

Step 5, push even harder.

△ **Step 6, burn, baby, burn.**

▷ **It's called "tire recycling."**

Today, many Corvette racetrack events have burnout contests and they are crowd-pleasing events. The winner may get (and need) a set of new tires.

The idea of a burnout is to get the rear tires turning so quickly that they spin on the road surface, rather than achieve the resistance needed to move the car. There are different procedures for doing burnouts, depending on whether a car has an automatic transmission or a manual transmission.

Bleach, detergent powder and even gasoline have been used to make burnouts easier to achieve. Who wants bleach or detergent powder shooting on their car's nice paint? Gasoline should be a definite no-no for safety reasons. A spark could send you to that "big burnout in the sky." Water makes tires slip easier, which is "friendlier" to your car.

Burnouts are exciting and will get the Corvette owner attention. They can also cause wear or damage to brakes, axles, transmissions, engines and other components. With a Corvette, that could mean some big bills!

Bowling Green Corvette Assembly Plant Tour

△ Corvettes are made in a special place.

◁ Exterior view of the Corvette Assembly Plant at Bowling Green, Kentucky.

Corvette Assembly is a special place. The cars we drive are made at the million-square-foot assembly plant in Bowling Green, Kentucky. The assembly line workers who built these great cars also feel the "pull" of the Corvette mystique.

Bob Breeding gives private guided tours at the plant and talks of the *camaraderie* of the workers there. Down-to-earth

△ This is the Corvette Assembly plant during the C5 era.

▷ Stacked in the foreground are "hydro-formed" side rails of the C5 Corvette frame.

▷ Here's another sub-assembly line. If you own a C5, this worker had a hand in assembling the doors.

▽ A proud Corvette assembly worker in the "body shop" gathers parts for sub-assembly of the uni-frame.

plant manager Wil Cooksey is "The Man." When you talk to Wil you get a warm, welcome feeling. "I'm not better than anybody else," he says and his attitude pervades at the plant. The other workers send out similar vibes.

Still, there's a special feeling of pride among Corvette workers. You see it in the looks and smiles and it's like they're saying, "We build Corvettes and we're glad you're here to see how we do it."

Corvette Assembly appears to be all it was cracked up to be — a real storybook land of happy workers building a marque with an equally storied past.

The basic concept of an assembly line is more complicated than the third-grade image most of us have of Ford workers building Model Ts. We tend to think you start out with a frame on a moving line and keep attaching parts until it becomes a car. Then, you fire up the car and drive it away.

◁ This part of the uni-frame is the seat back/tunnel assembly.

◁ Figuring out how the uni-frame is sub-assembled would take an engineering degree. Forty-eight robots weld along the frame, while welders do both MIG and spot welding.

△ Inside the green tunnel is a "Perceptron" system of laser cameras that check the uni-frame and body for dimensional integrity.

◁ The entire cockpit is sub-assembled in a separate line. Two workers install the radio at this station.

□ Workers in "Hysters" shuttle parts, like these seats, throughout the plant.

▽ One of the assembly line workers was a real ham . . . or cheese.

□ Corvette panels are painted separately while on a "truck" that holds them in their exact position on the car. This makes the robot paint patterns consistent on every panel.

◁ Here, a cockpit is lowered onto a built-up uni-frame assembly.

▽ A glass robot applies adhesive to the windshield.

△ Another sub-assembly line builds up the suspensions.

In Corvetteland, just over 1,000 employees build about 130 cars per day. They work eight-hour shifts running Monday through Friday from 6:12 am to 2:42 pm. After that, production closes for the day.

What's called "the line" is actually a network of conveyor systems that cover 7 miles. Breeding explained that the Corvette plant has four different departments: 1) body shop, 2) paint, 3) trim and 4) chassis, that comprise the assembly process.

◁ A hatch and rear deck lid go on the uni-frame.

▷ Two operators drop an engine into a chassis.

▽ The Corvette C5 chassis had a high-tech look.

There are various sub-assembly lines along the seven-mile path to a finished car. For example, there is a sub-assembly line for doors. There is also a chassis sub-assembly line. It consists of a motor line, a line to put together suspensions and a line that builds the drive train (including transaxle and the torque tube assembly). These are all separate lines.

△ **The transmission mounts at the rear of the Corvette, which helps evenly distribute the weight.**

The most dramatic part of assembly occurs when the body and the drive train come together in the "body marriage." Connecting the engine and drive train to the body takes 26 different attachments requiring about three minutes to complete.

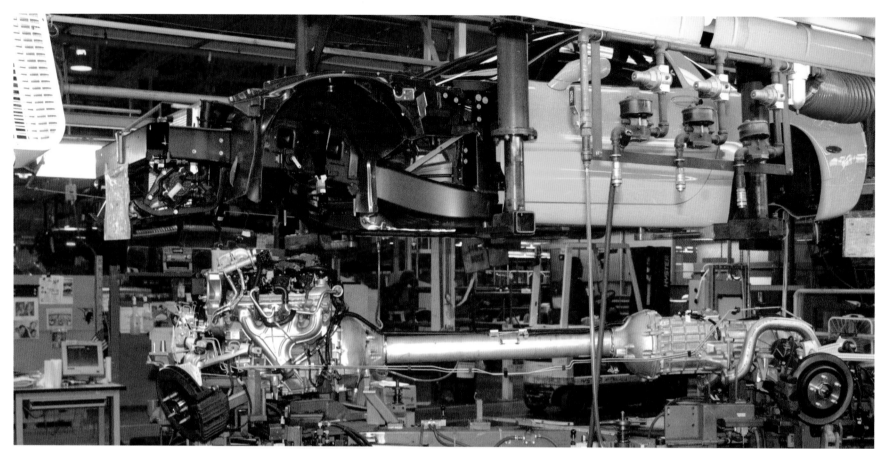

△ The body marriage is the most dramatic part of the assembly process.

▽ Operators drop a Corvette body onto the chassis.

▷ After body marriage, the parts and pieces really look like a car.

▷ The operator uses this complicated-looking machine to install the energy absorber for the front bumper.

▽ How's about putting a hood on next?

◁ On the side of the assembly line, we noticed this sub-assembly of the front fascia.

△ We're getting to the end of the line, now. The cars are complete.

▷ This is the end of the assembly line, where they fire up the engine and drive away.

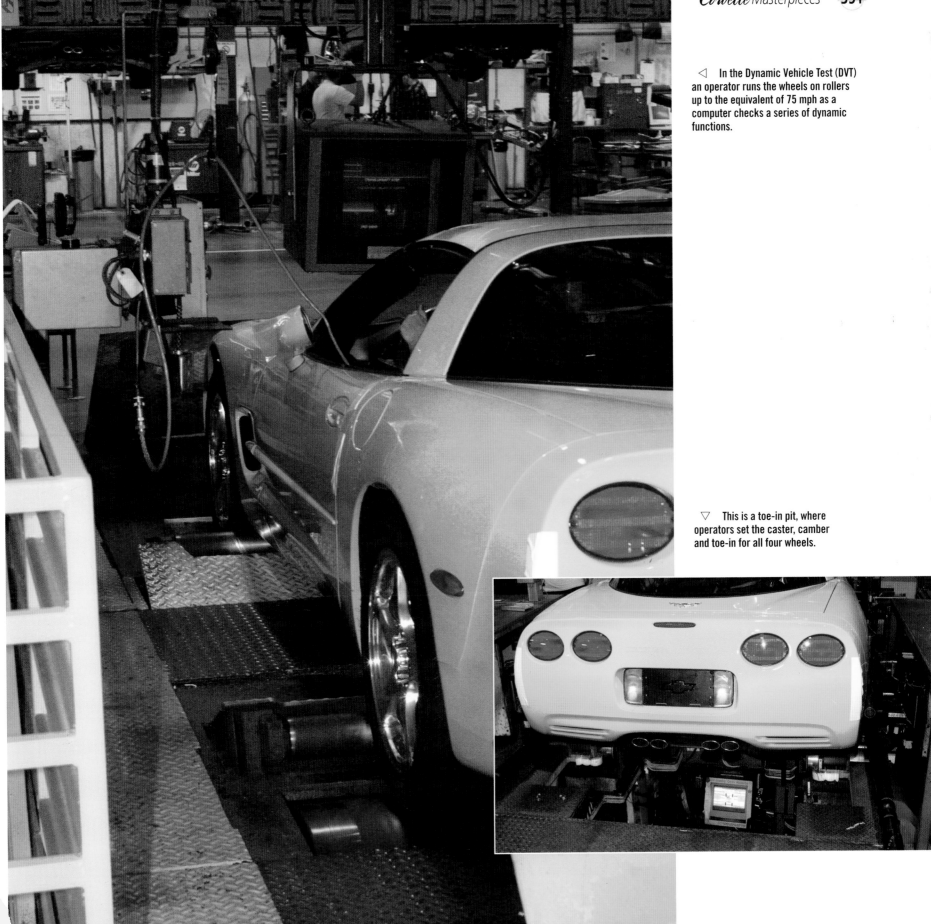

◁ In the Dynamic Vehicle Test (DVT) an operator runs the wheels on rollers up to the equivalent of 75 mph as a computer checks a series of dynamic functions.

▽ This is a toe-in pit, where operators set the caster, camber and toe-in for all four wheels.

▷ This is the "bump track" where operators drive Corvettes to listen for any squeaks or rattles.

 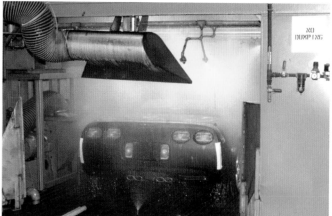

▷ Corvettes go through a four-minute monsoon. If there's a leak, Corvette Assembly wants to know.

△ Corvettes stack up in the yard outside the plant awaiting shipment.

Cars literally come to life on the assembly line. Parts are not produced there. Exactly 393 suppliers shipped 1,476 individual parts to Bowling Green to build the C5 Corvettes appearing on these pages.